CHALLENGE YOUR MIND

Math Games Throughout the Year

by

Jillayne Prince Wallaker

Cover Illustration
by
Vickie Lane

Inside Art
by
Randy Rider

Published by Instructional Fair
an imprint of
Frank Schaffer Publications®

Instructional Fair

Author: Jillayne Prince Wallaker
Editors: Linda Kimble, Wendy Roh Jenks, Elizabeth Flikkema
Cover Artist: Vickie Lane
Interior Designer: Pat Geasler
Interior Artist: Randy Rider

Frank Schaffer Publications®

Instructional Fair is an imprint of Frank Schaffer Publications.

Send all inquiries to:
Frank Schaffer Publications
3195 Wilson Drive NW
Grand Rapids, Michigan 49534

Challenge Your Mind Math Games—grades 6–8

ISBN: 1-56822-784-1

4 5 6 7 8 9 10 MAZ 10 09 08 07 06

Table of Contents

Common Factors Through Time

Name ______________________

As the year is completed and a new one has begun, it is time to consider the history of numbers. Erathosthenes, an ancient Greek mathematician, developed a method to determine prime numbers. His method for finding the 25 prime numbers between 1 and 100 is explained below. A prime number is a number with only two factors. Circle all prime numbers. Then cross out all composite numbers (those with more than two factors).

1	2	3	4	5	6	7	8	9	10
11	12	13	14	15	16	17	18	19	20
21	22	23	24	25	26	27	28	29	30
31	32	33	34	35	36	37	38	39	40
41	42	43	44	45	46	47	48	49	50
51	52	53	54	55	56	57	58	59	60
61	62	63	64	65	66	67	68	69	70
71	72	73	74	75	76	77	78	79	80
81	82	83	84	85	86	87	88	89	90
91	92	93	94	95	96	97	98	99	100

1. Cross out 1.
2. Circle the smallest prime number. What is it? ______
3. Cross out all multiples of this number.
4. Circle the next prime number. What is it? ______
5. Cross out all multiples of this number.
6. Circle the next prime number. What is it? ______
7. Cross out all multiples of this number.
8. Circle the next prime number. What is it? ______
9. Cross out all multiples of this number.
10. Circle the prime numbers.

THIS METHOD OF FINDING PRIME NUMBERS IS CALLED THE SIEVE OF ERATOSTHENES!

After-Holiday Sale!

Name ______________________

New Year's

No calculator. Show all work.

After the holidays, everything at Big Buys is discounted. From 9 A.M. to 9 P.M. nothing is full price! Calculate the discounts and subtract from the regular prices. Write the pre-tax prices on the sale tags.

$129.95
33% Off
portable sound system
____

$46.97
33% Off
telephone
____

$99.99
33% Off
camera
____

$85.29
55% Off
winter jacket
____

$25.14
55% Off
holiday craft kit
____

$99.99
55% Off
large stuffed bear
____

$37.89
25% Off
watch
____

$67.99
25% Off
hand-held game
____

$19.95
25% Off
latest VCR movie
____

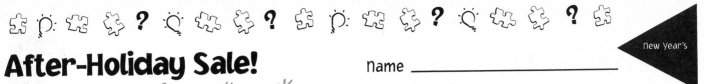

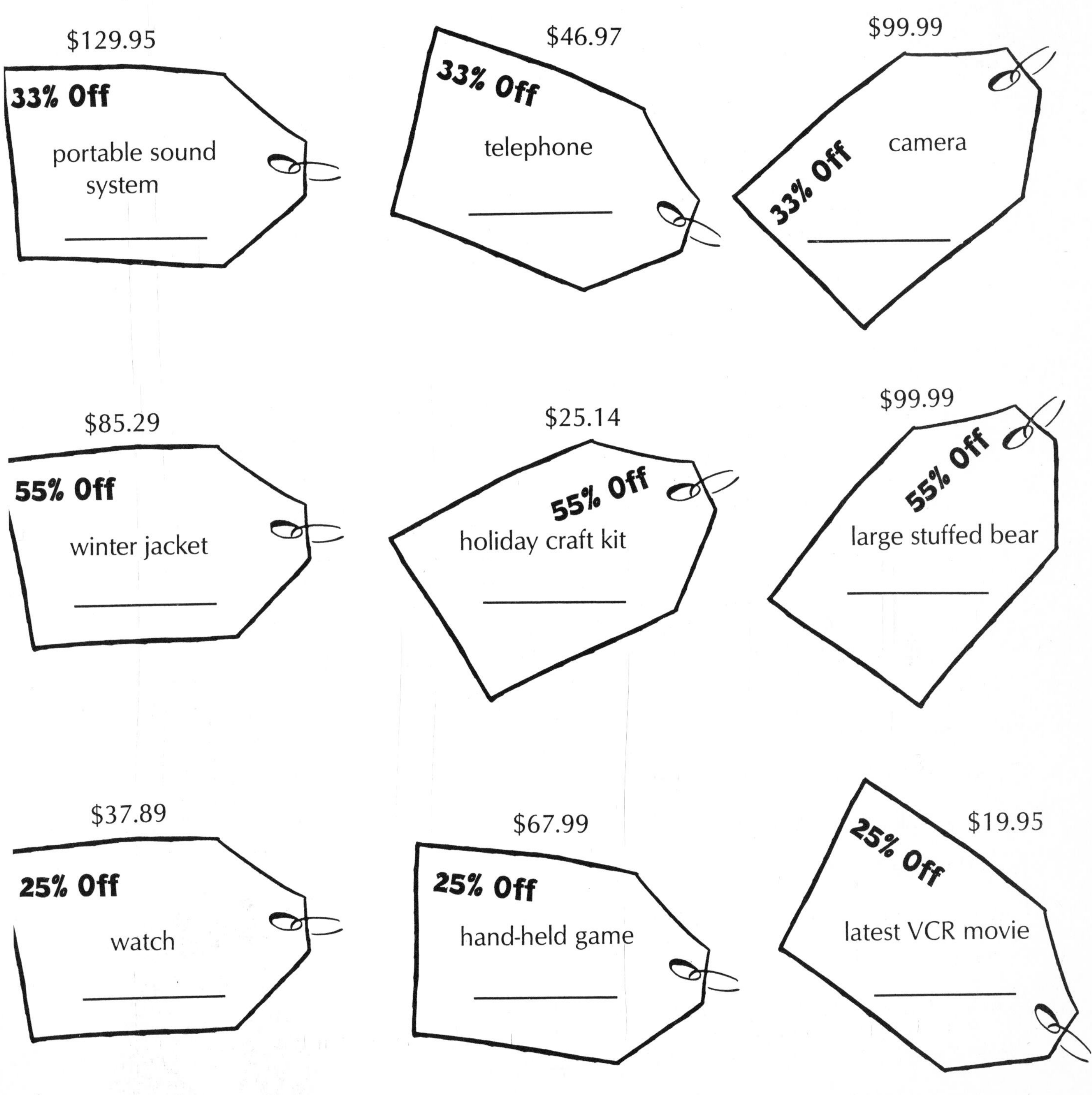

Holiday Cash

Name ____________________

No calculator. Show all work.

You received a total of $164.00 as gift money during the holiday season. Read each of the following situations and keep a running balance. Notice that each situation begins with the remaining balance of the previous situation; you do not begin with $164.00 each time. Show your work.

Beginning balance: $164.00

1. Your parents have decided that you must put 30% of your gift money into your savings account.

   remaining balance: __________

2. You lost your ski boots and you must replace them. They are normally $87.95, but are 35% off with the post-holiday sales.

   remaining balance: __________

3. You promised your brother you would buy him an action figure for helping you shovel the driveway. You can buy 3 for $7.00, but you want to buy only one.

   remaining balance: __________

4. Mom and Dad pay you $6.50 each time you shovel the driveway. You shoveled 4 times this week.

   new balance: __________

5. You went out for pizza with 7 friends. You split the cost of two pizzas with all of your friends. The pizzas, without beverages, cost $16.50. You also paid for two large drinks at $1.09 each.

   remaining balance: __________

Let It Snow

Name ______________________

Solve each problem. Use the corresponding letters in the code below to determine some words used for various types of snow. These words come from the Inuit Indians and the Lapps.

K

1. $\frac{2}{3} \times 1\frac{1}{8}$

O

2. $4\frac{1}{2} \times 2\frac{2}{3}$

I

3. $1\frac{2}{3} \times \frac{4}{5}$

A

4. $\frac{3}{4} \times 5\frac{1}{3}$

T

5. $5\frac{1}{4} \times 4\frac{2}{3}$

S

6. $\frac{1}{3} \times 3\frac{1}{2}$

Q

7. $4\frac{2}{5} \times 1\frac{3}{7}$

P

8. $4\frac{1}{12} \times 1\frac{3}{7}$

L

9. $2\frac{1}{5} \times 6\frac{1}{9}$

U

10. $5\frac{1}{3} \times 4\frac{1}{2}$

A

11. $3\frac{3}{5} \times 7\frac{1}{6}$

I

12. $2\frac{1}{6} \times 3\frac{1}{3}$

___ ___ ___ : The blanket of snow that insulates and covers the ground.

$25\frac{4}{5}$ $5\frac{5}{6}$ $1\frac{1}{3}$

___ ___ ___ ___ ___ : The bottom layer of snow that is melted by the earth and creates tunnels for mice and other small animals.

$5\frac{5}{6}$ 24 $\frac{3}{4}$ 4 $\frac{3}{4}$

___ ___ ___ ___ : Snow that blankets tree and bush branches; helps winter animals hide and pushes food into their reach.

$6\frac{2}{7}$ $25\frac{4}{5}$ $13\frac{4}{9}$ $7\frac{2}{9}$

___ ___ ___ ___ ___ : Snow that is wind-packed and hard; used to make igloos.

24 $5\frac{5}{6}$ $1\frac{1}{6}$ $1\frac{1}{3}$ $\frac{3}{4}$

___ ___ ___ ___ ___ ___ ___ ___ ___ : Snow with a crust on top, formed when melted snow refreezes.

$1\frac{1}{6}$ $7\frac{2}{9}$ $6\frac{2}{7}$ 12 $6\frac{2}{7}$ $24\frac{1}{2}$ 12 4 $6\frac{2}{7}$

Winter Fences

Name ______________________

Write the factors of each composite number below it on the fence post. Write the Greatest Common Factors (GCF) in the rungs between the posts. The first one is done for you.

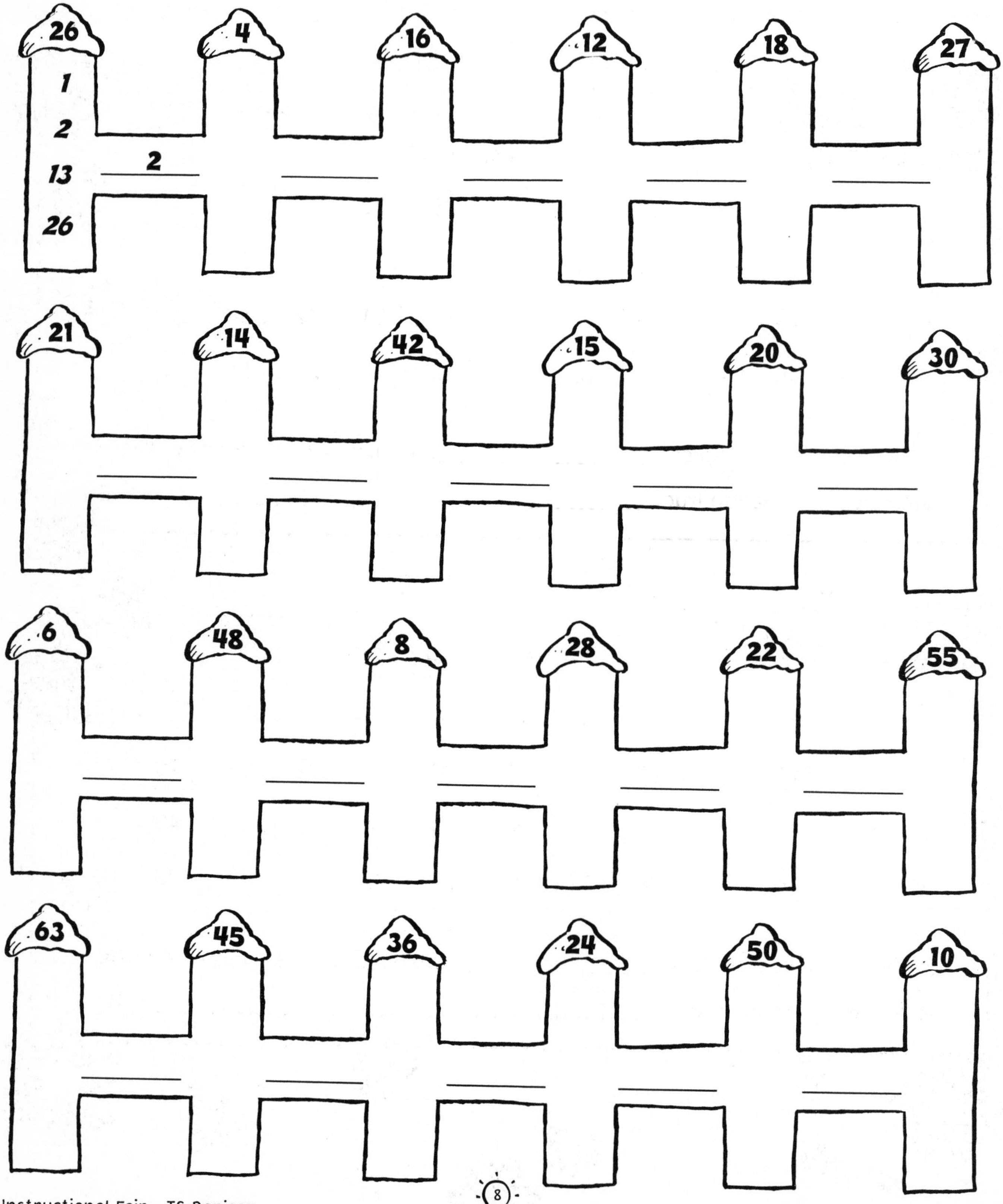

Through the Blizzard

Name ______________________

Wade through the blizzard of multiples. One number in each row of the chart is not a multiple of the given number. Circle it in each line. Arrange the circled numbers and follow the rules for order of operations to arrive at the given answer.

Number	Multiples									
2	10	4	2	7	8	26	32	12	14	16
3	15	3	24	6	12	21	9	26	30	18
6	46	18	36	12	48	6	24	42	54	30
9	36	72	9	63	18	45	15	27	54	81

List the incorrect multiples: ____ ____ ____ ____ Arrange these numbers to make the following equation true: ______________________________ = 160

Number	Multiples									
4	20	16	36	8	24	4	32	12	18	28
5	10	50	15	9	5	40	30	20	35	25
7	35	7	63	28	42	24	14	56	21	49
8	56	24	48	72	16	20	32	64	8	40

List the incorrect multiples: ____ ____ ____ ____ Arrange these numbers to make the following equation true: ______________________________ = 18

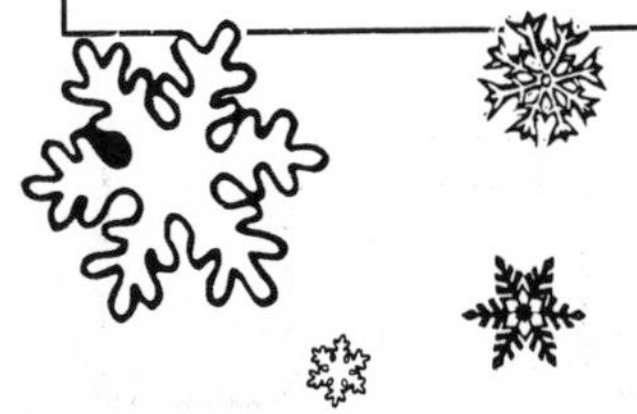

Build a Snowman

Name ____________________

Solve each addition problem.

1.
4.571
24.85
360.521
\+ .0391

2.
981.1
89.342
2.013
\+ 10.906

3.
108.61
3.386
51.105
\+ .009

4.
31.61
111.364
8.008
\+ 942.1

5.
.4632
50.11
9.0501
\+ 8.76

6.
833.3
68.89
361.275
\+ 5.687

7.
69.125
152.96
3.892
\+ 2,115.6

8.
.785
432.1
41.52
\+ 962.38

9.
36.54
147.02
6,205.6
\+ 8.699

10.
85.36
397.6
5,900.369
\+ 77.1205

11.
52.141
9.511
214.9
\+ 69.341

12.
27.99
713.24
58.378
\+ 464.8

13.
64.12
408.4
5.99
\+ 709.577

Look at each sum. Follow the directions.

1. Circle all 8s in the hundredths place. Draw one piece of coal for the mouth for each.
2. Underline all 1s in the tenths place. Draw one eye for each.
3. Put a triangle around each 5 in the ten-thousandths place. Draw one carrot nose for each.
4. Draw an arrow beneath each 3 in the thousandths place. Draw one stick arm for each.
5. Put a box around each 6 in the tens place. Draw one charcoal button for each.
6. Underline each 3 in the ten-thousandths place. Draw one hat for each.

Tic-Tac-Toe Is Cool

Name ____________________

Solve each subtraction problem. Then locate each answer in the tic-tac-toe games. Replace the traditional Xs and Os with snowmen and mittens. Draw a snowman over the answer of each even-numbered difference and a mitten over the odd-numbered differences.

1. $\frac{1}{3} - \frac{1}{12} =$
2. $\frac{5}{8} - \frac{1}{4} =$
3. $\frac{9}{10} - \frac{3}{4} =$

$\frac{3}{8}$	$\frac{1}{5}$	$\frac{3}{20}$
$\frac{7}{18}$	$\frac{7}{12}$	$\frac{1}{4}$
$\frac{1}{6}$	$\frac{4}{7}$	$\frac{1}{8}$

4. $\frac{5}{8} - \frac{1}{2} =$
5. $\frac{3}{4} - \frac{1}{6} =$
6. $\frac{2}{3} - \frac{1}{2} =$
7. $\frac{5}{9} - \frac{1}{6} =$
8. $\frac{4}{5} - \frac{1}{2} =$
9. $\frac{13}{14} - \frac{6}{7} =$

$\frac{3}{10}$	$\frac{1}{14}$	$\frac{2}{3}$
$\frac{2}{15}$	$\frac{4}{15}$	$\frac{2}{5}$
$\frac{5}{12}$	$\frac{1}{18}$	$\frac{7}{12}$

10. $\frac{2}{3} - \frac{1}{4} =$
11. $\frac{4}{5} - \frac{2}{3} =$
12. $\frac{5}{6} - \frac{1}{4} =$
13. $\frac{1}{3} - \frac{5}{18} =$
14. $\frac{13}{15} - \frac{3}{5} =$
15. $\frac{2}{3} - \frac{4}{7} =$

$\frac{13}{28}$	$\frac{2}{7}$	$\frac{3}{5}$
$\frac{1}{16}$	$\frac{1}{3}$	$\frac{3}{4}$
$\frac{1}{2}$	$\frac{1}{9}$	$\frac{2}{21}$

16. $\frac{12}{15} - \frac{1}{5} =$
17. $\frac{3}{4} - \frac{2}{7} =$
18. $\frac{5}{6} - \frac{1}{2} =$
19. $\frac{2}{3} - \frac{1}{6} =$
20. $\frac{7}{9} - \frac{2}{3} =$
21. $\frac{5}{8} - \frac{9}{16} =$

Let It Snow...

name ______________________

Bryan and Mikaela collected data regarding snow types that fell during January. They collected a snow sample on a 2″ by 2″ piece of black cloth from 3:00 to 3:15 P.M. each time it snowed on school days. Use the frequency table to answer the questions. Use the data to make a graph.

Bryan and Mikaela's Frequency Table

Snow Crystals	Frequency
hexagonal plate	456
stellar dendrite	364
column	203
needle	289
tsuzumi	0

1. What is the greatest number in the frequency table? __________

2. What is the least number in the frequency table? __________

3. Name a numerical scale with equal intervals that you believe is appropriate for graphing the given data. ________

WAVELIKE RIDGES OF SNOW ARE KNOWN AS SASTRUGI!

50
25
0

hexagonal plate | stellar dendrite | column | needle | tsuzumi

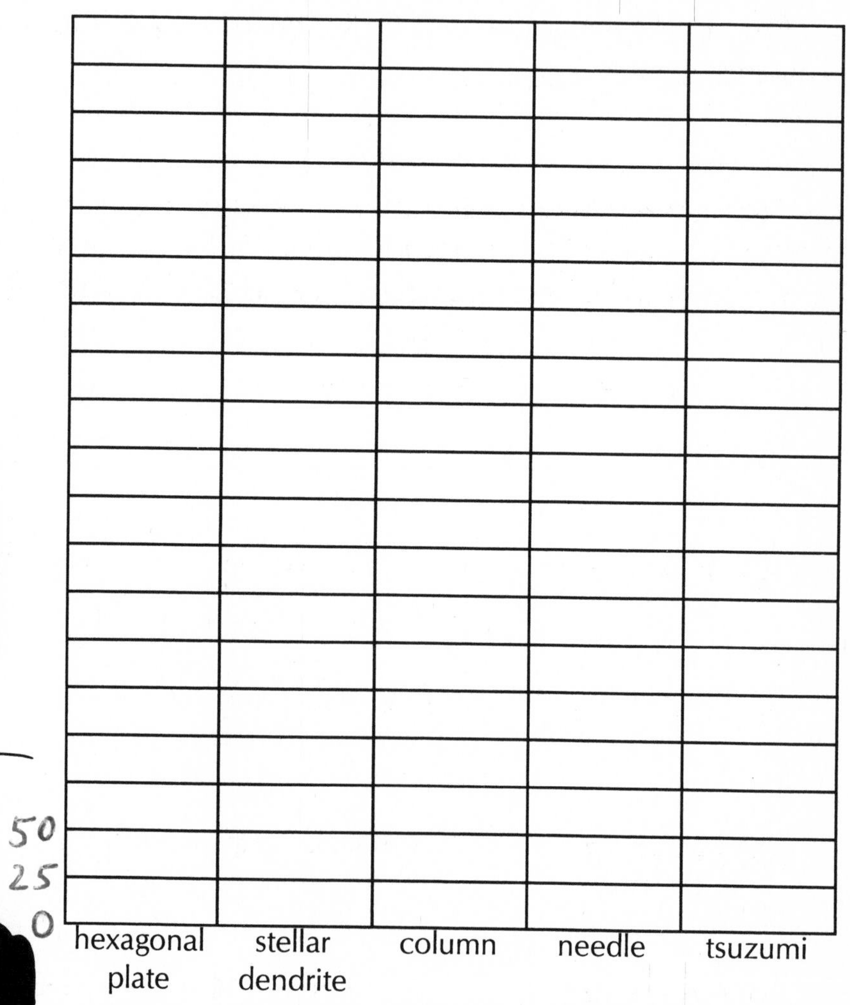

It's Freezing Out There!

name ______________________

Solve each temperature problem.

1. It was 5°C outside at noon. Four hours later, the temperature had dropped 8 degrees. What was the temperature outside at 4:00? ________

2. It was -6°F outside at Kevin's house. His friend Jan called to say it was 32°F outside at his house. How much colder is it at Kevin's house than at Jan's? ________

3. At 3:00, it was -6°F outside. The windchill made it feel like -10°F. How much colder did the windchill make the temperature seem? ________

4. The air temperature was -7°C. The water temperature was 4°C. How much warmer is the water temperature? ________

5. Solve the equations below. Write the sums and differences in order from least to greatest. Write the corresponding letters in the same order. The letters will spell the answer to the following question: What measurement tool is used with temperature?

___ ___ ___ ___ ___ ___ ___ ___ ___ ___ ___ ___

-4 – +3 =	T	+6 + -10 =	H	+8 – -2 =	R
-5 – -7 =	O	-9 + -3 =	A	+6 + -6 =	R
+2 + +5 =	T	-1 + +9 =	E	+13 + -7 =	E
+4 + -6 =	E	-3 – -8 =	M	-8 + +9 =	M

THE TEMPERATURE ONCE DROPPED 101° F IN A 24-HOUR PERIOD IN BILLINGS, MONTANA... BRRR!

Snowball Buildings

Name ______________________

Winter

Build the snow pyramids. Some blocks are missing. Use your addition skills to fill them in. Each pyramid adds to the top.

1.

$10\frac{1}{3}$

___ ___

___ ___ ___

___ ___ ___ ___

$\frac{1}{3}$ $\frac{5}{6}$ $\frac{1}{2}$ $\frac{3}{4}$ $\frac{2}{3}$

2.

___

___ ___

___ ___ ___

___ ___ ___ ___

$\frac{1}{2}$ $\frac{5}{8}$ $\frac{3}{4}$ $\frac{1}{12}$ $\frac{1}{6}$

3.

___

___ ___

___ ___ ___

___ ___ ___ ___

$\frac{1}{6}$ $\frac{5}{9}$ $\frac{3}{18}$ $\frac{1}{2}$ $\frac{3}{4}$

4.

___

$\frac{63}{12}$ ___

___ $\frac{29}{12}$ $\frac{18}{12}$

___ ___ $\frac{11}{12}$ ___

___ $\frac{5}{6}$ ___ ___ $\frac{1}{3}$

5.

$9\frac{3}{16}$

___ $\frac{38}{8}$

___ $\frac{19}{8}$ ___

___ $\frac{9}{8}$ ___ ___

___ ___ $\frac{3}{4}$ ___ ___

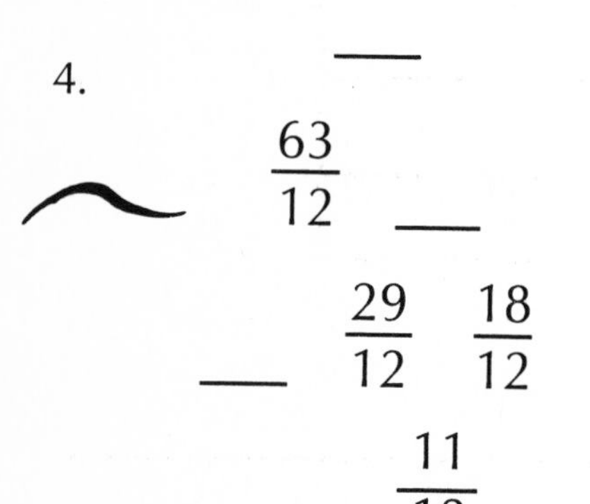

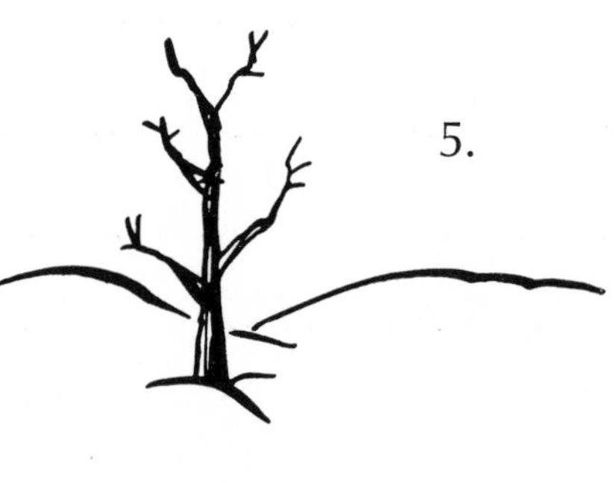

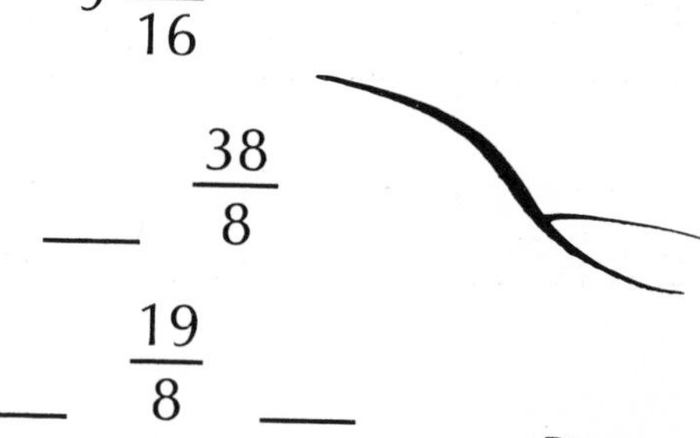

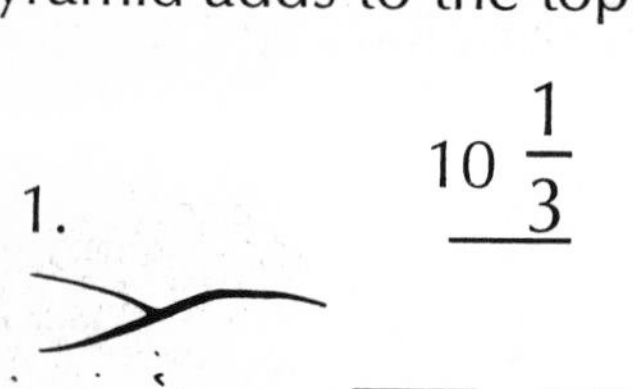

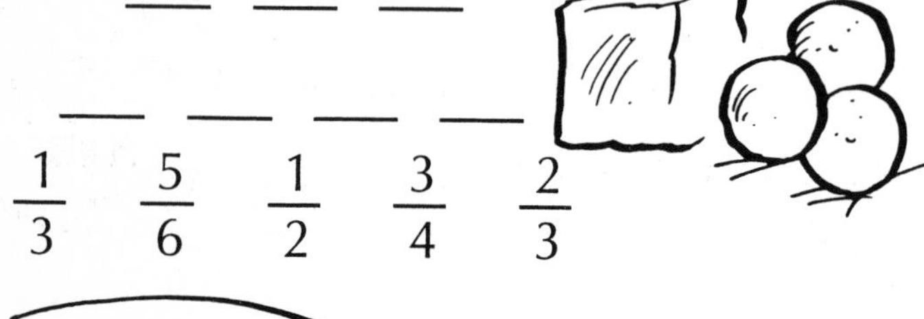

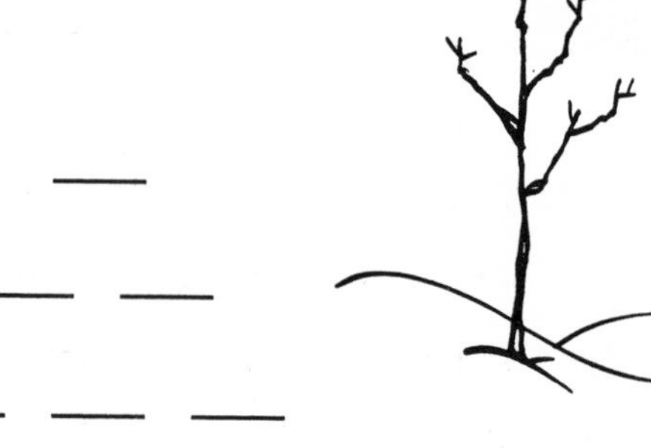

What's Your Favorite Winter Sport?

Name ______________________

Determine the favorite winter sport of each of seven Internet pen pals. Use the clues and matrix to determine who likes each winter sport.

WHAT ABOUT HOCKEY?

1. Denzel lives in Hawaii and enjoys water sports.
2. Manny loves snow country.
3. Ulf does not like downhill skiing.
4. Judy needs a board to enjoy her water sport.
5. Ione had to wait for the pond to freeze before she could enjoy her sport.
6. Quinn grabs a backpack and heads into the Arizona desert.
7. Whitney had to fix the engine of her sport vehicle last week.

	Cross-country skiing	Down-hill skiing	Hiking	Ice-Skating	Snow-mobiling	Surfing	Swim-ming
Denzel							
Ione							
Judy							
Manny							
Quinn							
Ulf							
Whitney							

Denzel enjoys ______________________

Ione enjoys ______________________

Judy enjoys ______________________

Manny enjoys ______________________

Quinn enjoys ______________________

Ulf enjoys ______________________

Whitney enjoys ______________________

A Solemn Pledge

Name ____________________

Inauguration Day

Every four years, the president is sworn in on January 20 by the Chief Justice of the U.S. Supreme Court. Solve each problem. Convert any improper fractions. Then use the answers and the key to write "The Presidential Oath of Office." The problem numbers are written below the blanks.

"

____ 19	____ 9	____ 18	____ 2	____ 14
____ 19	____ 13	____ 16	____ 4	____ 1
____ 24	____ 12	____ 20	____ 12	____ 3
____ 17	____ 10,	____ 15	____ 13,	____ 8
____ 1	____ 7	____ 12	____ 22	____ 23,
____ 6,	____ 11,	____ 15	____ 21	____ 3
____ 5	____ 12	____ 1	____ 17	____ 10."

ability	16/35	do	1 1/3	of	3/5	solemnly	8/15	the	4/5
and	6 1/8	execute	3/11	office	5 1/4	States	5/6	to	1 1/9
best	1 1/7	faithfully	1 4/7	preserve	3/4	swear	1 1/14	United	7/10
Constitution	3/7	I	2/15	President	1	that	3 1/3	will	2/3
defend	1 1/2	my	7/18	protect	1 1/5				

Show work on back or separate sheet of paper.

1. $\frac{2}{3} \div \frac{5}{6} =$
2. $\frac{6}{7} \div \frac{4}{5} =$
3. $\frac{1}{2} \div \frac{5}{8} =$
4. $\frac{1}{4} \div \frac{11}{12} =$
5. $\frac{1}{3} \div \frac{7}{9} =$
6. $\frac{1}{3} \div \frac{4}{9} =$
7. $\frac{6}{7} \div \frac{3}{4} =$
8. $\frac{5}{6} \div \frac{3}{4} =$
9. $\frac{8}{9} \div \frac{2}{3} =$
10. $\frac{5}{8} \div \frac{3}{4} =$
11. $\frac{9}{10} \div \frac{3}{4} =$
12. $\frac{1}{5} \div \frac{1}{3} =$
13. $\frac{8}{21} \div \frac{4}{7} =$
14. $\frac{5}{7} \div \frac{3}{14} =$
15. $\frac{7}{8} \div \frac{1}{7} =$
16. $\frac{6}{7} \div \frac{6}{11} =$
17. $\frac{14}{25} \div \frac{4}{5} =$
18. $\frac{2}{9} \div \frac{5}{12} =$
19. $\frac{1}{9} \div \frac{5}{6} =$
20. $\frac{6}{15} \div \frac{2}{5} =$
21. $\frac{1}{6} \div \frac{1}{9} =$
22. $\frac{1}{3} \div \frac{6}{7} =$
23. $\frac{2}{7} \div \frac{5}{8} =$
24. $\frac{3}{8} \div \frac{1}{14} =$

Famous Black Americans

name ____________________

Solve each problem. Use the answers to decode the names of famous people who contributed to our history.

1. +5 + -3 =	2. -10 − -4 =	3. -1 + -7 =	4. -4 − -9 =
5. -4 + +7 =	6. +2 + +9 =	7. +6 − +7 =	8. -7 + -5 =
9. -14 − -15 =	10. +6 + -9 =	11. -9 + +15 =	12. +5 + -9 =
13. -10 − -14 =	14. +16 + -6 =	15. -2 + -3 =	16. -4 − +5 =
17. +6 − -3 =	18. -10 − -8 =	19. -16 − -6 =	20. -7 + +14 =

A +2	D +9	G +4	J -1	M -5	P +7	T +5
B -4	E +1	H -6	K -8	N +3	R -3	U +11
C -12	F -10	I -9	L +6	O +10	S -2	

First black woman astronaut:

__ __   __ __ __   __ __ __ __ __ __ __
17 10   15 1 9   7 9 15 16 18 14 5

Talented opera singer:

__ __ __ __ __ __   __ __ __ __ __ __ __ __
15 1 10 16 14 5   1 5 17 9 10 18 14 5

First African American baseball player to play for the major leagues:

__ __ __ __ __ __   __ __ __ __ __ __ __ __
7 1 8 3 16 9   10 14 12 16 5 18 14 5

First African American Supreme Court justice:

__ __ __ __ __ __ __ __   __ __ __ __ __ __ __ __
4 2 6 10 13 14 14 17   15 1 10 18 2 1 11 11

Teacher who founded Kwanzaa:

__ __   __ __ __ __ __ __ __   __ __ __ __ __ __ __
17 10   15 1 6 11 1 5 1   3 1 10 9 5 13 1

Woman who refused to give up her seat to a white person on a public bus:

__ __ __ __   __ __ __ __ __
10 14 18 1   20 1 10 3 18

Super Scientist

Name ____________________

Black History Month

In 1946, Congress designated January 5 as a day to honor a famous scientist. This agricultural scientist developed over 200 ways to use the peanut and sweet potato. Who is this scientist? Solve for each letter. Write the letter in caps above each corresponding answer.

___ ___ ___ ___ ___ ___
2.45 6.2 2.56 .65 .15 .73

___ ___ ___ ___ ___ ___ ___ ___ ___ ___
.78 .61 .56 .25 .88 .36 .899 .98 .87 .66

___ ___ ___ ___ ___ ___
.51 .11 .413 2.6 9.45 .47

HE EARNED HIS COLLEGE TUITION BY WORKING AS A COOK!

1. $350h = 87.5$

   h =

2. $3.12 + r = 3.77$

   r =

3. $t \div .4 = 2.45$

   t =

4. $1r^2 = .2209$

   r =

5. $465 \div g = 3100$

   g =

6. $e - .578 = 8.872$

   e =

7. $o(.13) = .3328$

   o =

8. $77/a = 700$

   a =

9. $6.12 - g = 3.67$

   g =

10. $.652 + a = 1.262$

    a =

11. $1.512 \div n = 4.2$

    n =

12. $r + 4.87 = 5.283$

    r =

13. $n(.23) = .1518$

    n =

14. $4.6 - w = 3.82$

    w =

15. $e9 = 55.8$

    e =

16. $4.61 + g = 5.509$

    g =

17. $v - 1.54 = 1.06$

    v =

18. $4.21i = 3.7048$

    i =

19. $o + 5.68 = 6.55$

    o =

20. $.1938/c = .38$

    c =

21. $6e = 4.38$

    e =

22. $1.848/3.3 = s$

    s =

Groundhog Day

Name ______________________

On Groundhog Day, the groundhog looks for its shadow to predict winter's length. Look at the shadows on this page. Determine the *shadowed* area of each figure.

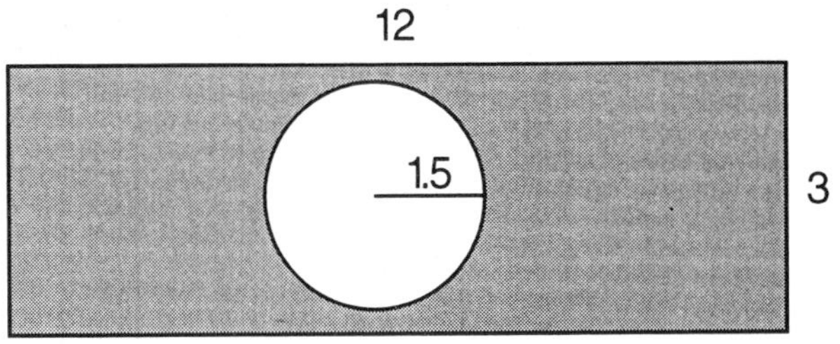

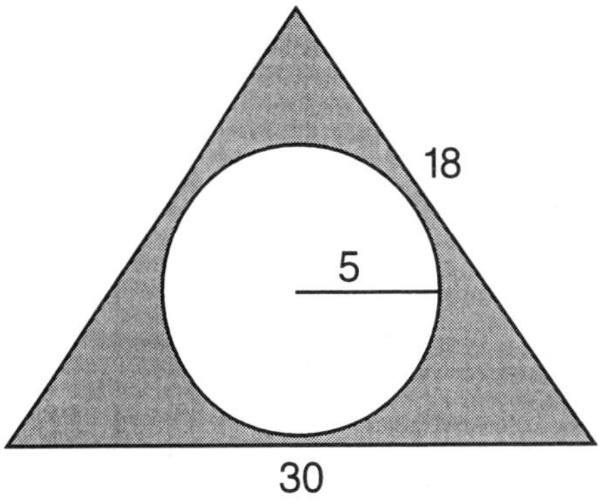

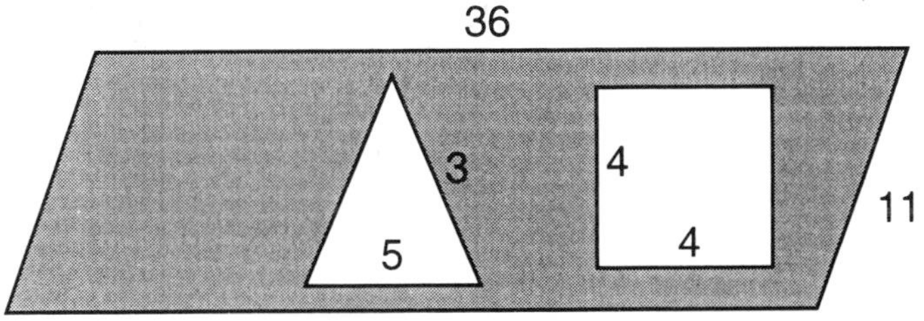

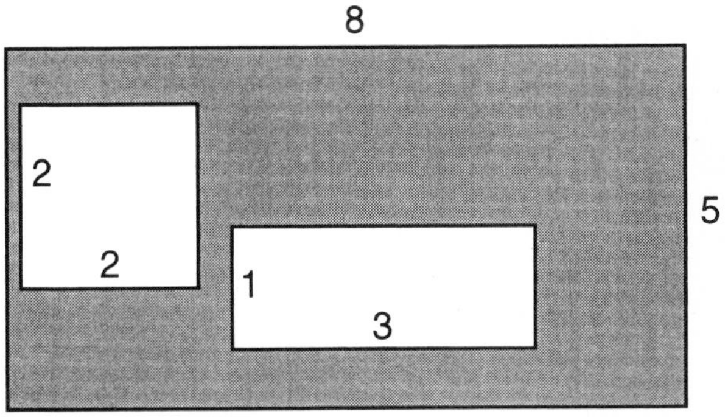

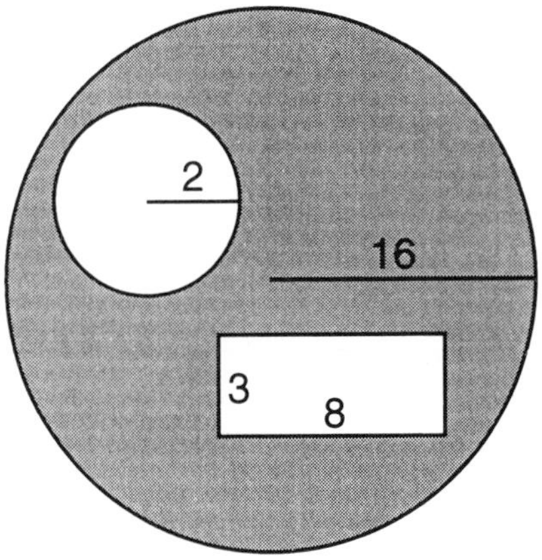

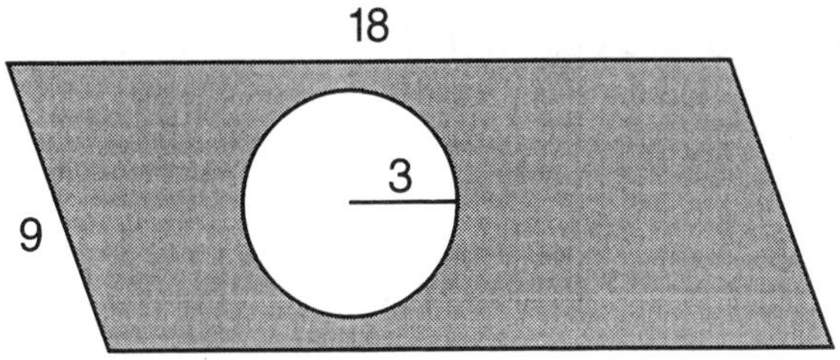

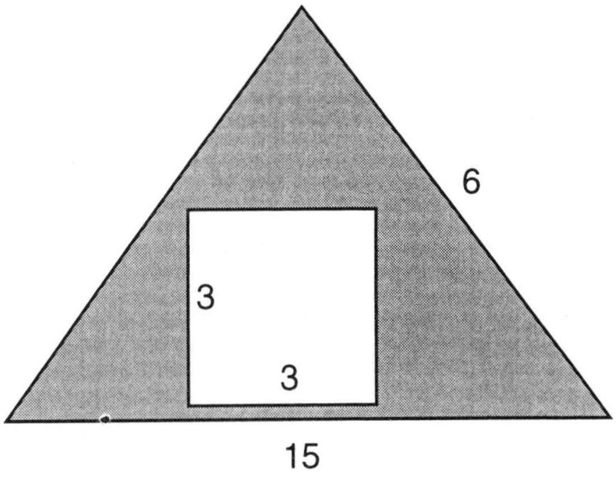

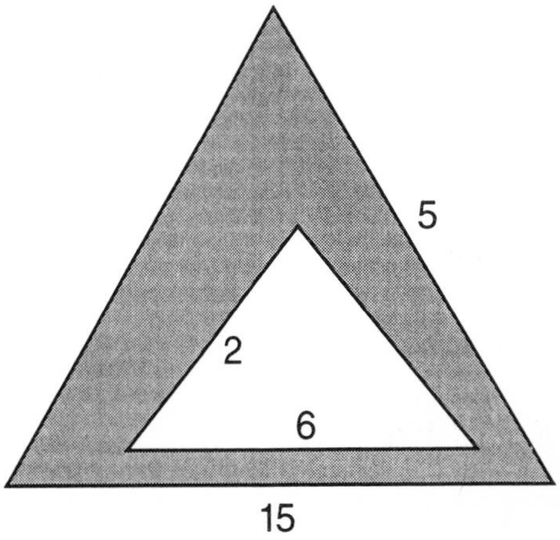

Report Card Time

Name ____________________

Ms. Phreye grades on improvement. Before determining semester grades, she eliminates the lowest of the first four test scores. Then she places the highest of the last three scores in the highest score column. Using Ms. Phreye's system, find the mean, or average, of each student's scores. Use the eight unmarked scores, including the one in the highest score column, to find the mean. Round the mean score to the nearest whole number and record it in the last column. The first one is done for you. Answer the questions based on this table.

	Weekly Test Scores								Highest Score	Mean Score
Edrea	78	93	~~62~~	92	86	89	91	96	96	90
Nevin	75	80	89	75	95	86	90	89		
Philippa	50	87	93	87	87	87	98	94		
Quinn	95	100	100	98	95	96	100	89		
Ramiro	87	94	35	64	50	100	36	50		
Tessa	89	93	88	97	100	100	97	100		
Zedra	55	60	56	72	43	52	60	70		

Use the students' cumulative scores to answer the following questions.

1. What is the mean of all the cumulative scores? __________
2. What is the range of these scores? __________
3. What is the mode of these scores? __________
4. What is the median of these scores? __________.

Use individual student's scores to answer the following questions.

5. What is the range of Ramiro's scores? __________
6. What is the mode of Philippa's scores? __________
7. What is the median of Nevin's scores? __________

Look at Those Test Grades name ______________________

End of Semester

Ms. Prince recorded the following grades for the unit test. Each of her tests has bonus points built in and identified. Read the data in the stem-and-leaf plot then answer the questions.

11	1	3	4	4	4	5	6	9					
10	0	0	0	1	1	3	4	5	5	8	9		
9	3	4	5	5	5	5	5	6	7	7	8	9	9
8	1	1	2	3	4	5	6	6	7	8	9	9	
7	1	2	5	7	8	8							
6	2	3	3	4	7	9	9						
5	0	2	6	9									
4	1	6	8										

Grading Scale

A+	105+
A	96–104
A-	90–95
B	80–89
C	70–79
Retake	< 69

...THINK I'LL MAKE LIKE A TREE AND LEAF...

1. How many students took the test? ________
2. What percentage of students earned an A- or better? _____
3. What percentage of students had to retake the test? _____
4. What is the range of grades? __________
5. What is the mode? ________________
6. Cal took the test. What is the probability that he had to retake the test? ______________
7. Sasha took the test. What is the probability that she passed the test? _____________
8. How many students earned the following grades:

A+ ___________ A ___________

A- ___________ B ___________

C ___________ Retake ___________

9. What is the probability that Tony earned a B or a C? ______________________
10. Did more students pass, or did more students need to retake the test? Explain _____________

____

____

Name That Inventor

Name ______________________

Famous Inventor's Birthday

Solve each problem. Use the code to find out which inventor was born on February 11, 1847. Among this inventor's 1,300 plus patents are the carbon telephone transmitter, the phonograph, and the incandescent lamp. Who is this famous inventor?

3,741	197	243	518	268	669	864	635	5,410	725	299	411
A	D	E	H	I	L	M	N	O	S	T	V

1. 66 $\overline{)246,906}$
2. 42 $\overline{)11,256}$
3. 97 $\overline{)524,770}$
4. 55 $\overline{)34,925}$
5. 38 $\overline{)15,618}$
6. 61 $\overline{)31,598}$
7. 13 $\overline{)8,697}$
8. 94 $\overline{)18,518}$
9. 71 $\overline{)21,229}$
10. 76 $\overline{)18,468}$
11. 18 $\overline{)15,552}$
12. 25 $\overline{)18,125}$

THIS GUY HAD ONLY THREE MONTHS OF FORMAL SCHOOLING!

___ ___ ___ ___ ___ ___　　___ ___ ___ ___　　___ ___ ___ ___ ___ ___
 9　 6　 3　 11　 1　 12　　 1　 7　 5　 1　　 10　 8　 2　 12　 3　 4

Valentine's Day

Message to a Sweetheart

Name ____________________

SHOW WORK!

Solve the problems. Find the answers in the Coordinate Box. Write the grid coordinates in the blanks above the problem numbers, then find them on the grid. Connect the points in order. Complete the grid by connecting the grid coordinates listed to the right of the grid. You'll discover a valentine message.

1. $\frac{4}{5} \times \frac{15}{16} =$

2. $\frac{6}{7} \times \frac{7}{12} =$

3. $\frac{2}{3} \times \frac{9}{16} =$

4. $\frac{5}{18} \times \frac{9}{10} =$

5. $\frac{16}{21} \times \frac{7}{8} =$

6. $\frac{12}{25} \times \frac{15}{16} =$

7. $\frac{4}{9} \times \frac{6}{10} =$

8. $\frac{6}{15} \times \frac{5}{6} =$

9. $\frac{8}{9} \times \frac{3}{20} =$

10. $\frac{7}{20} \times \frac{4}{7} =$

11. $\frac{7}{16} \times \frac{6}{21} =$

Coordinate Box

(4, 6)	$\frac{1}{2}$	(7, 8)	$\frac{1}{3}$	(5, 9)	$\frac{1}{5}$	(9, 9)	$\frac{9}{20}$	(7, 4)	$\frac{3}{8}$
(4, 8)	$\frac{3}{4}$, $\frac{3}{24}$	(8, 9)	$\frac{4}{15}$	(6, 9)	$\frac{2}{15}$	(10, 6)	$\frac{1}{4}$	(10, 8)	$\frac{2}{3}$

(___, ___)1 (___, ___)2 (___, ___)3 (___, ___)4 (___, ___)5

(___, ___)6 (___, ___)7 (___, ___)8 (___, ___)9 (___, ___)10 (___, ___)11

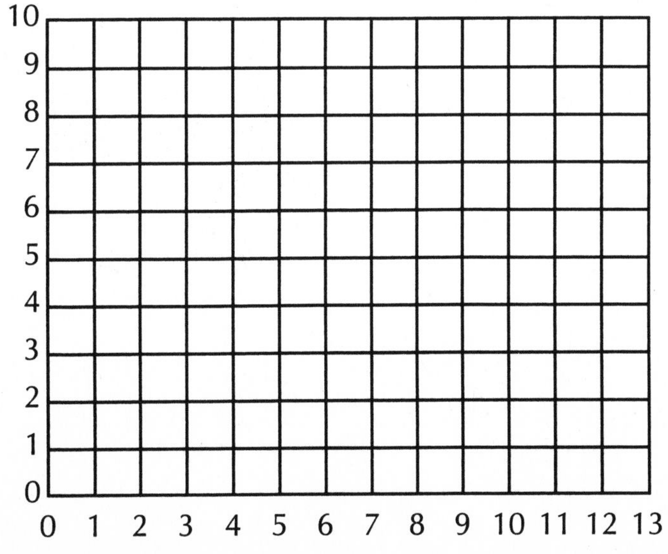

(1, 2), (1, 1), (2, 1), (2, 3), (1, 3), (1, 2), (2, 2) stop

(4, 1), (3, 1), (3, 3), (4, 3), (3, 2) stop

(8, 1), (8, 3), (7, 2), (6, 3), (6, 1) stop

(9, 1), (9, 3) stop

(10, 1), (10, 3), (11, 1), (11, 3) stop

(12, 2), (13, 3), (12, 3), (12, 1), (13, 1) stop

Valentine Rhyme

Valentine's Day

Name ____________________________

Solve each problem. Circle the word in each row with the corresponding answer. Read the words top to bottom and write the rhyme on the lines below.

1. $6 + 2 \times 3 - 6 \div 2$	3 I	21 Love	9 Roses
2. $(5 - 2) \div (2 + 1)$	1 Are	5 Is	$4\frac{1}{3}$ Am
3. $12 \div 4 + 2 \times 5$	10 In	13 Red	$\frac{6}{7}$ A
4. $(4 + 6 \div 2) - (10 \div 2 - 5)$	5 Many	7 Violets	$-2\frac{2}{3}$ Love
5. $2 \times (3 + 4 - 5) - 10$	−5 Splendor	−1 With	−6 Are
6. $(10 \div 2 + 10) \div 3$	$\frac{1}{6}$ Thing	$7\frac{2}{3}$ Blue	5 White
7. $2 \times 2 \times 5 \times 4 - 6$	74 Mathematics	−40 Sugar	56 I
8. $(16 \div 2 - 6) \times 12$	−64 Love	24 Is	−48 Am
9. $7 \times 6 - 10 \times 8 \div 2$	−112 Sweet	128 You	2 Fun
10. $8 \times 8 \div 2 + -4 \times 5$	12 Both	−160 Do	$-6\frac{2}{5}$ And
11. $(42 - 20) \div 11 + 8$	$1\frac{3}{19}$ You	$43\frac{1}{19}$ So	10 Day
12. $(8 - 2 \times 2) \times 20 \div 5$	16 And	12 Are	48 Love
13. $(5 \times 5 - 10) \div 5$	−1 Me?	23 You!	3 Night!

FOOTBALLS ARE BROWN,
GOLF BALLS ARE WHITE,
TO DO THIS PAGE MIGHT
TAKE YOU ALL NIGHT!

Valentine Message:

____

____

Presidents

Presidents' Day

Name ______________________

Use the clues to complete the matrix and determine each president's term of office.

1. Lyndon B. Johnson became president when President John Kennedy was shot. He finished Kennedy's term and was elected for an additional four years.
2. John Adams was the second president of the United States.
3. Ulysses S. Grant and Theodore Roosevelt were both elected to two terms.
4. Andrew Johnson was the seventeenth president. He was elected just after Abraham Lincoln, the sixteenth president, and just before Ulysses S. Grant, the eighteenth president.
5. Millard Fillmore was the thirteenth president. He resided in the White House when the first bathtub with running water was installed.

	John Adams	Millard Fillmore	Ulysses S. Grant	Andrew Johnson	Lyndon B. Johnson	Theodore Roosevelt	William H. Taft
1797–1801							
1850–1853							
1865–1869							
1869–1877							
1901–1909							
1909–1913							
1963–1969							

John Adams: ______________________

Millard Fillmore: ______________________

Ulysses S. Grant: ______________________

Andrew Johnson: ______________________

Lyndon B. Johnson: ______________________

Theodore Roosevelt: ______________________

William Howard Taft: ______________________

It's Still Winter

name ______________________

1. $4\frac{1}{3} \div 2\frac{8}{9} =$

2. $2\frac{1}{5} \div 1\frac{1}{10} =$

3. $5\frac{1}{4} \div 2\frac{1}{3} =$

4. $4\frac{1}{6} \div 1\frac{2}{3} =$

5. $2\frac{1}{7} \div 1\frac{2}{9} =$

6. $3\frac{8}{9} \div 8\frac{1}{3} =$

7. $4\frac{1}{2} \div 2\frac{8}{9} =$

8. $2\frac{2}{3} \div 4\frac{2}{3} =$

9. $2\frac{3}{4} \div 4\frac{1}{8} =$

10. $9\frac{3}{7} \div 5\frac{1}{2} =$

11. $3\frac{3}{4} \div 2\frac{1}{2} =$

12. $5\frac{1}{3} \div 2\frac{2}{15} =$

Code

E	$1\frac{1}{2}$	**T**	$2\frac{1}{2}$
I	$\frac{4}{7}$	**V**	$1\frac{58}{77}$
n	$2\frac{1}{4}$	**W**	$\frac{2}{3}$
O	2	**y**	$\frac{7}{15}$
R	$1\frac{1}{3}$		
S	$1\frac{5}{7}$		

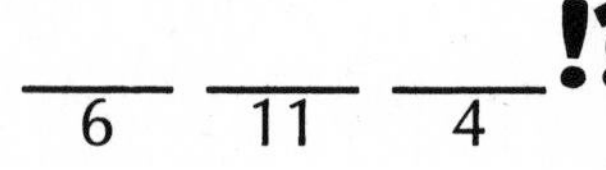

SCIENTIFIC FACT NO. 33: IT'S USUALLY COLDER IN THE WINTER!

___ ___ ___ ___ ,
8 10 3 4

___ ___ ___ ___ ___ ___
9 8 3 12 11 7

___ ___ ___ ___   ___ ___ ___ !?
2 5 1 7   6 11 4

Leprechaun's Gold

Name ______________________________

Find the products. Then shade the corresponding pieces of gold to find out which leprechaun has the most gold.

1. $\frac{2}{5} \times \frac{3}{8} =$

2. $\frac{4}{7} \times \frac{1}{8} =$

3. $\frac{3}{5} \times \frac{5}{6} =$

4. $\frac{8}{9} \times \frac{3}{10} =$

5. $\frac{2}{9} \times \frac{6}{7} =$

6. $\frac{1}{5} \times \frac{10}{11} =$

7. $\frac{4}{13} \times \frac{1}{8} =$

8. $\frac{14}{15} \times \frac{5}{6} =$

9. $\frac{4}{9} \times \frac{3}{4} =$

10. $\frac{2}{3} \times \frac{9}{10} =$

11. $\frac{4}{5} \times \frac{1}{4} =$

12. $\frac{15}{16} \times \frac{2}{5} =$

13. $\frac{7}{9} \times \frac{9}{28} =$

14. $\frac{3}{8} \times \frac{4}{9} =$

15. $\frac{9}{14} \times \frac{2}{3} =$

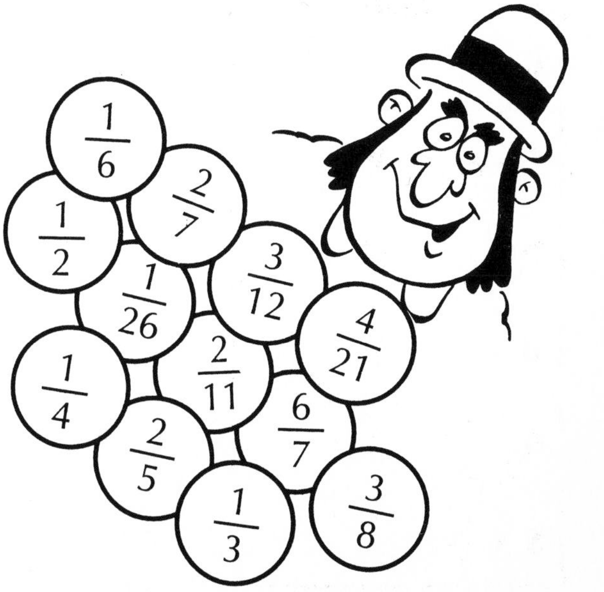

Hide and Seek

Name ___________________________

St. Patrick's Day

The leprechauns have hidden more than gold. Find the following mathematical terms in the puzzle. If a math term consists of more than one word, it can change direction at the space. Words can be found →, ←, ↗↙, ↕. They can be spelled forward or backward.

addend	liter	mass	quotient
area	ordered pair	mean	range
average	order of operations	median	rate
bar graph	prime number	percent	ratio
factor tree	square root	perimeter	meter
fraction	tree diagram	probability	sum
gram	greatest common factor	product	mode
numerator	least common denominator	proportion	unit rate
integers	least common multiple		

Q	U	O	T	I	E	N	T	O	P	E	R	A	T	I	O	N	S	T	A
M	D	I	A	G	R	A	M	F	N	U	M	E	R	A	T	F	M	E	A
P	R	E	G	R	A	T	I	O	O	R	D	T	N	E	C	R	E	P	R
I	N	E	M	R	V	L	I	R	E	D	R	O	R	D	E	A	R	E	M
Y	N	R	E	P	E	R	I	M	E	T	E	R	A	N	G	C	O	M	M
T	E	T	E	R	R	A	N	N	U	N	U	M	E	R	A	T	O	R	S
I	I	L	E	T	A	R	T	A	N	G	L	E	M	E	D	I	A	N	Q
L	I	T	E	G	G	N	D	E	N	O	M	I	N	A	T	O	R	T	U
I	N	T	E	R	E	Q	O	M	S	E	S	Q	U	A	R	N	I	O	A
B	L	E	A	S	T	R	Q	M	G	T	C	O	M	M	O	N	U	O	R
A	R	M	E	T	C	O	S	N	M	E	D	I	A	S	Q	F	M	R	E
B	A	B	I	O	A	S	A	P	R	O	D	U	C	T	I	A	E	M	T
O	T	N	M	E	E	R	T	R	O	T	C	A	F	L	S	C	E	N	A
R	I	M	R	A	R	Q	L	E	A	S	T	M	U	S	M	T	R	O	R
P	O	A	P	R	I	M	B	A	R	G	R	A	P	H	E	O	Q	C	T
N	U	M	B	E	A	N	O	I	T	R	O	P	O	R	P	R	D	R	I
M	U	L	T	I	P	L	E	S	R	E	B	M	U	N	U	E	C	E	N
A	D	D	E	N	D	E	R	E	D	R	O	S	Q	E	M	I	R	P	U

Four-Leaf Clovers

Name ____________________

Multiply the numbers in each cloverleaf by the number in its center. Shade each clover whose four products add up to a number > 4,000. These are the genuine four-leaf clovers.

15.69 36.9
24
65.4 47.04

87.234 5.739
16.5
111.5 209.42

9.356 45.62
82.1
6.444 17.5

8.43 3.68
301.4
.45 1.418

.087 .152
2,349
.008 1.013

45.91 2.89
44
100.7 .0245

72.08 63.16
9.88
258.04 140.08

467.2 8,560.5
.099
9,369 7,305.6

How Could It Be True?

Name ______________________________

Don't be fooled by these challenging problems! Complete the base table which is continued at the bottom of the page. Then use both tables to find the correct base to make each problem true.

base 10	1	2	3	4	5	6	7	8	9	10	11	12	13	14	15	16	17
base 7	1	2	3	4	5	6	10	11	12	13	14	15	16	20	21	22	23
base 5	1	2	3	4	10	11	12	13	14	20	21	22	23	24	30	31	32
base 4	1	2	3	10	11	12	13	20	21	22	23	30	31	32	33	100	101
base 3	1	2	10	11	12	20	21	22	100	101	102	110	112	112	120	121	122

1. 10__ + 21__ = 101__
2. 101__ - 20__ = 21__
3. 5__ x 3__ = 21__
4. 11__ + 23__ = 100__
5. 1,022__ ÷ 21__ = 12__
6. 111__ - 24__ = 32__
7. 2__ x 14__ = 31__
8. 41__ ÷ 3__ = 12__
9. 1,020__ - 221__ = 22__
10. 20__ x 3__ = 110__
11. 23__ + 102__ = 131__
12. 13__ x 2__ = 31__
13. 102__ ÷ 3__ = 14__
14. 40__ - 33__ = 4__
15. 1,002__ - 21__ = 211__

base 10	18	19	20	21	22	23	24	25	26	27	28	29	30	31	32	33	34
base 7													42				
base 5										102							
base 4						113											
base 3																1020	

Spring's Upon Us

Name ____________________

Color the squares as indicated. Use the grid coordinates to discover a sign of spring.

	1	2	3	4	5	6	7
A							
B							
C							
D							
E							
F							
G							
H							
I							
J							
K							
L							

Color Key

B = color blue

O = color orange

G = color green

Coordinates

B A-3, A-5, D-4, E-1, E-7, G-3, H-1, H-2, H-3, H-4, H-6, H–7, I-1, I-2, I-3, I-6, J-1, J-2, J-3, J-5, K-1, K-2, K-3, L-1, L-2, L-3, L-7

B \ O B-1, C-2, G-6

O \ B A-2, B-3, E-6, F-7

O / B B-7, C-6, F-3, G-2

B / O A-6, B -5, E-2, F-1

O A-1, A-4, A-7, B-2, B-4, B-6, C-3, C-4, C-5, D-1, D-2, D-3, D-5, D-6, D-7, E-3, E-4, E-5, F-2, F-4, F-6, G-1, G-4, G-7

G \ O F-5

G G-5, H-5, J-4, J-7, K-4, K-5, K-6, L-4, L-5

G / B I-5, K-7, L-6

B / G I-4, I-7, J-6

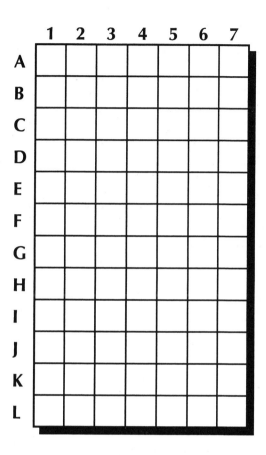

SCIENTIFIC FACT NO. 1372: SPRING IS A GREAT TIME TO START A BASEBALL SEASON!

April Showers

Name ______________________________

Springtime

April showers bring May flowers. Write the numbers that are on the petals in order on the rain-drops to arrive at the answer in the center of the flower. Use order of operations.

___ − ___ + ___ x ___ − ___ ÷ ___ − ___

Flower: center 11; petals 2, 4, 5, 6, 8, 11, 22

___ ÷ ___ + ___ ÷ ___ − ___ + ___ x ___

Flower: center 19; petals 2, 5, 6, 7, 6, 10, 36

___ ÷ ___ + ___ + ___ ÷ ___ − ___ x ___

Flower: center 0; petals 2, 3, 6, 9, 10, 21, 24

___ x ___ ÷ ___ + ___ x ___ ÷ ___ − ___

Flower: center 6; petals 2, 4, 5, 7, 8, 9, 10

___ ÷ ___ x ___ ÷ ___ + ___ − ___ + ___

Flower: center 4; petals 1, 2, 4, 5, 9, 6, 18

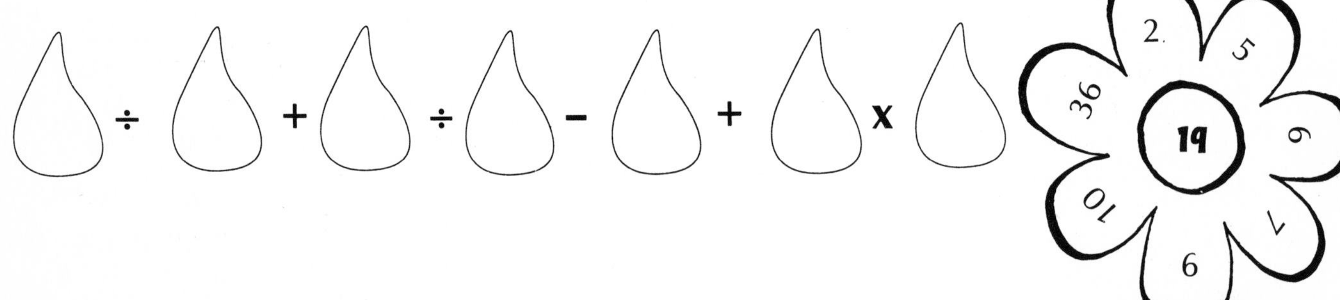

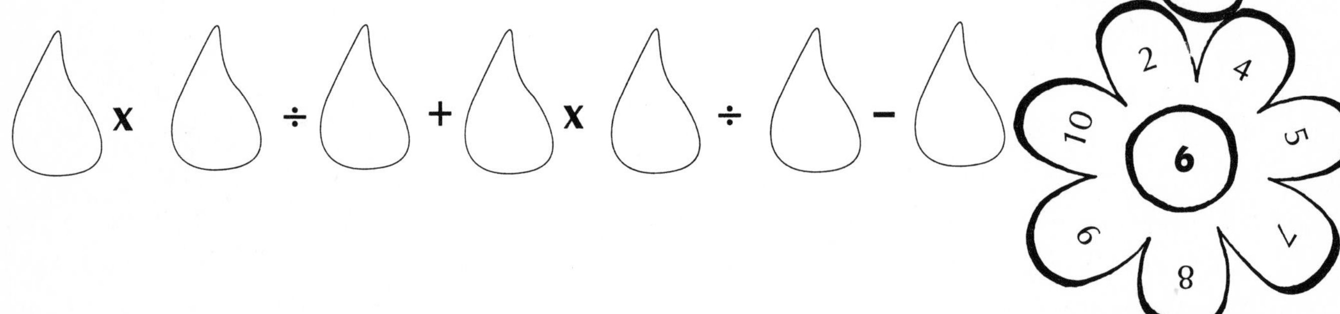

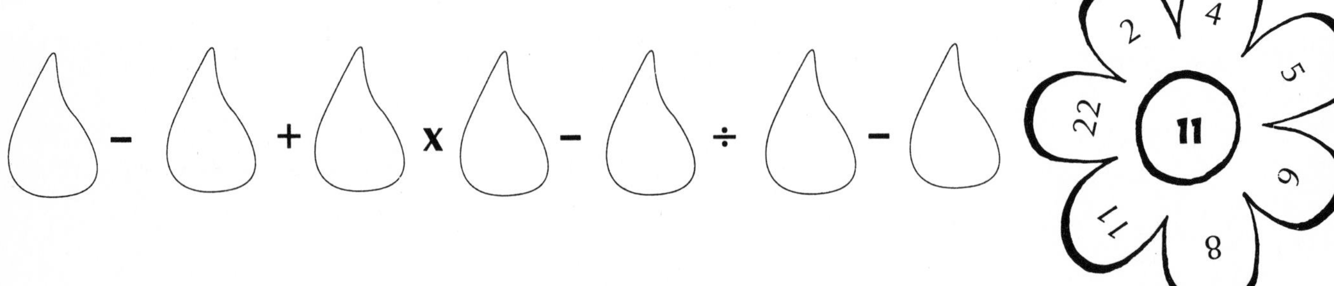

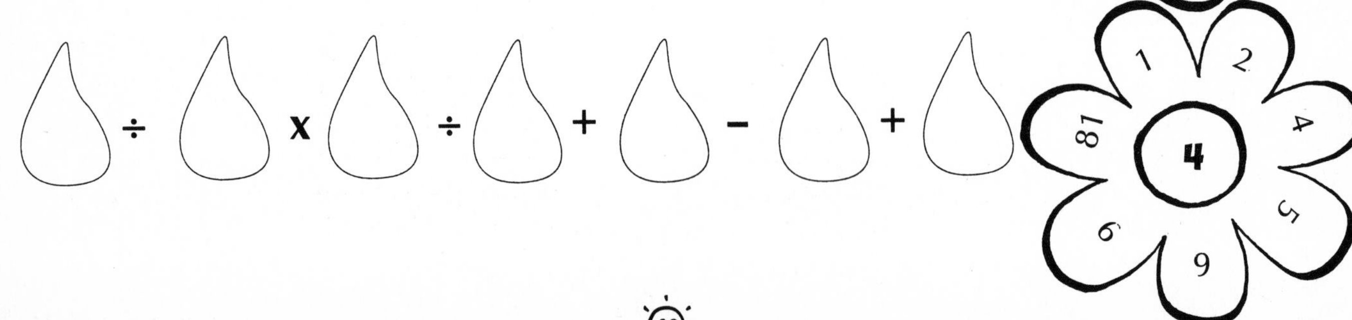

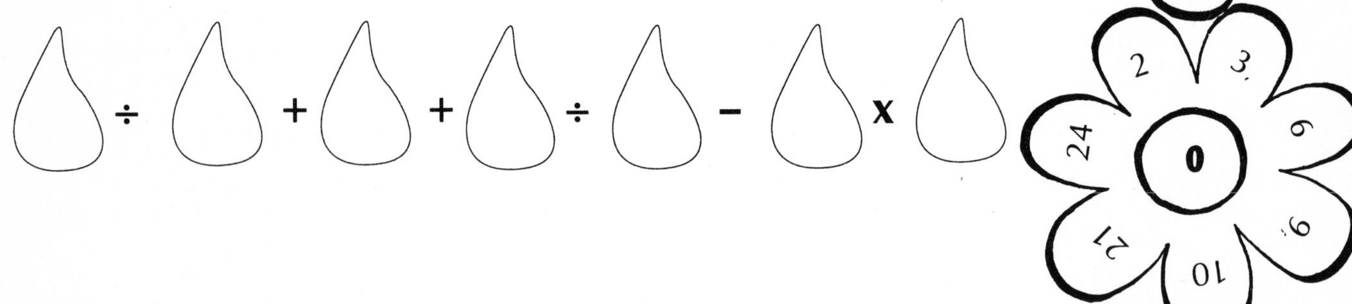

Springtime

Water the Flowers

Name ______________________

Solve each problem. Find the answers in the tic-tac-toe boards at the bottom of the page. Draw a raindrop on the answers of the odd-numbered problems and a flower on the answers of the even-numbered problems. Who won each game?

1. $2\frac{1}{3} + 7\frac{1}{6}$

2. $8\frac{4}{5} + 1\frac{4}{15}$

3. $7\frac{3}{4} - 2\frac{1}{6}$

4. $1\frac{6}{7} + 5\frac{1}{2}$

5. $8\frac{3}{8} - 5\frac{3}{4}$

6. $4\frac{1}{4} - 1\frac{2}{3}$

7. $1\frac{5}{6} + 1\frac{8}{9}$

8. $10\frac{1}{2} - 6\frac{2}{3}$

9. $2\frac{5}{6} + 4\frac{1}{3}$

10. $1\frac{3}{8} + 1\frac{3}{4}$

11. $5\frac{1}{8} - 3\frac{3}{4}$

12. $3\frac{5}{16} + 2\frac{5}{8}$

13. $2\frac{3}{5} + 3\frac{2}{3}$

14. $6\frac{1}{4} - 1\frac{4}{5}$

15. $11\frac{13}{15} - 9\frac{1}{5}$

$5\frac{7}{12}$	$9\frac{1}{2}$	$7\frac{5}{14}$
$4\frac{1}{2}$	$3\frac{13}{18}$	$2\frac{5}{8}$
$2\frac{7}{12}$	$3\frac{5}{6}$	$10\frac{1}{15}$

$7\frac{1}{6}$	$5\frac{15}{16}$	$1\frac{3}{8}$
$2\frac{2}{3}$	$4\frac{9}{20}$	$1\frac{5}{7}$
$6\frac{4}{15}$	$3\frac{5}{9}$	$3\frac{1}{8}$

Gardens

name ______________________

Hy plans gardens. He needs to know the area and perimeter of each plot to determine the number of plants he needs and the amount of edging or fencing needed. Help him calculate the perimeter and area of the following plots.

1. area ______________

   perimeter ______________

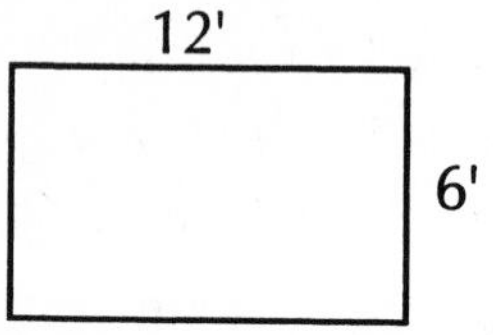

2. area ______________

   perimeter ______________

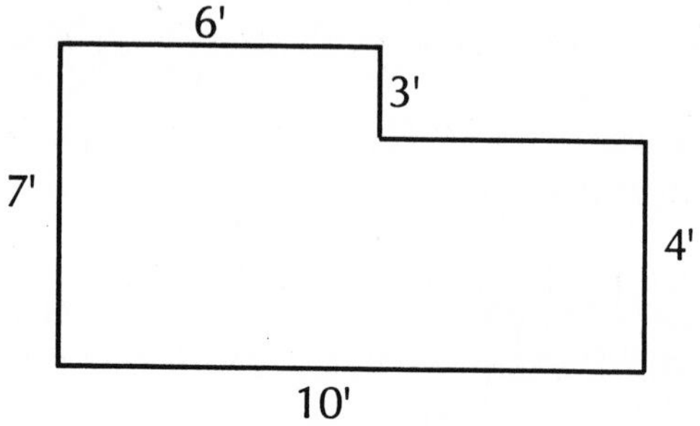

3. area ______________

   perimeter ______________

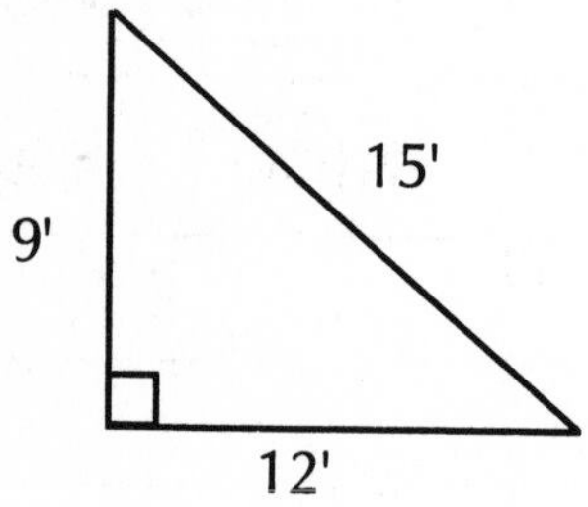

4. area ______________

   perimeter ______________

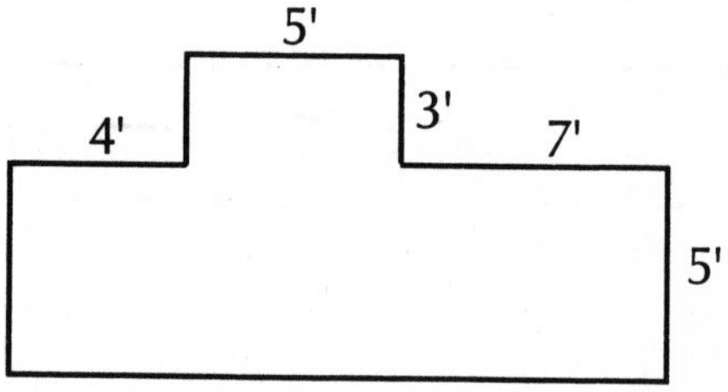

5. area ______________

   perimeter ______________

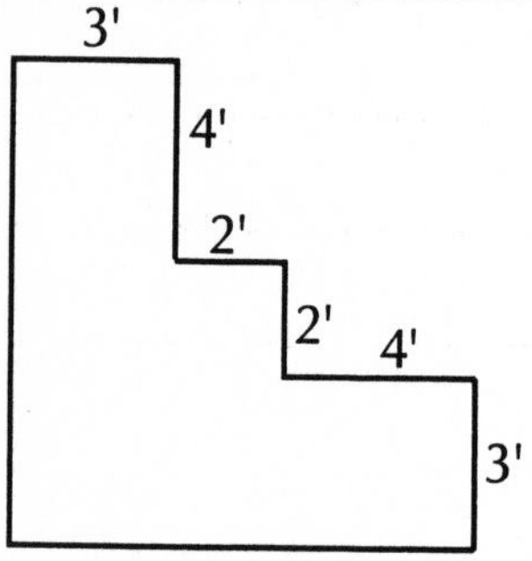

6. area ______________

   perimeter ______________

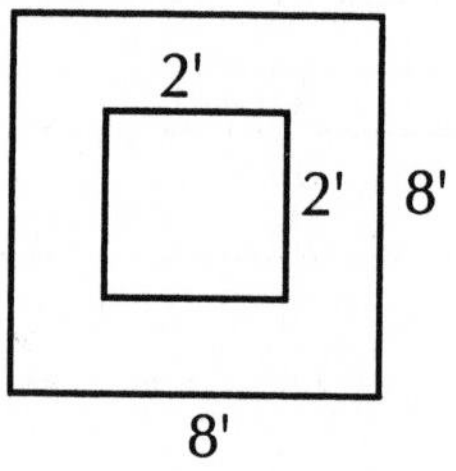

Do all figures with the same area have the same perimeter? ______________
Prove your answer here:

Do all figures with the same perimeter have the same area? ______________
Give evidence to support your answer:

Gardening

Name ______________________

Each of seven students was in charge of planting and caring for a different plant in the greenhouse. Use the matrix to determine who grew each item.

1. Alix planted a root vegetable.
2. The edible part of Zora's plant is green.
3. Paz's plant grew to be a leaf you can eat on a sandwich or in a salad.
4. Hal planted neither an edible root nor an edible flower.
5. The mature plant Isla tends is a seed you can eat.
6. Lev's plant is not a carrot, but it is a root vegetable.

DID YOU KNOW THAT FORMER PRESIDENT GEORGE BUSH *REALLY* DOESN'T LIKE BROCCOLI!

	broccoli	carrots	cauliflower	celery	corn	lettuce	radishes
Alix							
Ean							
Hal							
Isla							
Lev							
Paz							
Zora							

Alix grew ______________________

Ean grew ______________________

Hal grew ______________________

Isla grew ______________________

Lev grew ______________________

Paz grew ______________________

Zora grew ______________________

Tree Planting

Name ______________________

Arbor Day

The three grades at High Marks Middle School planted trees for Arbor Day. Below is a table with the data regarding the trees. Use the table to answer the probability questions.

Trees Planted on Arbor Day by High Marks Middle School

Grade	Spruce	Maple	Dogwood	Total
6	67	46	97	210
7	87	62	41	190
8	50	74	86	210
Totals				

SCIENTIFIC FACT NO. 2173: SOME TREES GROW REALLY BIG!

1. What is the probability that a sixth grader planted a spruce tree?

   ____

2. What is the probability that a seventh grader planted a maple or dogwood tree?

   ____

3. Terry is in eighth grade. What is the probability that she planted a dogwood tree?

   ____

4. Ashur is a sixth-grade student. What is the probability that he planted a spruce or maple?

   ____

5. What is the probability that a sixth-, seventh-, or eighth-grade student planted a

   dogwood tree? ______________

   a maple tree? ______________

The sixth graders were each able to take a tree home in a pot. Make a tree diagram to find out the choices.

clay pot	spruce
plastic pot	maple
cardboard pot	dogwood

What is the probability that a sixth grader . . .

- took home a spruce in a clay pot?____________
- took home a plastic pot? ______________
- took home a maple or dogwood? ____________
- took home a maple or a spruce in a clay pot? ___________

Who Planted More?

Name ______________________

Arbor Day

On Arbor Day, two classes planted trees. Shade the answers on the trees to find out which class planted the most.

Mr. Larson's Homeroom

755.87
.579
5.628
6.2197
474.64
58.559
6.512
644.74
32.571
226.839

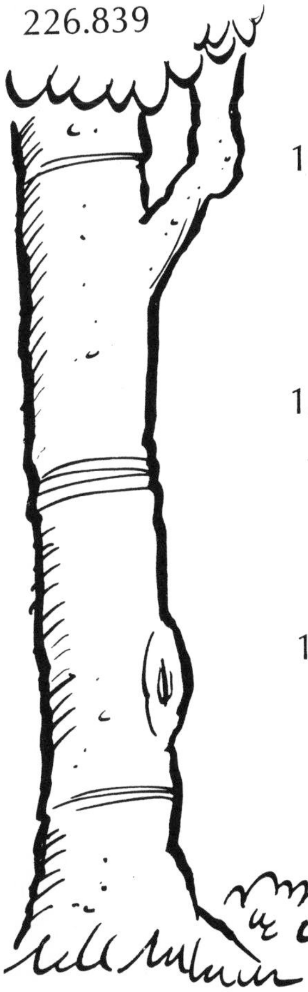

Ms. Young's Homeroom

709.69
290.479
4.9032
17.445
1.1148
329.059
755.87
350.738
302.54
1.6148

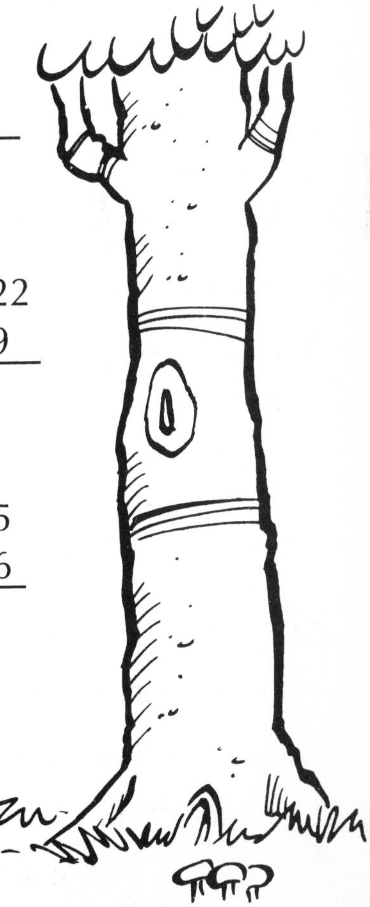

1. 276.2 − 49.361

2. 84.66 − 52.089

3. 653.64 − 8.9

4. 2.3004 − .6856

5. 375.4 − 72.86

6. 351.3 − .562

7. 8.26 − 1.748

8. 65.018 − 6.459

9. 942.06 − 186.19

10. 427.21 − 98.151

11. 1.738 − .6232

12. 548.3 − 73.66

13. 12.647 − 6.4273

14. 24.663 − 7.218

15. 6.8022 − 1.899

16. 333.2 − 42.721

17. 12.111 − 6.483

18. 2.055 − 1.476

Trees in the Ground

Arbor Day

Name ______________________

These seven friends each planted a different tree for Arbor Day. Use the matrix to determine who planted which tree.

1. Brier planted an evergreen.
2. Flint planted a fruit tree.
3. Guy planted a deciduous tree that does not bear edible fruit.
4. Jackie planted a fruit tree that grows in the northern United States.
5. Pam will be able to make pancake syrup from the sap of the tree she planted.
6. Ranee planted a tree brought across the United States by John Chapman.
7. Tyrone did not plant a spruce.

	Apple	Ash	Hemlock	Maple	Orange	Plum	Spruce
Brier							
Flint							
Guy							
Jackie							
Pam							
Ranee							
Tyrone							

Brier planted ______________________

Guy planted ______________________

Pam planted ______________________

Tyrone planted ______________________

Flint planted ______________________

Jackie planted ______________________

Ranee planted ______________________

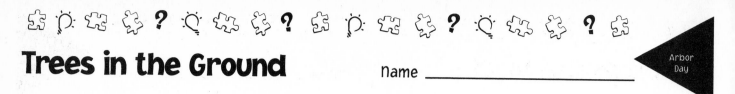

Through the Mud and Ooze

Name ______________________

Find the missing term in each proportion. Use cross products to make the ratios equivalent.

1. $\frac{6}{8} = \frac{d}{12}$ $d =$
2. $\frac{1}{c} = \frac{3}{6}$ $c =$
3. $\frac{p}{7.2} = \frac{5}{12}$ $p =$
4. $\frac{3}{9} = \frac{y}{21}$ $y =$
5. $\frac{3}{h} = \frac{4}{6}$ $h =$
6. $\frac{12}{4} = \frac{r}{12}$ $r =$
7. $\frac{2}{k} = \frac{10}{25}$ $k =$
8. $\frac{2}{7} = \frac{6}{m}$ $m =$
9. $\frac{4}{9} = \frac{r}{27}$ $r =$
10. $\frac{3}{8} = \frac{9}{z}$ $z =$
11. $\frac{6}{2} = \frac{12}{w}$ $w =$
12. $\frac{5}{3} = \frac{r}{6}$ $r =$
13. $\frac{g}{4} = \frac{7}{2}$ $g =$
14. $\frac{6}{4} = \frac{12}{s}$ $s =$
15. $\frac{25}{a} = \frac{5}{3}$ $a =$
16. $\frac{7}{p} = \frac{6}{36}$ $p =$
17. $\frac{5}{16} = \frac{10}{k}$ $k =$
18. $\frac{n}{4} = \frac{22}{8}$ $h =$
19. $\frac{2}{h} = \frac{4}{26}$ $h =$
20. $\frac{57}{u} = \frac{19}{2}$ $u =$
21. $\frac{8}{3} = \frac{j}{6}$ $j =$
22. $\frac{26}{y} = \frac{40}{8}$ $y =$
23. $\frac{4}{8.5} = \frac{8}{f}$ $f =$
24. $\frac{4}{6} = \frac{r}{5.85}$ $r =$
25. $\frac{s}{6} = \frac{9}{3}$ $s =$
26. $\frac{5}{4} = \frac{25}{g}$ $g =$
27. $\frac{2}{m} = \frac{6}{69}$ $m =$
28. $\frac{4}{3} = \frac{h}{21}$ $h =$

It's a muddy May. Use the answers to find the coordinates of the stepping stones in the mud and ooze. Using one color for the answers to the odd problems and another color for the even problems, shade each stone. Four stones in a row; horizontally, vertically, or diagonally; is one point. How many points do even and odd each get?

2	(2,4)	13	(4,3)
3	(4,5)	14	(5,3)
3.9	(0,3)	15	(5,6)
4	(5,5)	16	(6,5)
4.5	(3,6)	17	(2,5)
5	(5,4)	18	(4,2)
5.2	(2,3)	20	(1,2)
6	(0,2)	21	(1,2)
7	(4,4)	23	(3,1)
8	(3,3)	24	(2,6)
9	(4,6)	28	(0,1)
10	(3,5)	32	(3,2)
11	(1,3)	36	(3,4)
12	(6,3)	42	(6,6)

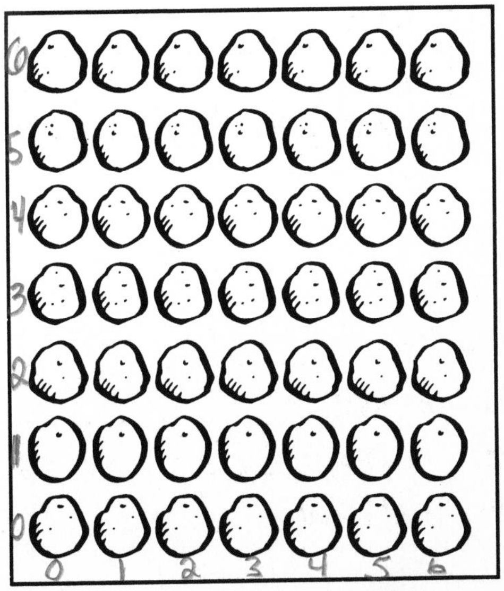

To Market, to Market

name ____________________

At the store, you noticed that prices vary greatly, and most items come in a variety of package sizes. A wise shopper finds the unit rate or unit price, then bases purchasing decisions on the best prices. Find the unit rate of each item. Circle the best deal.

Potato Chips—14-oz. package of Brand A for $2.66	14-oz. package of store brand for $1.96
8-oz. package of cream cheese for $1.84	8-oz. package of store brand for $1.36
Ice cream—2 quarts of Brand B for $5.00	2 quarts of Brand C for $3.20
Apple Juice—64 ounces of Brand M for $2.56	64 ounces of Brand T for $1.92
32 ounces of taco chips for $1.76	32 ounces of Brand T for $1.12
Microwave Popcorn—3 packages of Brand P for $3.36	4 packages of Brand S for $1.47
3 packages of snack crackers for $2.07	6 packages of Brand P crackers for $5.76

SCIENTIFIC FACT NO. 8167:
POPCORN AND SODA POP GO WELL
WITH LATE NIGHT MONSTER MOVIES!

Phone Bill

name ______________________

Mom and Dad were quite upset by the last phone bill and all the calls you made during the month of May. After a family discussion, it was decided that you would begin paying for your own calls. Your parents have decided to charge 6¢ for each local call (includes each time you hook up to the Internet) and 15¢ a minute for long-distance calls. Complete the phone record to determine how much you owe the "phone bank" after one week.

Date	Call Placed to	Local	Long Distance	Start	Stop	Total Time
5/6	Geena	/				
5/6	Tyler		/	5:05	5:15	
5/6	Internet	/				
5/6	Jill	/				
5/6	Geena	/				
5/6	Casilda		/	7:21	7:57	
5/6	Geena	/				
5/7	Taisha	/				
5/7	Internet	/				
5/7	Dane	/				
5/7	Fred	/				
5/7	Casilda		/	9:12	9:23	
5/8	Internet	/				
5/8	Tyler		/	6:03	6:14	
5/8	Geena	/				
5/8	Robyn		/	7:32	7:48	
5/9	Internet	/				
5/9	Grandma	/				
5/9	Casilda			6:44	6:58	
5/9	Internet	/				
5/9	Robyn		/	8:03	8:24	
5/10	Geena	/				
5/10	Jill	/				
5/10	Internet	/				
5/10	Taisha	/				
5/10	Fred	/				
5/11	Internet	/				
5/11	Tyler		/	5:36	5:55	
5/11	Robyn		/	6:12	6:19	
5/11	Internet	/				
5/12	Ty	/				
5/12	Casilda		/	7:38	7:44	
5/12	Geena	/				
5/12	Jill	/				
5/12	Internet	/				

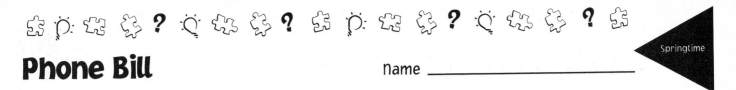

THE INTERNET STARTED AS A MILITARY PROJECT!

How much would you owe if your parents charged 10¢ a local call and 10¢ per minute for long-distance calls?

Measurements

Name ______________________

Use the metric units to answer the following spring gardening questions.

thousands	hundreds	tens	ones	tenths	hundredths	thousandths
kilo-	hecto-	deka-	base unit	deci-	centi-	milli-

1. a kilogram = ____________ grams
2. a milliliter = ____________ liters
3. a centimeter = ____________ meters
4. a hectoliter = ____________ liters
5. a decigram = ____________ grams
6. a dekameter = ____________ meters

7. Antonio needs a plant stake that is 1 meter high. The store measures them by the centimeter. How many centimeters long is the plant stake that Antonio needs to buy? __________

8. Jenna wants to buy 2.36 kilograms of seed. The seed comes in 20-gram packages. How many packages does she need to buy? __________

9. Tangie planted 100 grams of seed. Tell how many of each she planted:

   ______ mg ______ cg ______ hg ______ kg

10. The plants grew an average of 25 centimeters in 2 weeks. Convert to the following:

    ______ mm ______ dm ______ m ______ km

11. Each plant needs 2.5 liters of water. Sulu has a deciliter container. How many deciliter containers does he need to fill for each plant? __________

12. Each row has 8 plants. Each plant needs 2.5 liters of water. How many dekaliters of water are needed per row? __________

Coordinate Planes

Name ______________________

Use the coordinate planes to answer questions about and give ordered pairs.

Always start at (0, 0). Give directions to each location and name the ordered pair.

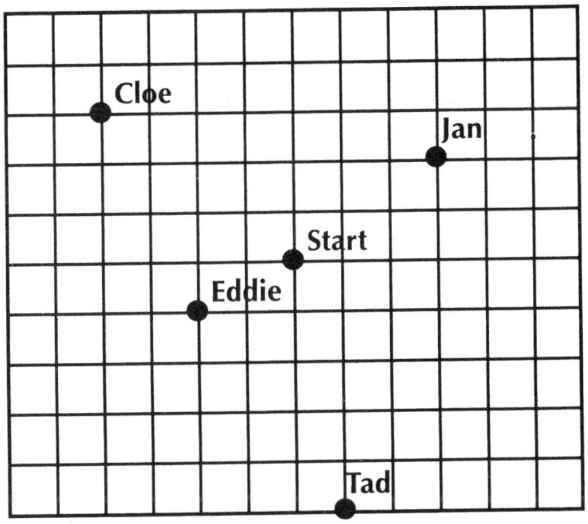

1. Jan's house:
   3 blocks east, 2 blocks north (3, 2)
2. Tad's house:
   ____
3. Cloe's house:
   ____
4. Eddie's house:
   ____

Plot each house (point) and name the ordered pair.

5. Meg's house: 4 blocks west, 5 blocks south (___ , ___)
6. John's house: 1 block east, 2 blocks south (___ , ___)
7. Fatima's house: 2 blocks east, 3 blocks north (___ , ___)
8. Dawnte's house: 2 blocks west, 4 blocks north (___ , ___)

Plot each set of points. Connect them in order. Label each shape.

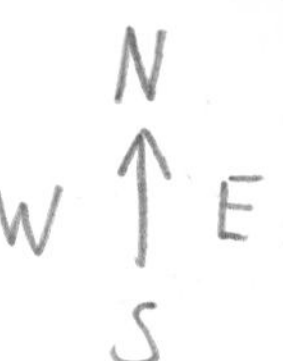

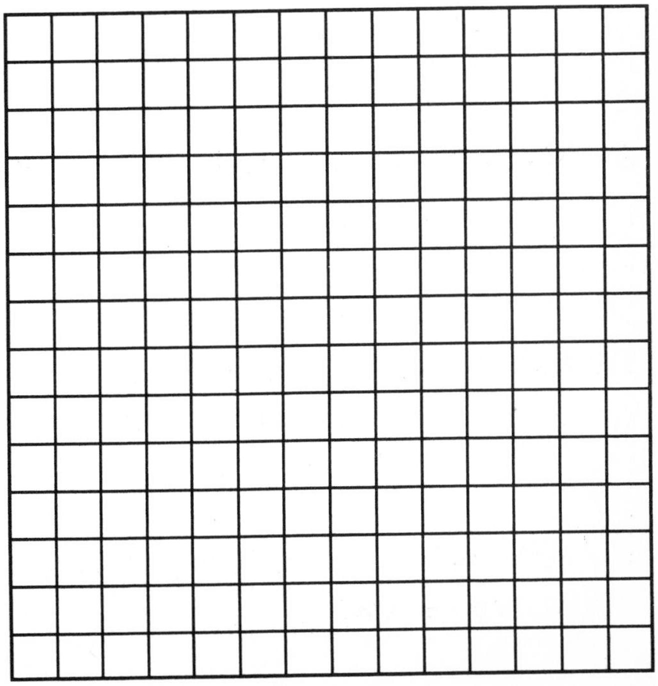

9. (3, 3) (3, -1) (5, -1)
   ____
10. (4, 0) (-4, 0) (0, 7)
   ____
11. (2, 2) (-1, 4) (-2, 0) (1, -2)
   ____
12. (1, 1) (-3, 1) (-3, -1) (1, -1)
   ____
13. (-2, -2) (6, -2) (6, 6) (-2, 6)
   ____
14. (1, -3) (2, -4) (2, -5) (1, -6) (0, -6) (-1, -5) (-1, -4) (0, -3) ______________________

Science Grades

Third Marking Period

Name ____________________

Mrs. Wall's grading scale uses points based on effort and quality. All assignments have built-in extra-credit points, so a student can earn more points than required. Use Mrs. Wall's scoring system to determine Jayde's grade for science this marking period. Her individual scores are printed below.

Science—Seeds and Plants
Teacher Mrs. Wall
Seeds and Plants Unit Grade ___

Grade #1—Vocabulary and Questions Assignments Score: ______

____ NHI* ____ F (0–49) ____ D (50–59) ____ C (60–69) ____ B (70–79) ____ A (80+)

Grade #2—Projects and Assignments Total Score: ______

____ F (0–190) ____ D (191–224) ____ C (225–260) ____ B (261–280) ____ A (281 +)

a) Edible Plant Parts homework (36 pts.**) ______ NHI* score ______
b) Plant Cycle (60 pts.**) ______ NHI* score ______
c) Leaf Rubbings and Information (60 pts.**) ______ NHI* score ______
d) Plants Parts drawing (25 pts.**) _____ NHI* score ______
e) Farmers' Market homework (50 pts.**) _____ NHI* score ____
f) Bean Parts poster (30 pts.**) _____ NHI* score ____
g) Bonus Work _____ NHI* score ______

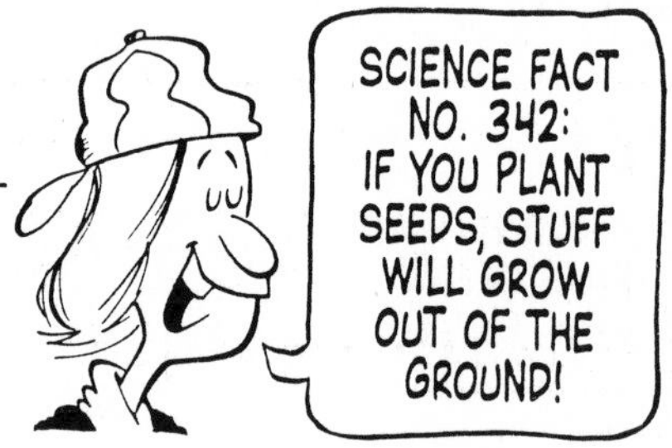
SCIENCE FACT NO. 342: IF YOU PLANT SEEDS, STUFF WILL GROW OUT OF THE GROUND!

Grade #3—Final Test (103 pts.) Score ____ Grade ____

____ F (<59) ____ D (60-79) ____ C (80-94)
____ B (90-105) ____ A (106+)

*NHI—not handed in (0 points)
**If minimum requirements were met

1. Jayde completed her vocabulary and questions assignments with a total of 35 points for vocabulary and 68 points for the questions.
2. Jayde did not hand in her Farmers' Market or her Edible Plant Parts homework assignments.
3. She did extra leaf rubbings with information about each tree type and its growing needs. She received 84 points for this assignment.
4. Jayde earned 36 points on her Bean Parts poster and 28 points on her Plant Parts assignment.
5. The Plant Cycle was top quality work for which Jayde earned 75 points.
6. Jayde designed and executed a scientific plan to determine the fertilizer preferences of green beans. When complete, she reported to the class and received 100 points for this.
7. Her final test was 127 points.

Let's Go Bowling

Name ____________________

Who won the bowling match? Use the following information to fill out the scoring sheet. The first two frames have been done for you.

- A ***frame*** consists of two consecutive balls thrown at the same 10 pins.
- Add the total from both balls thrown to the score of the previous frame to arrive at the total for that frame. The score of the first ball thrown in a frame is recorded to the left of the small top square, and the score of the second ball thrown is recorded in the small square. The accumulated score is recorded in the lower portion of the frame.
- Draw an **X** in the small square to record a strike. Add 10 points plus the score for the next two balls to that frame.
- Draw a / to record a spare. Add 10 points to that frame plus the score of the next ball.

Family Bowling Center

111 Main Street
Anywhere, Michigan
555-555-1234

	Name	1	2	3	4	5	6	7	8	9	10	Total
1	Hye	5 4 9	7 1 17									
2	Theddy	3 / 16	6 1 23									

Hye			Theddy		
Frame	**Ball 1**	**Ball 2**	**Frame**	**Ball 1**	**Ball 2**
1	5 pins down	4 pins down	1	3 pins down	7 pins down
2	7 pins down	1 pin down	2	6 pins down	1 pin down
3	3 pins down	7 pins down	3	9 pins down	1 pin down
4	5 pins down	0 pins down	4	8 pins down	1 pin down
5	10 pins down		5	7 pins down	3 pins down
6	8 pins down	1 pin down	6	10 pins down	
7	4 pins down	6 pins down	7	10 pins down	
8	10 pins down		8	9 pins down	0 pins down
9	6 pins down	2 pins down	9	8 pins down	2 pins down
10	3 pins down	5 pins down	10	10 pins down	
11			11	8 pins down	1 pin down

Golfing

name ______________________

Springtime Fun

Who won the 9 holes of golf? The person with the lowest score wins. Use the following golf information to fill out the scorecard and determine the winner.

Triple Bogey	par + 3	Birdie	par -1
Double Bogey	par +2	Eagle	par -2
Bogey	par + 1	Double Eagle	par -3
Par	expected score for the hole		

Scorecard for Golf Meadows

Hole Par	1 4	2 4	3 5	4 4	5 3	6 5	7 4	8 3	9 4	Out 36	Over/ Under Par
Rick											
Ernie											
Willie											
Ian											

Rick:

hole 1 = double bogey
hole 2 = triple bogey
hole 3 = bogey
hole 4 = par
hole 5 = bogey
hole 6 = birdie
hole 7 = par
hole 8 = double bogey
hole 9 = bogey

Ernie:

hole 1 = bogey
hole 2 = bogey
hole 3 = par
hole 4 = double bogey
hole 5 = par
hole 6 = triple bogey
hole 7 = bogey
hole 8 = par
hole 9 = birdie

Willie:

hole 1 = par
hole 2 = par
hole 3 = eagle
hole 4 = bogey
hole 5 = double bogey
hole 6 = par
hole 7 = birdie
hole 8 = bogey
hole 9 = par

Ian:

hole 1 = birdie
hole 2 = par
hole 3 = bogey
hole 4 = birdie
hole 5 = double bogey
hole 6 = bogey
hole 7 = bogey
hole 8 = par
hole 9 = birdie

Outdoor Fun

name ______________________

Solve each problem. Refer to the Coordinate Key to complete the code and make the diagram. Find out what the plans are for this weekend. Complete the problems at the bottom of the page to solve the letter code.

1. $\frac{1}{2} \times \frac{4}{5} =$

2. $4\frac{1}{5} \times 3\frac{4}{7} =$

3. $2\frac{2}{3} \div 2\frac{2}{9} =$

4. $2\frac{5}{8} + 4\frac{1}{2} =$

5. $6\frac{1}{3} - 4\frac{2}{3} =$

6. $\frac{6}{7} - \frac{1}{3} =$

7. $\frac{1}{5} + \frac{2}{3} =$

8. $6\frac{2}{3} \times 2\frac{7}{10} =$

Coordinate Key

(1, 1)	$\frac{2}{5}$
(3, 1)	$1\frac{1}{5}$
(3, 4)	$\frac{11}{21}$ and 15
(5, 1)	$7\frac{1}{8}$ and 18
(7, 5)	$1\frac{2}{3}$
(9, 2)	$1\frac{5}{9}$

___ ___ ___ ___ ___ ___ ___ ___
3 6 1 8 2 5 7 4

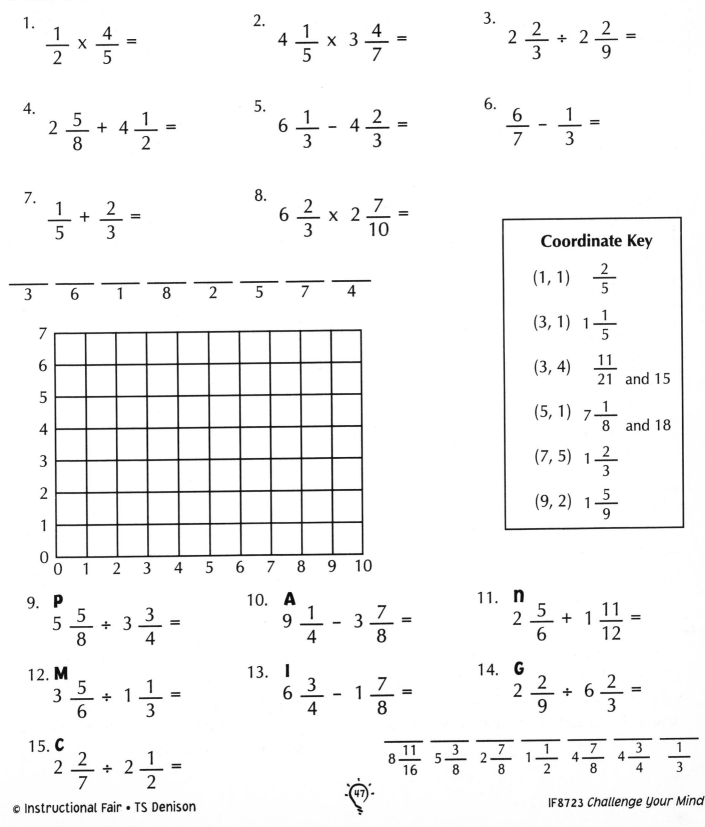

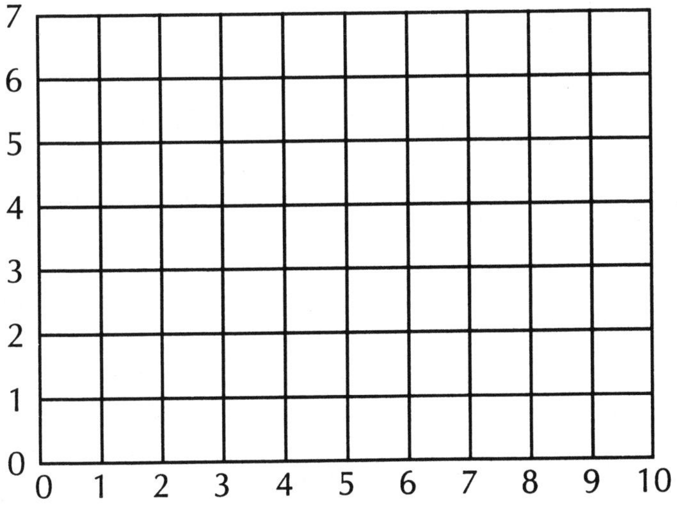

9. **P** $5\frac{5}{8} \div 3\frac{3}{4} =$

10. **A** $9\frac{1}{4} - 3\frac{7}{8} =$

11. **N** $2\frac{5}{6} + 1\frac{11}{12} =$

12. **M** $3\frac{5}{6} \div 1\frac{1}{3} =$

13. **I** $6\frac{3}{4} - 1\frac{7}{8} =$

14. **G** $2\frac{2}{9} \div 6\frac{2}{3} =$

15. **C** $2\frac{2}{7} \div 2\frac{1}{2} =$

___ ___ ___ ___ ___ ___ ___
$8\frac{11}{16}$ $5\frac{3}{8}$ $2\frac{7}{8}$ $1\frac{1}{2}$ $4\frac{7}{8}$ $4\frac{3}{4}$ $\frac{1}{3}$

Fishing

Springtime Fun

name ______________________

Multiply the numbers in the small fish and circle each correct answer in the largest fish to determine the "keepers."

634.82 x 2.93 =

31.547 x .68 =

8.6291 x 77.9 =

57.81 x 6.74 =

1860.0226

672.20689

6272.06

18600.226

386.9394

21.45196

389.6394

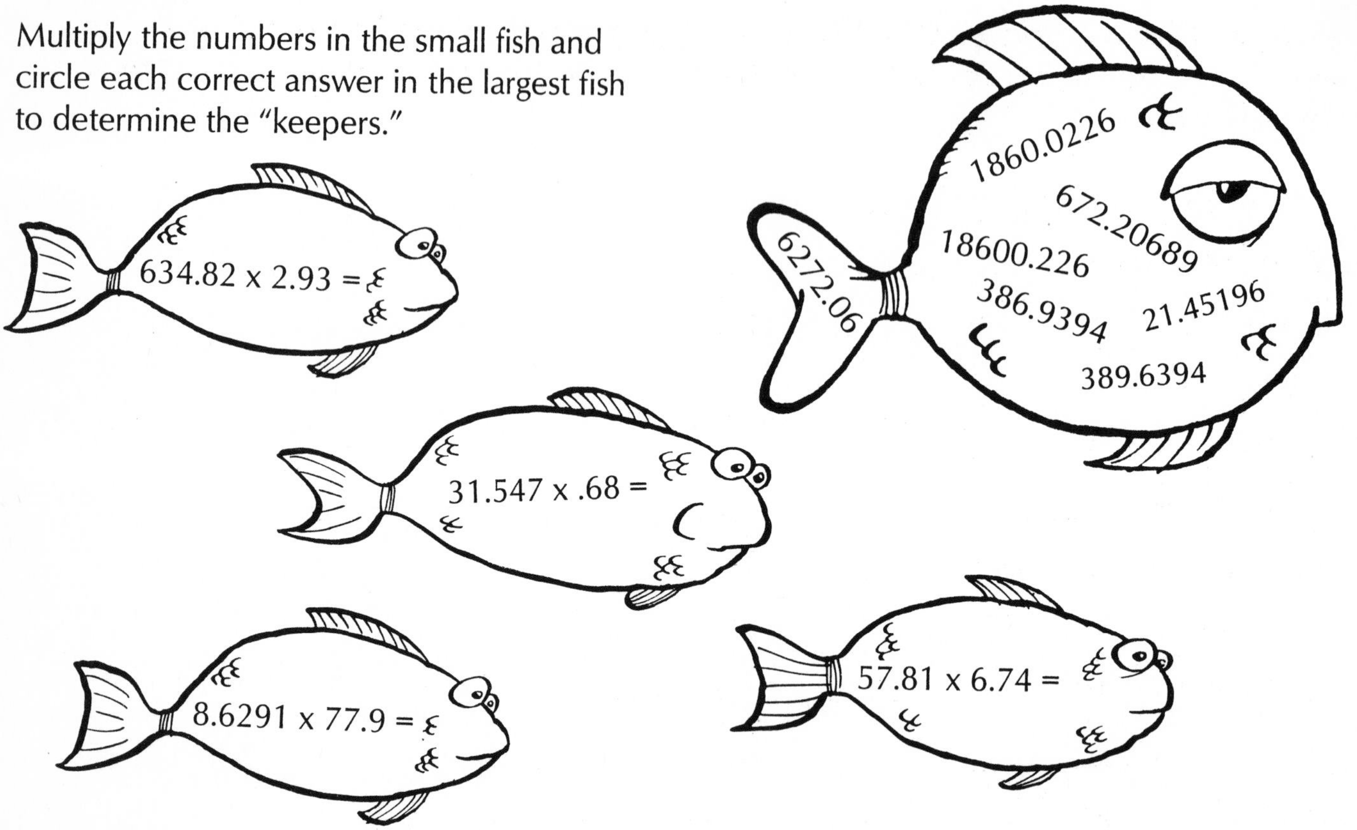

Divide the numbers in each small fish and circle the correct answers in the large fish.

.948315 ÷ .015 =

1.42298 ÷ 26 =

33.2648 ÷ 4.3 =

218.688 ÷ 6.7 =

5.473

326.4

32.64

0.05473

7.736

63.221

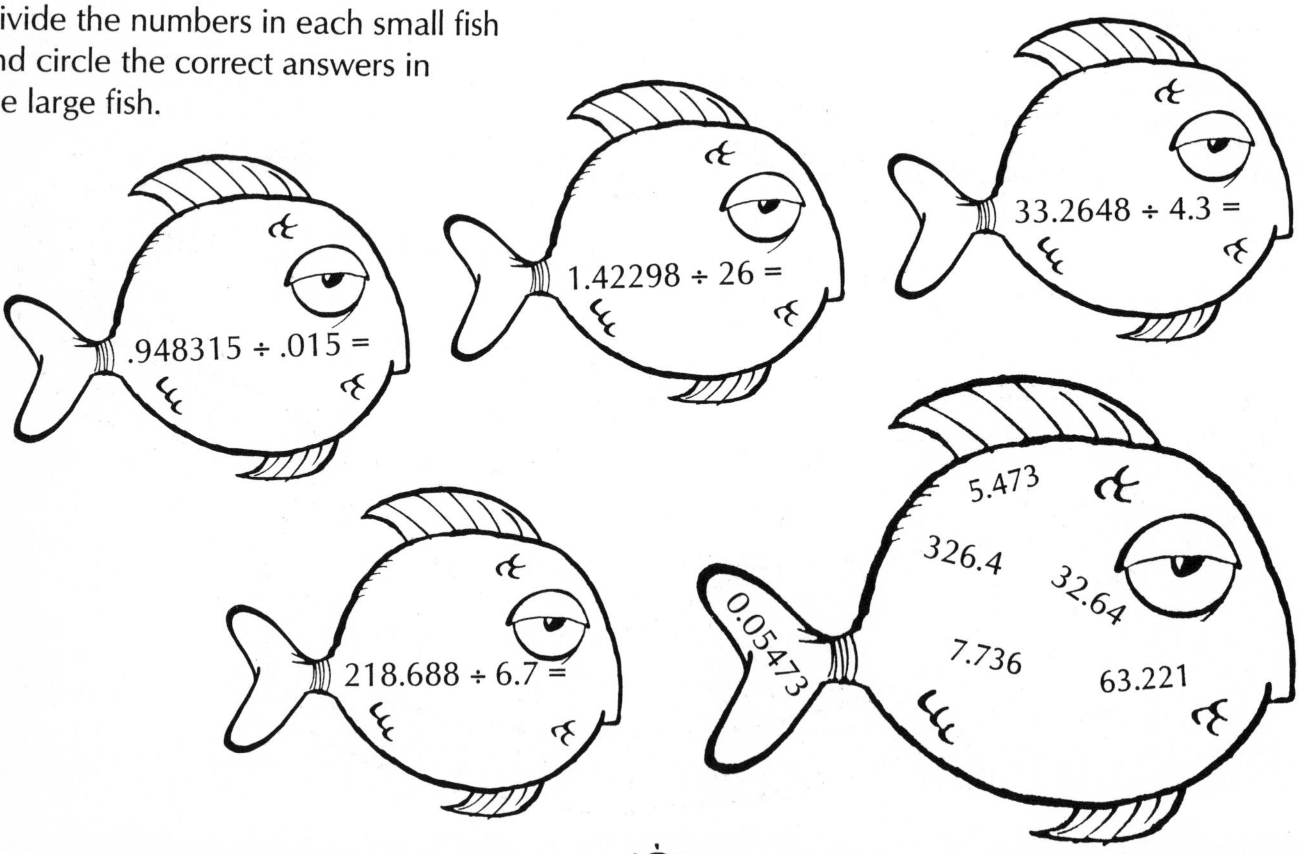

Jump into the Pool

Name ______________________

Solve the problems and place each answer in the appropriate "pool" of the Venn diagram. Remember, Venn diagrams have an outside set. Place a star next to each problem whose answer goes in the outside set.

1. 3,467,931 + 4,813,566 = ______________________
2. 2,791,342 x 27 = ______________________
3. 6,943,782 – 2,395,824 = ______________________
4. 3,890,688 ÷ 68 = ______________________
5. 8,206,512 ÷ 34 = ______________________
6. 28 x 358,491 = ______________________
7. 3,695,842 + 1,783,395 = ______________________
8. 8,213,234 – 3,846,709 = ______________________
9. 6,054,001 – 1,968,157 = ______________________
10. 1,972,501 x 36 = ______________________
11. 8,100,569 + 1,939,854 = ______________________
12. 10,442,813 ÷ 29 = ______________________

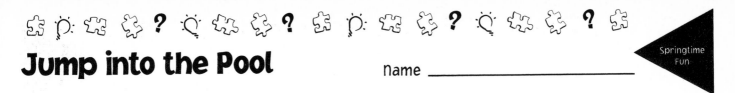

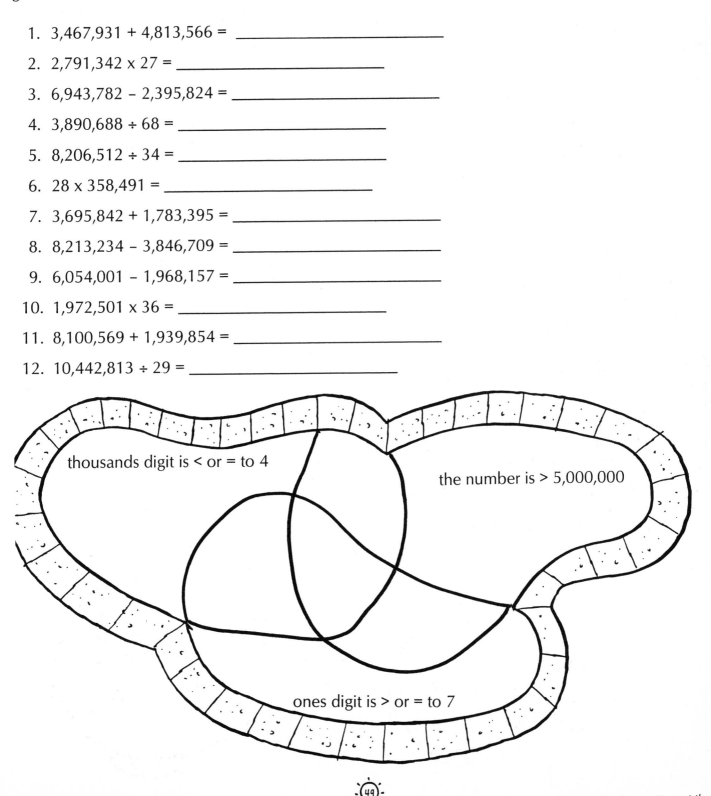

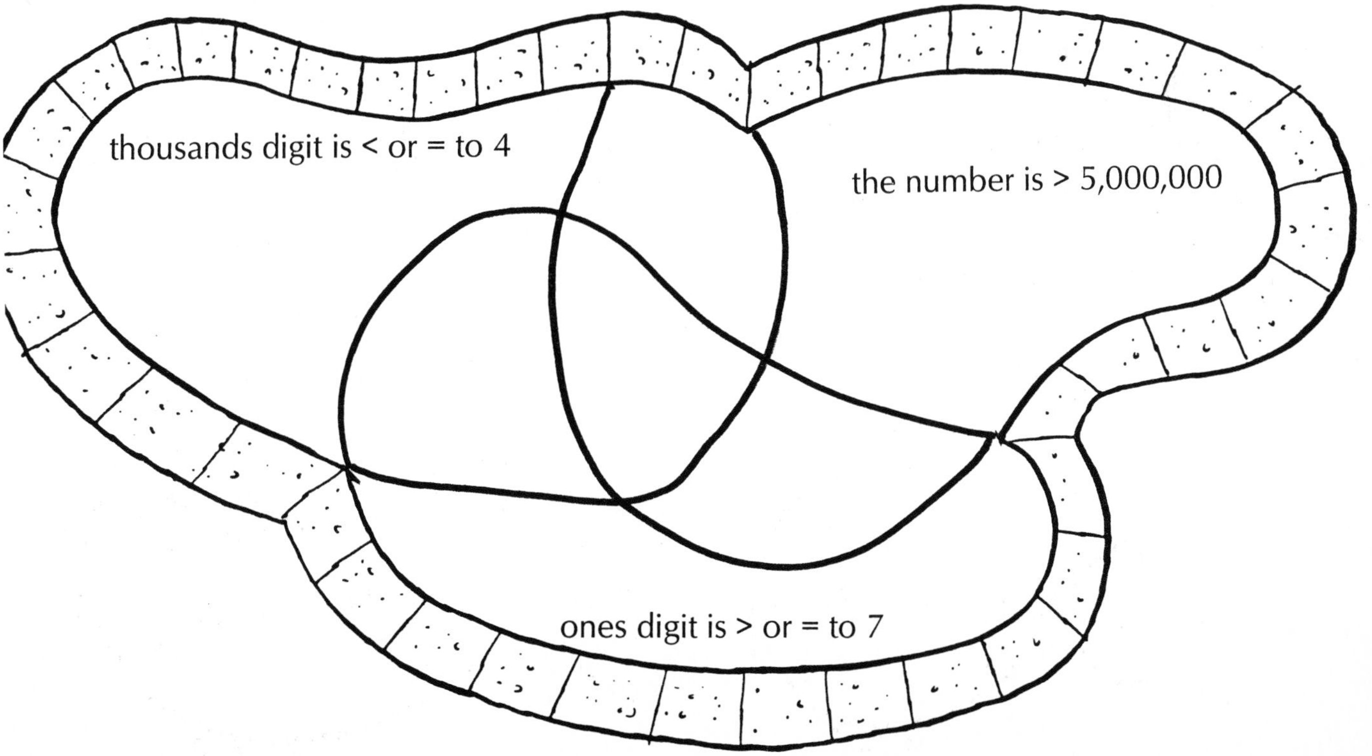
thousands digit is < or = to 4
the number is > 5,000,000
ones digit is > or = to 7

Amusement Park Map

Name ____________________

Springtime Fun

Before leaving on the class trip, each student was required to make a map of the amusement park using the coordinates given. Locate, label, and outline each item on the map.

Entrance A
A–11, A–12

Tilt-A-Whirl
G–15, G–16, H–15, H–16

Log Jam
D–1, E–1, F–1, F–2, F–3

Spiral Coaster
P–19, P–20, Q–19, R–16, R–19, R–20, S–16, S–17, S–20, T–17, T–18, T–19, T–20

Ferris Wheel
I–6, I–7, I–8, I–9, J–6, J–7, J–8, J–9

Wave Runner
N–1, N–2, N–5, N–6, O–2, O–3, O–4, O–5

Submarine
H–1, H–2, I–1, J–1, K–1, L–1

Drop Off
D–17, E–16, E–17

Rest Rooms
T–1, T–2; A–14, A–15; G–5, G–6; N–14, N–15

Entrance B
Q–1, R–1

Water Ride
B–1, B–2, B–3, C–3

Roller Coaster
R–9, S–5, S–7, S–8, S–9, T–5, T–6, T–7

Cliff Drop
A–19, A–20, B–19, B–20, C–19

Fun House
A–5, A–6, A–7, A–8, A–9, B–9, C–9, D–9, E–9, F–9

Arcade
E–19, E–20, F–20, G–20, H–20, I–20, J–19, J–20

Whip-A-Round
E–12, E–13, F–12, F–13

Bumper Cars
I–12, I–13, J–12, J–13, K–12, K–13

Food
A–16, A–17, B–15, B–16; E–5, E–6, F–5, F–6; N–10, N–11, N–12, N–13, O–10, O–11, O–12, O–13, O–14, O–15

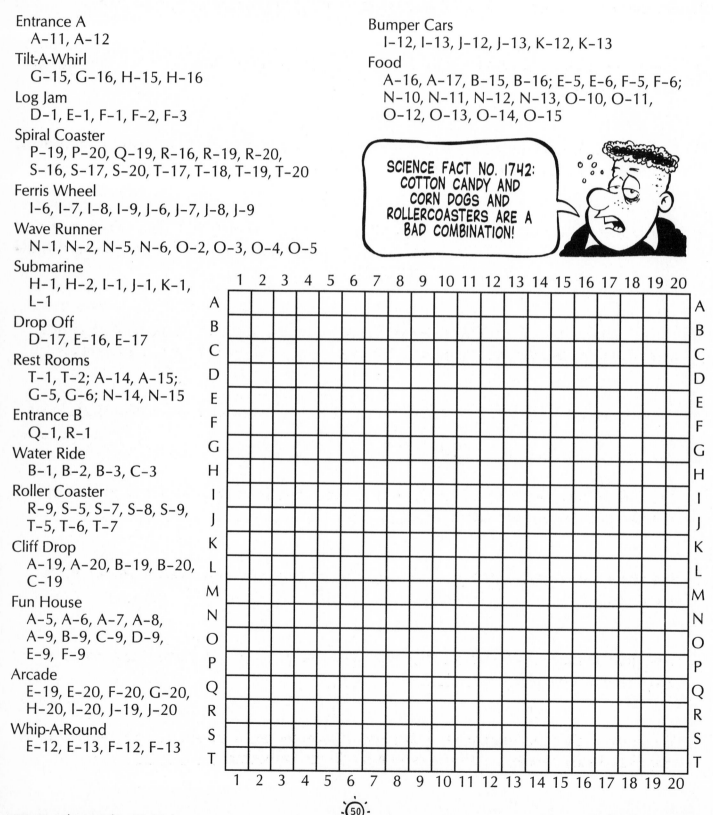

	1	2	3	4	5	6	7	8	9	10	11	12	13	14	15	16	17	18	19	20	
A																					A
B																					B
C																					C
D																					D
E																					E
F																					F
G																					G
H																					H
I																					I
J																					J
K																					K
L																					L
M																					M
N																					N
O																					O
P																					P
Q																					Q
R																					R
S																					S
T																					T
	1	2	3	4	5	6	7	8	9	10	11	12	13	14	15	16	17	18	19	20	

Amusement Park Ratios and Proportions

Name ____________________

Use ratios and proportions to answer each question about the amusement park field trip.

1. One of the buses traveled 133 miles and used 19 gallons of gas. How many miles per gallon did the bus get? __________

2. Each turnstile can admit 36 people per minute. There are 8 turnstiles at entrance A. How many people can enter the park at this entrance in one minute? __________

3. Each student was given an amusement park drink cup for attending as a group. Each time it is filled, the beverage costs 6¢ per ounce. You filled this 16-ounce cup to the top. How much did you pay? __________ How much to fill it 4 times? __________

4. The Whip-A-Round spins five times every 3 seconds. If you go on the minute-and-a-half ride (besides feeling like you are going to vomit) how many times will you have spun around? _____

5. One vendor sells fruit salad for $4.16 a pound. You want 6 ounces. How much will you pay? __________

6. The Cliff Drop can accommodate 720 people each hour. There are 444 people in front of you. How long until you get to ride? __________

7. The Wave Runner cycles 240 gallons of water per minute. How many gallons does it cycle each second? __________ Each hour? __________

8. One gear on the Spiral Coaster turns 7 revolutions each second. How many revolutions on each minute and a half ride? __________

9. You are in line for the Submarine. A sign says 15 minutes and there are 330 people in front of you. How many people per minute does this ride accommodate? __________

Class Trip

Name ____________________

Springtime Fun

After a class trip to an amusement park, the following data was collected. Use the data from each table to find the range, mean, median, and mode.

Students on buses

bus number	*number of students*
251	75
216	73
172	74
135	73
228	72

range: __________ median: __________
mean: __________ mode: __________

Money spent to nearest dollar

name	*amount*
Petra	$5.00
Torrie	$25.00
Clark	$16.00
Yates	$2.00
Xenia	$5.00

range: __________ median: __________
mean: __________ mode: __________

Number of photographs taken

name	*number of photos*
Zale	0
Maisie	15
Hyatt	7
Irma	32
Kyle	24
Larkin	0
Willie	16

range: __________ median: __________
mean: __________ mode: __________

Number of rides

name	*number of rides*
Aisla	16
Armani	22
Calvin	____
Ernie	25
Judy	15

range: __________ median: __________
mean: ____*20*____ mode: __________

Summer School

Take a Class

Name ______________________

Use the data given on this page to answer the questions about summer school experiences.

1. Make a tree diagram to show all of the possible combinations for advanced summer classes.

Health	**Academic**	**Application**
swimming	adv. mathematics	internship
hiking	adv. science	lab
golf	adv. writing	computer
		partnership

2. How many choices are there? __________

3. What is the probability that Julie will take golf and lab? __________

4. What is the probability that August will take advanced science? __________

5. What is the probability that May will take hiking and internship or hiking and computer?

____

6. What is the probability that June will take advanced mathematics? __________

The advanced science class measured trees in a lot. They make the following stem-and-leaf plot. Answer the questions regarding this data.

Tree Height in Feet

4	0	3	3	5	6	7	7	8						
3	1	1	1	2	2	4	5	5	5	7	9	9	9	9
2	0	0	2	2	6	8	8	9						
1	1	2	5	5	5	6	8							
0	2	2	2	3	3	4	5	5	6	7	7	8	9	

7. How many trees grew in the lot? __________

8. What is the range of tree heights? __________ The mode? __________

9. What percent of trees are over 34 feet tall? __________

10. What is the probability that a tree was less than or equal to 12 feet? __________

11. How many trees were greater than or equal to 49 feet? __________

12. What percent of trees were 20 to 25 feet tall? __________

Cross-Number Puzzle

Name ____________________

Summer School

Solve each problem. Then write each product in the cross-number puzzle. Each decimal will take a box.

1. 146.4 x .3
2. .827 x .61
3. 265.05 x .07
4. 93.02 x 413
5. 50.07 x .68
6. 60.82 x .6
7. .342 x 528
8. 505.05 x 97
9. 46.941 x .8
10. 56.3 x .004
11. 49.9 x .65
12. 4.475 x .32
13. 21.41 x 3
14. 78.1 x .07

SCIENCE FACT NO. 342: TOO MUCH MATH WILL TURN YOUR HAIR BLUE!

3.
6.
7.
2.
1.
13.
8.
11.
10.
14.
4.
12.
5.
9.

Let's Visit

name ______________________

These eight students each chose a different national park or national monument on which to research and report. Use the clues and matrix to determine who researched each location.

1. Dan chose a location east of the Mississippi River.
2. Fay and Joe chose parks without manmade monuments.
3. Neither Abi nor Joe chose the Grand Canyon.
4. Eli studied an active glacier in this Alaska Park.
5. Fay's report did not include a geyser, but Moe's report did.
6. Ian reported that panthers, crocodiles, snakes, and pelicans lived in this park.
7. Lee reported that his is the tallest manmade monument in the U.S.

THE GATEWAY ARCH IN ST. LOUIS IS ON THE ORIGINAL RIVERFRONT TOWN SITE!

	Abi	Dan	Eli	Fay	Ian	Joe	Lee	Moe
Everglades								
Gateway Arch								
Grand Canyon								
Kenai Fjords								
Mt. Rushmore								
Sequoia								
Yellowstone								
Washington Monument								

Abi studied ______________________

Dan studied ______________________

Eli studied ______________________

Fay studied ______________________

Ian studied ______________________

Joe studied ______________________

Lee studied ______________________

Moe studied ______________________

What Am I?

Name ____________________

U.S. Independence Day

I was a gift from France for America's 100th birthday. My crown has seven spikes, which represent the world's seven continents.

Solve each equation. Locate the answer to the problem in the code below. Write the correct letter above the answer.

Letter Key	1	2	3	4	5	6	7	8	9	10	11	12
	A	B	E	F	I	L	O	R	S	T	U	Y

1. $\frac{3}{5} + \frac{1}{3} + \frac{8}{15} =$

2. $\frac{1}{2} + \frac{3}{4} \times \frac{2}{3} =$

3. $3\frac{2}{3} - \frac{5}{6} \div \frac{5}{8} =$

4. $(\frac{1}{2} - \frac{1}{3}) \times \frac{2}{3} =$

5. $\frac{2}{9} \div (\frac{5}{6} + \frac{4}{9}) =$

6. $\frac{1}{5} \div (\frac{1}{5} + \frac{3}{4}) =$

7. $(\frac{2}{3} + \frac{2}{5}) \div 1\frac{3}{5} =$

8. $\frac{1}{2} \div \frac{3}{4} \times \frac{9}{10} =$

9. $2\frac{7}{10} + \frac{1}{4} \div \frac{5}{6} =$

10. $2\frac{2}{9} \times \frac{3}{8} - \frac{1}{3} =$

11. $6 \div \frac{2}{3} \times \frac{5}{18} =$

12. $6\frac{1}{3} - 3\frac{1}{3} \div 1\frac{1}{4} =$

THIS FAMOUS MONUMENT IS 150.9 FEET HIGH!

____ ____ ____ ____ ____ ____   ____ ____

3 $\frac{1}{2}$ $1\frac{7}{15}$ $\frac{1}{2}$ $2\frac{1}{2}$ $2\frac{1}{3}$ $\frac{2}{3}$ $\frac{1}{9}$

____ ____ ____ ____ ____ ____ ____

$\frac{4}{19}$ $\frac{4}{23}$ 1 $2\frac{1}{3}$ $\frac{3}{5}$ $\frac{1}{2}$ $3\frac{2}{3}$

First Flight

Name ______________________

Find each sum. Then follow the directions below.

1.
```
   762,489
     5,628
 6,562,899
+2,258,364
```
R

2.
```
 7,986,140
   628,309
 1,421,602
+   26,876
```
A

3.
```
    62,927
 6,291,673
   982,735
+  468,098
```
A

4.
```
 4,634,923
   848,577
     2,698
+1,249,864
```
R

5.
```
 1,840,294
   728,166
 5,050,671
+3,615,800
```
E

6.
```
 1,650,205
    95,364
 1,079,643
+  346,725
```
T

7.
```
 34,925,635
 55,869,722
+ 9,182,528
```
A

8.
```
 86,624,690
  6,518,315
+ 4,003,189
```
M

9.
```
 44,649,417
  8,155,627
+24,318,243
```
L

10.
```
 2,612,536
   905,428
 4,183,620
+1,009,087
```
H

11.
```
 13,421,673
  2,730,948
    457,831
+41,173,996
```
I

12.
```
    997,173
 26,321,730
     84,651
+ 1,256,788
```
A

13.
```
 53,601,717
  4,183,552
  8,234,606
+13,976,378
```
E

Who tried to fly around the world at the equator?

Order the sums from greatest to least and write the letters of the problems in that order below to learn the pilot's name. One sum is the date the flight began. Can you find it? Write the date here. ______________________

___ ___ ___ ___ ___ ___

___ ___ ___ ___ ___ ___ ___

Scientific Find

Special Days

name ______________________

In November 1996, scientists in China found something very special that may prove dinosaurs were the ancestors of birds. Solve each problem. Circle the word by each corresponding answer to determine this event.

1.	6,428,921 − 619,563	The 5,809,358	Cave 6,211,442	65 5,819,441
2.	234,896 − 159,347	paintings 125,551	trillion 75,551	150 75,549
3.	7,640,358 −3,732,947	million 3,907,411	year 4,112,611	depicting 4,907,511
4.	9,631,400 −6,298,261	old 3,433,239	year 3,333,139	feathered 3,467,261
5.	4,125,634 − 943,573	DNA 4,822,141	old 3,182,061	dinosaurs 3,882,161
6.	8,341,087 −2,915,149	fossil 5,425,938	flying 6,634,142	with 5,434,942
7.	1,842,573 −1,296,499	and 554,074	of 546,074	gene 654,426
8.	3,664,715 −2,579,806	gliding 1,125,111	strands 1,085,119	feathered 1,084,909
9.	2,671,482 − 843,594	for 1,832,882	Sinosauropteryx 1,827,888	through 2,232,112
10.	5,963,117 −2,695,528	space 3,332,411	Prima 3,267,589	feathers 3,267,411

Wild Animals in Our World

Name ____________________

These ten students each chose a different wild animal to research. Use the matrix to determine who researched each animal.

1. Roe, Van, and Web studied water animals.
2. Lou and Zoe studied birds.
3. Nat and Lou saw their black and white animals at a zoo.
4. Bud studied the only extinct animal listed. It once lived on the island of Mauritius.
5. Kay studied one of the larger mammals on earth.
6. Pam said her water mammal was a slow-moving herbivore, often referred to as a sea cow.
7. Roe did not study a reptile.
8. Van studied the largest marine mammal listed.

	Bud	Kay	Lou	Nat	Pam	Roe	Tye	Van	Web	Zoe
dodo										
dolphin										
elephant										
humpback whale										
leatherback turtle										
manatee										
panda										
parrot										
penguin										
tiger										

Bud studied ____________________

Kay studied ____________________

Lou studied ____________________

Nat studied ____________________

Pam studied ____________________

Roe studied ____________________

Tye studied ____________________

Van studied ____________________

Web studied ____________________

Zoe studied ____________________

In the Stars

name ____________________

During the time of slavery in the United States, those escaping through the Underground Railroad used stars and directional songs to help them travel north to safety. Find the sums. Match the problem number to the coordinates given and draw the constellation in the grid.

1. $\frac{3}{4} + \frac{3}{4}$

2. $\frac{5}{8} + \frac{1}{8}$

3. $\frac{4}{7} + \frac{6}{7}$

4. $\frac{5}{9} + \frac{8}{9}$

5. $\frac{1}{5} + \frac{2}{5}$

6. $\frac{1}{2} + \frac{5}{8}$

7. $\frac{2}{3} + \frac{4}{9}$

8. $\frac{1}{6} + \frac{2}{3}$

VINCENT VAN GOGH PAINTED "THE STARRY NIGHT" IN JUNE, 1889!

Connect the (x, y) coordinates in the order of the answers.

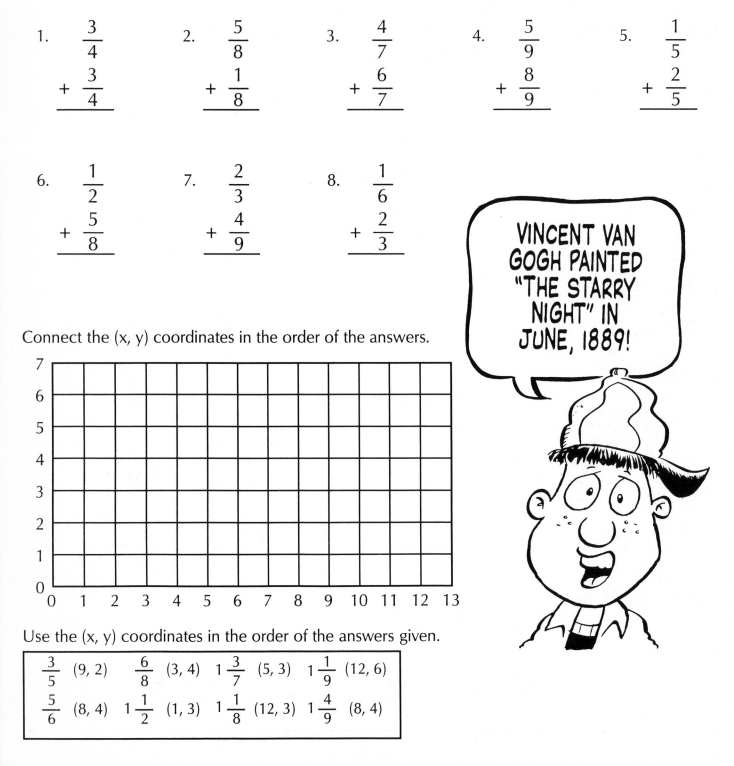

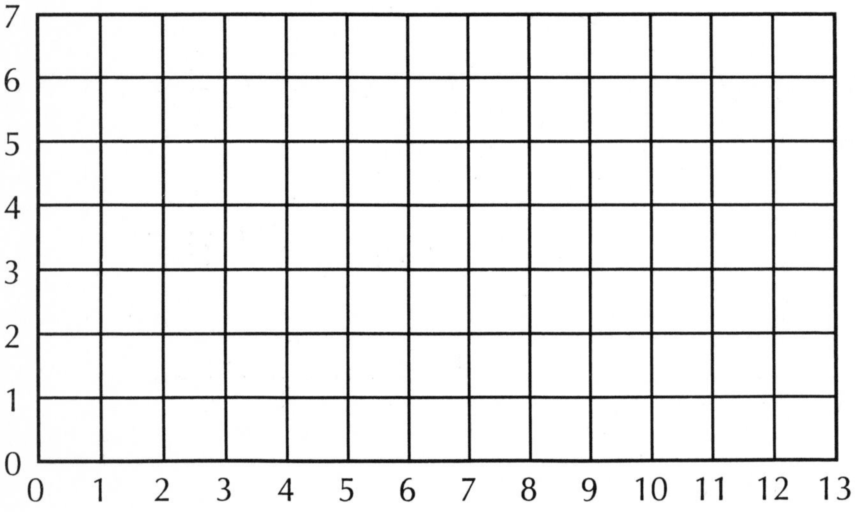

Use the (x, y) coordinates in the order of the answers given.

$\frac{3}{5}$	(9, 2)	$\frac{6}{8}$	(3, 4)	$1\frac{3}{7}$	(5, 3)	$1\frac{1}{9}$	(12, 6)
$\frac{5}{6}$	(8, 4)	$1\frac{1}{2}$	(1, 3)	$1\frac{1}{8}$	(12, 3)	$1\frac{4}{9}$	(8, 4)

New Planet

Name ____________________

In 1996, scientists discovered a new planet larger than Jupiter and 17 times larger than Earth. It was discovered 600 trillion miles away from Earth, outside of our solar system in the constellation Cygnus. Something is very unusual about this planet. Solve each problem and use the Letter Bank and code to determine what is so unusual about this planet.

Letter Bank

A. $1\frac{1}{2}$	**H.** $1\frac{9}{14}$	**N.** $1\frac{11}{18}$	**S.** $1\frac{11}{24}$
B. $1\frac{5}{8}$	**I.** $1\frac{7}{15}$	**O.** $1\frac{7}{20}$	**T.** 2
G. $1\frac{11}{12}$	**L.** $1\frac{13}{16}$	**R.** $1\frac{11}{21}$	

SCIENCE FACT NO. 675: 600 TRILLION MILES IS PRETTY FAR!

1. $\frac{1}{3} + \frac{3}{4} + \frac{5}{6} =$

2. $\frac{1}{2} + \frac{6}{7} + \frac{2}{7} =$

3. $\frac{5}{8} + \frac{3}{4} + \frac{1}{8} =$

4. $\frac{3}{8} + \frac{1}{4} + \frac{5}{6} =$

5. $\frac{5}{7} + \frac{2}{3} + \frac{1}{7} =$

6. $\frac{2}{3} + \frac{1}{2} + \frac{5}{6} =$

7. $\frac{4}{9} + \frac{5}{6} + \frac{1}{3} =$

8. $\frac{3}{5} + \frac{1}{3} + \frac{8}{15} =$

9. $\frac{5}{8} + \frac{1}{4} + \frac{15}{16} =$

10. $\frac{3}{4} + \frac{3}{8} + \frac{1}{2} =$

11. $\frac{1}{4} + \frac{1}{2} + \frac{3}{5} =$

___ ___   ___ ___ ___   ___ ___
8 6   2 3 4   3 7

___ ___ ___ ___ ___ ___   ___ ___ ___ ___ ___
11 10 9 11 7 1   11 5 10 8 6

Nine Planets?

Name ______________________

Summer Skies

Subtract the mixed numbers. Use the answers in the code to name eight planets in our solar system. **Bonus:** Which planet is missing? ____________________

1. $5\frac{1}{3} - 1\frac{2}{3}$
2. $7\frac{1}{5} - 4\frac{4}{5}$
3. $11\frac{2}{7} - 8\frac{5}{7}$
4. $6\frac{4}{9} - 5\frac{5}{9}$
5. $15\frac{5}{8} - 10\frac{7}{8}$
6. $9\frac{1}{4} - 2\frac{3}{4}$
7. $12\frac{7}{12} - 6\frac{9}{12}$
8. $14\frac{1}{2} - 11\frac{5}{6}$
9. $3\frac{2}{5} - 1\frac{3}{5}$
10. $2\frac{1}{3} - 1\frac{7}{12}$
11. $9\frac{3}{5} - 4\frac{7}{10}$
12. $8\frac{1}{3} - 5\frac{5}{6}$
13. $16\frac{5}{7} - 13\frac{18}{21}$
14. $11\frac{2}{3} - 7\frac{7}{9}$
15. $6\frac{1}{8} - 1\frac{3}{4}$

Letter Box

$1\frac{4}{5}$	$\frac{8}{9}$	$3\frac{2}{3}$	$6\frac{1}{2}$	$2\frac{1}{2}$	$2\frac{4}{7}$	$3\frac{8}{9}$	$2\frac{2}{3}$
A	**E**	**H**	**I**	**J**	**L**	**M**	**N**
$2\frac{6}{7}$	$2\frac{2}{5}$	$\frac{3}{4}$	$4\frac{3}{8}$	$4\frac{3}{4}$	$5\frac{5}{6}$	$4\frac{9}{10}$	
O	**P**	**R**	**S**	**T**	**U**	**V**	

Find the letter for each answer and write it on the corresponding line below.

___ ___ ___ ___ ___
4 9 10 5 1

___ ___ ___ ___ ___ ___ ___
12 7 2 6 5 4 10

___ ___ ___ ___   ___ ___ ___ ___ ___ ___ ___
14 9 10 15   8 4 2 5 7 8 4

___ ___ ___ ___ ___   ___ ___ ___ ___ ___ ___
2 3 7 5 13   15 9 5 7 10 8

___ ___ ___ ___ ___ ___   ___ ___ ___ ___ ___
7 10 9 8 7 15   11 4 8 7 15

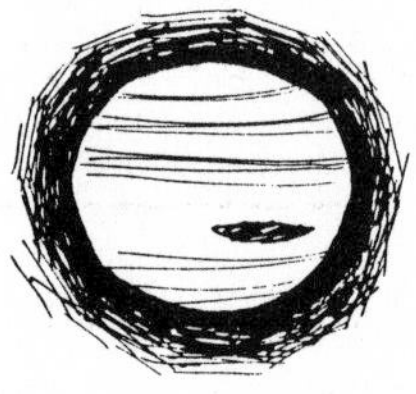

How Will You Labor?

Name ____________________________

Students were given a Labor Day assignment to poll 100 classmates to learn what they "wanted to be when they grew up." The results were to be shown in a pie graph.

Tallie polled 100 students, grouped the responses, and made this information chart. Answer the questions and design a pie graph to display her data.

Category	Number of Students
business	20
health	15
science	10
education	5
government	5
entertainment	30
other	15

1. What category did the greatest number of students choose? ____________________________
2. What is the range for these categories? ________________
3. If you were one of the students polled by Tallie, what is the probability that you told her you wanted to have a job in the field of science? ____________________

Jennie polled another 100 students. She made the following information chart. Answer the questions and design a pie graph to display her data.

Category	Number of Students
business	15
health	25
science	25
education	5
government	15
entertainment	10
other	5

4. If you were one of the students polled by Jenny, what is the probability that you told her you wanted to have a job in the field of science? ____________________
5. Whose information is more valid? ______________ Explain: ____________________________

____

____

6. Combine Tallie and Jenny's data. Make a pie graph on the back of this sheet showing the information regarding the 200 students.,

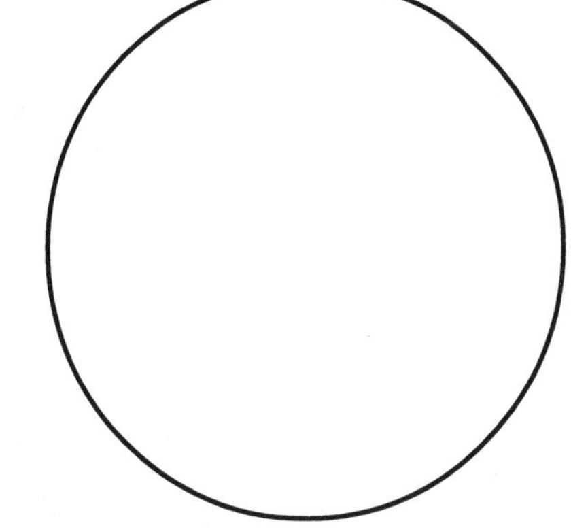

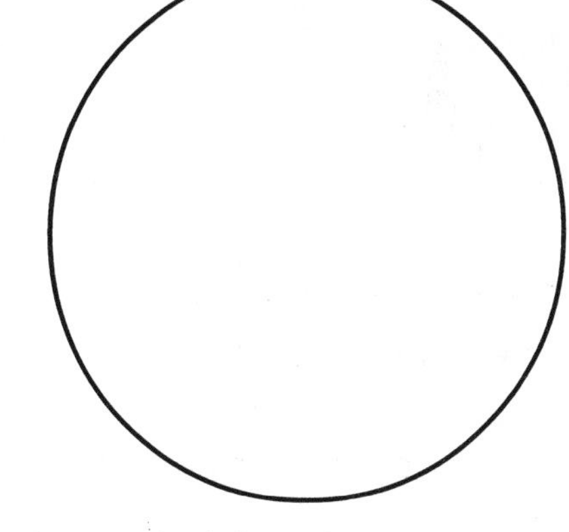

Back to Order

Name ______________________

Show wo

As school begins, procedures and schedules start again. These math problems each have their own procedure. Use the order of operations rules to solve each number sentence.

1. $6 + 7 \times 2 - 5 =$
2. $4 - 3 + 10 \div 2 =$
3. $(4 - 1) \times 5 - 10 =$
4. $6 \times 6 - 5 \times 4 =$
5. $9 \div 3 + (8 - 2 \times 3) =$
6. $14 \div 2 - 6 + 10 =$
7. $(3 + 1) \times (2 + 8) =$
8. $(4 + 5) \times 6 \div 3 =$
9. $(5 + 4 \times 4) \div 7 =$
10. $8 + 27 \div 3 =$
11. $(12 \div 4 + 5) \times 6 =$
12. $4 \times (5 + 1) \div 2 =$

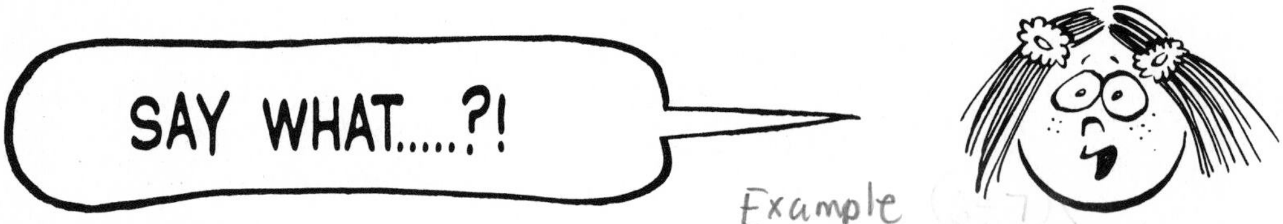

13. Rewrite problem #1 so the answer is 21. Example $(6+7) \times 2 - 5 = 21$
14. Rewrite problem #4 so the answer is 24. ______________________
15. Rewrite problem #7 so the answer is 13. ______________________
16. Rewrite problem #11 so the answer is 33. ______________________

Use the number 3 four times for problem #s 17–20. Use the order of operations to organize the threes to get the given answers.

Example

17. $(3+3)(3+3)$ $= 36$ — $(6)(6) = 36$
18. ______________________ $= 7$
19. ______________________ $= 3$
20. ______________________ $= 27$

Start of School

Where's That Locker?

name ______________________

Solve to find each difference. Then add the digits in each answer and shade the sums in the grid to find the route from the classroom to the lockers. The first one is done for you.

1. 9,522,519 − 2,893,026 = 6,629,493 = 39

2. 5,050,671 − 321,263

3. 6,291,673 − 3,186,849

4. 6,291,673 − 826,496

5. 7,986,140 − 92,685

6. 4,634,923 − 2,468,537

7. 3,947,621 − 52,366

8. 5,281,923 − 1,165,737

9. 6,562,899 − 648,920

10. 9,747,507 − 9,269,628

11. 4,235,403 − 536,926

12. 8,485,577 − 6,499,038

13. 4,634,923 − 9,355

14. 7,934,846 − 2,689,572

15. 4,053,803 − 2,144,735

35	23	19	45	31	50
42	17	56	48	34	41
29	37	41	21	36	12
49	52	43	30	32	25
28	53	33	46	27	16
51	49	22	44	39	40

DOES IT GET ANY BETTER THAN THIS? HOO-BOY!

Schedules

Name ______________________

1. Draw tree diagrams on a separate sheet of paper to show all of the possible combinations for first and second hour. Use them to answer the questions.

First Hour	Second Hour
general math English social studies band	physical education study hall music general science

THE SCIENCE OF DATING EVENTS AND STRUCTURES USING TREE RINGS IS KNOWN AS DENDROCHRONOLOGY!

2. How many combinations are there? __________
3. What is the probability that Abbey will have band first hour and physical education second hour? __________
4. What is the probability that Chessa will have general math first hour? __________
5. What is the probability that Beck will have study hall first hour? __________
6. What is the probability that Darnell will have English first hour and music or general science second hour? __________

Use the data below to answer the following questions about sixth graders at Open Middle School.

Sixth-Grade Course Selections at Open Middle School					
Mathematics		**Science**		**Fine Arts**	
general	*advanced*	*chemistry*	*earth*	*music*	*drama*
175	*25*	*66*	*134*	*98*	*102*

7. Which math class is Tait most likely in ? __________

   Why did you choose your answer? __________

8. Which science class is Ingrid least likely to be enrolled in? __________

   How did you come up with this conclusion? __________

9. Which three classes is Juan probably taking? __________

   What evidence do you have to support this? __________

Jesse Owens's Birthday

Jesse Owens

name ______________________

Jesse Owens, born on September 12, 1915, won four gold medals in the 1936 Olympics. To find out his winning events, solve each problem for the missing digits. Then tally the number of times you filled in a given digit. The event with the most tallies is the one in which Jesse Owens won his gold medals. Circle the event.

1.
62,153,64□
3,4□1,890
+ 1□,35□,677
75,973,□15

2.
31,045,387
,98□,4□0
+ 53,004,83□
85,0□2,708

3.
9,475,0□6
25,601,672
+ 20,□6□,013
5□,745,□71

4.
84,795,□61
□2,□67,192
+ 51,8□8,66□

5.
87,□0□,205
− □3,637,□3□
7□,769,067

6.
50,239,□21
− □5,□09,18□
1□,93□,341

7.
2,894,□97
□7,□□6,95□
+ 25,182,673
9□,40□,227

8.
14,93□,502
□9,□12,8□1
+ □,466,070
62,9□3,42□

9.
55,851,64□
1,□3□,2□8
+ 20,145,509
□7,9□3,424

10.
34,9□5,772
− □9,86□,52□
1□,056,□44

11.
64,624,□90
− □8,□49,823
2□,77□,86□

12.
44,318,243
− □□□36,□1□
5,58□,230

ON MAY 25, 1935, JESSE OWENS ACHIEVED THE BEST ONE-DAY SHOWING IN TRACK HISTORY!

Digits	Event	Tally	Total
0,5	swimming and diving		
1,6	lifting		
2,7	parallel bars and horse		
3,8	track and field		
4,9	ice-skating		

Picking a Way Through the Orchard

Name ______________________

Harvest Time

Solve each percentage problem. Then refer to the Coordinate Key to find the coordinate location of a tree in the orchard. Using one color for the answers to the odd-numbered problems and another color for the even-numbered problems, shade each tree. Four trees in a row; horizontally, vertically, or diagonally; is one point. How many points does each team earn?

1. 3% of 900 =	2. 12% of 150 =	3. 50% of 68 =	4. 30% of 40 =
5. 4% of 400 =	6. 15% of 460 =	7. 60% of 80 =	8. 16% of 50 =
9. 33% of 200 =	10. 60% of 400 =	11. 10% of 910 =	12. 90% of 60 =
13. 2% of 50 =	14. 7% of 300 =	15. 25% of 68 =	16. 70% of 120 =
17. 55% of 160 =	18. 45% of 80 =	19. 12% of 200 =	20. 75% of 12 =
21. 12% of 800 =	22. 50% of 6 =	23. 80% of 25 =	24. 2% of 300 =
25. 10% of 70 =	26. 25% of 140 =	27. 50% of 98 =	28. 20% of 70 =

Coordinate Key

1 (3,4)	18 (3,2)	49 (6,0)
3 (5,3)	20 (5,5)	54 (4,5)
6 (5,2)	21 (4,6)	66 (1,1)
7 (5,1)	24 (1,3)	69 (1,4)
8 (0,5)	27 (2,1)	84 (3,6)
9 (5,4)	34 (2,2)	88 (4, 0)
12 (2,3)	35 (2,5)	91 (4,2)
14 (0,3)	36 (6,6)	96 (6,3)
16 (4,1)	48 (3,1)	240 (5,6)
17 (4,3)		

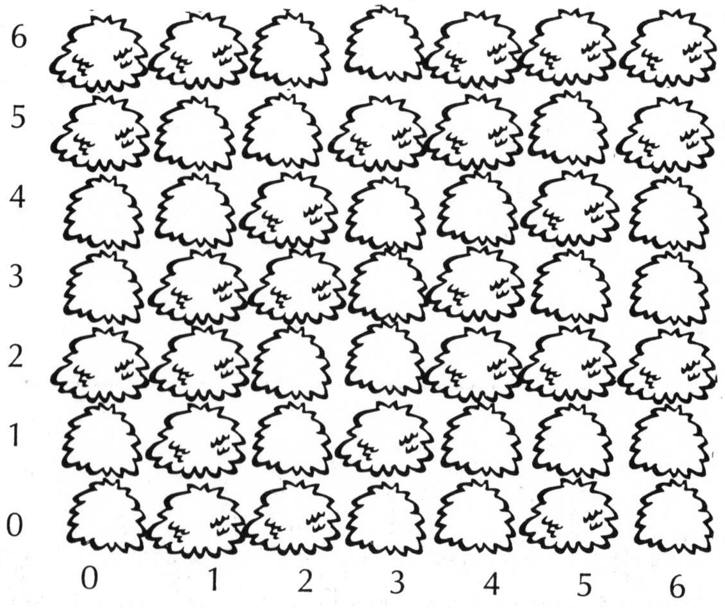

Points: __________ even __________ odd

Through the Orchard

Name ______________________

Solve each problem. Shade each box whose answer has a 4 in the hundredths place to find the pathway through the orchard.

Start

36.021 x .251	50.596 x 1.25	325.14 x .022	67.381 x .36
92,394 x .145	243.69 x 46	30.145 x .0082	4,723 x .08
81.89 x 3.7	6523.1 x .12	20.046 x 44	1.392 x 45
952.1 x 2.4	37,114 x .06	43.64 x 8.2	4,806 x .074
768.11 x .008	52,123 x .007	354.01 x 2.5	82.235 x .09

Plant Those Apple Trees!

Name ______________________

Harvest Time

Solve each problem and order the sums from least to greatest. Write the letter of each problem in the same order on the lines below. Find out which historical character is responsible for planting apple trees across the United States.

1.
```
  4,269,812
      6,922
+   358,189
```
J

2.
```
  1,620,803
  2,811,249
+ 4,053,525
```
P

3.
```
  3,405,000
  1,598,762
+    46,909
```
H

4.
```
    985,136
  6,168,523
+     6,508
```
H

5.
```
  3,641,805
     56,123
+   983,057
```
O

6.
```
     58,921
  7,934,600
+   846,773
```
M

7.
```
  1,843,277
  3,462,915
+     3,610
```
n

8.
```
    867,426
  1,473,916
+ 7,406,205
```
n

9.
```
  6,235,403
     62,407
  1,548,522
+   136,403
```
A

10.
```
  3,947,601
     89,053
    624,109
+ 4,861,756
```
A

11.
```
     66,385
  5,281,923
        801
+   942,564
```
C

HE ALSO PLANTED MANY HEALING HERBS!

____ ____ ____ ____

____ ____ ____ ____ ____ ____ ____

Scarecrows

Name ____________________

Circle the scarecrows head that you predict will translate to the fraction $\frac{1}{5}$. After you complete the page, shade the head, body, and legs that go with the fraction $\frac{1}{5}$. Write each as a decimal.

1. thirty-five hundredths
3. twenty-hundredths
5. fifteen-hundredths
2. twenty-four hundredths
4. sixty-eight hundredths
6. ten-hundredths

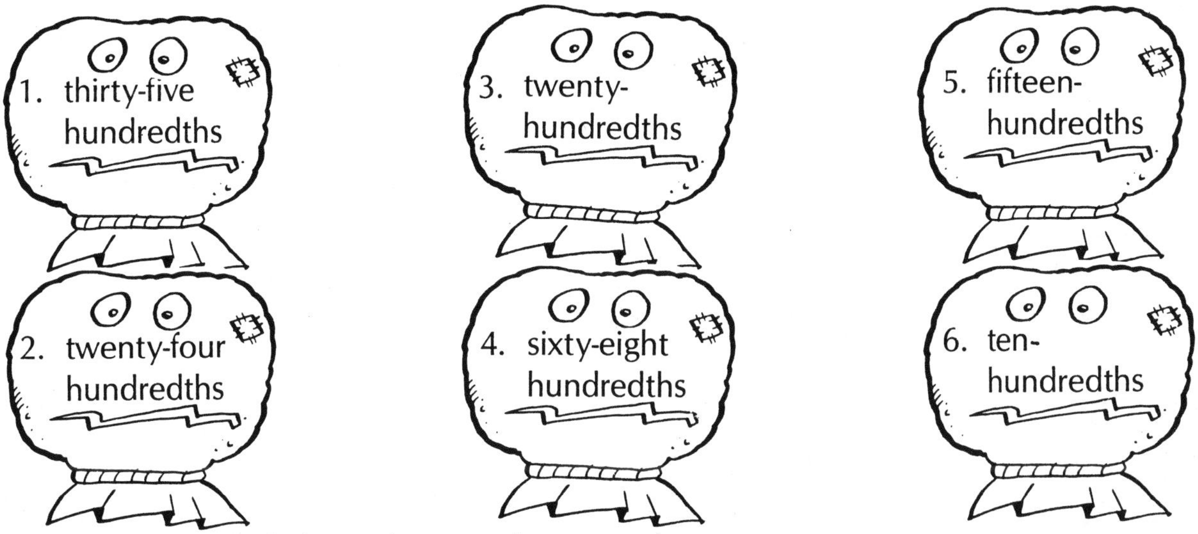

Copy the decimals from above and convert them to percents.

1. .35 = 35%
3. ________ = ________
5. ________ = ________
2. ________ = ________
4. ________ = ________
6. ________ = ________

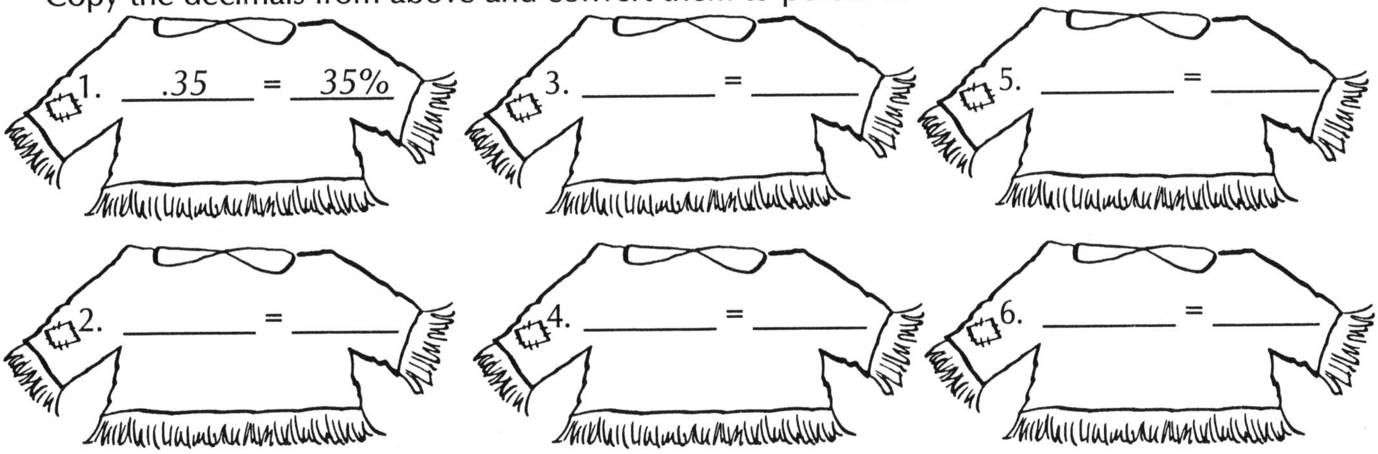

Write the above percents as fractions. Simplify to lowest terms.

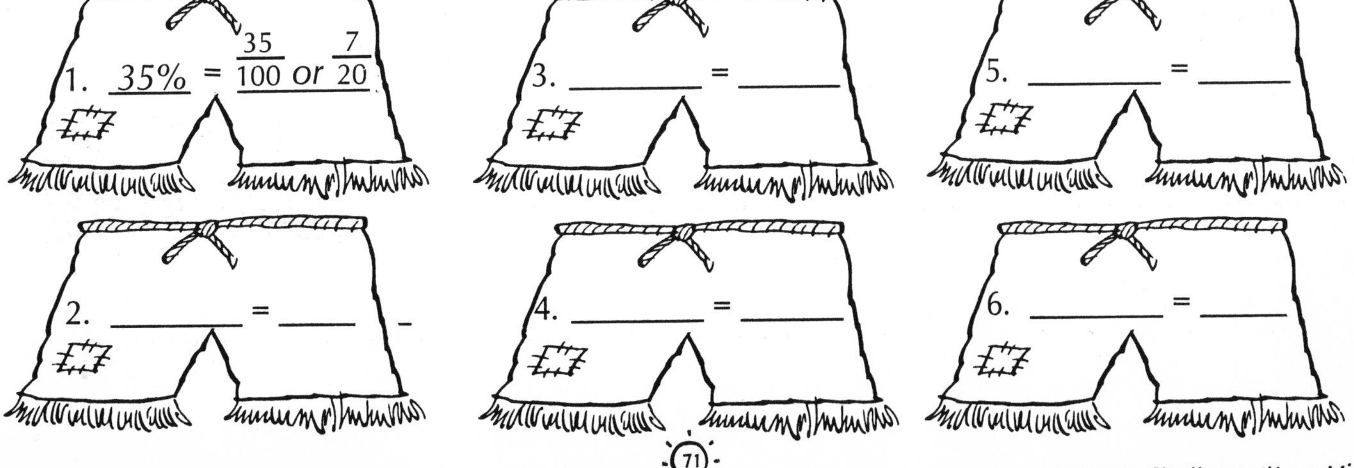

Great Food

Name ______________________

Harvest Time

Find the square roots. Write the corresponding letter with the matching answer below to answer the question.

1. $\sqrt{.49}$ ____ B	2. $\sqrt{.0196}$ ____ H	3. $\sqrt{729}$ ____ L	4. $\sqrt{2.89}$ ____ A	5. $\sqrt{1.44}$ ____ R
6. $\sqrt{.0081}$ ____ G	7. $\sqrt{121}$ ____ Y	8. $\sqrt{2.25}$ ____ S	9. $\sqrt{1,024}$ ____ E	10. $\sqrt{.25}$ ____ A
11. $\sqrt{144}$ ____ M	12. $\sqrt{.36}$ ____ D	13. $\sqrt{169}$ ____ N	14. $\sqrt{529}$ ____ I	15. $\sqrt{.0064}$ ____ E
16. $\sqrt{6.25}$ ____ V	17. $\sqrt{676}$ ____ F	18. $\sqrt{8,100}$ ____ T	19. $\sqrt{.16}$ ____ U	20. $\sqrt{.0004}$ ____ S

What did the farmer harvest?

MORE THAN HALF OF THE WORLD'S POPULATION IS ENGAGED IN FARMING!

___ ___ ___   ___ ___ ___ ___ ___ ___ ___ ___ ___
.02 .14 .08   .14 .5 1.2 2.5 32 1.5 90 .08 .6

___ ___ ___ ___   ___ ___ ___ ___ ___ ___
12 .5 13 11   26 1.2 .4 23 90 1.5

___ ___ ___   ___ ___ ___ ___ ___ ___ ___ ___ ___ ___
1.7 13 .6   2.5 .08 .09 32 90 1.7 .7 27 .08 .02

Compare the Harvest

Name ______________________

Solve each problem. Write the difference in the correct portion of the Venn diagram. Don't forget to use the outside set.

1. 887.245 − 265.9
2. 567.597 − 541.256
3. 857.445 − 256.104
4. 647.258 − 321.144
5. 561.9353 − 25.8941
6. 367.996 − 341.55
7. 1,132.425 − 483.125
8. 461.477 − 325.446
9. 847.191 − 246.25
10. 234.8315 − 225.8899
11. 688.778 − 542.818
12. 308.6191 − 254.3651
13. 762.96 − 130.554
14. 1,021.232 − 56.1859
15. 941.509 − 250.168
16. 965.415 − 520.694

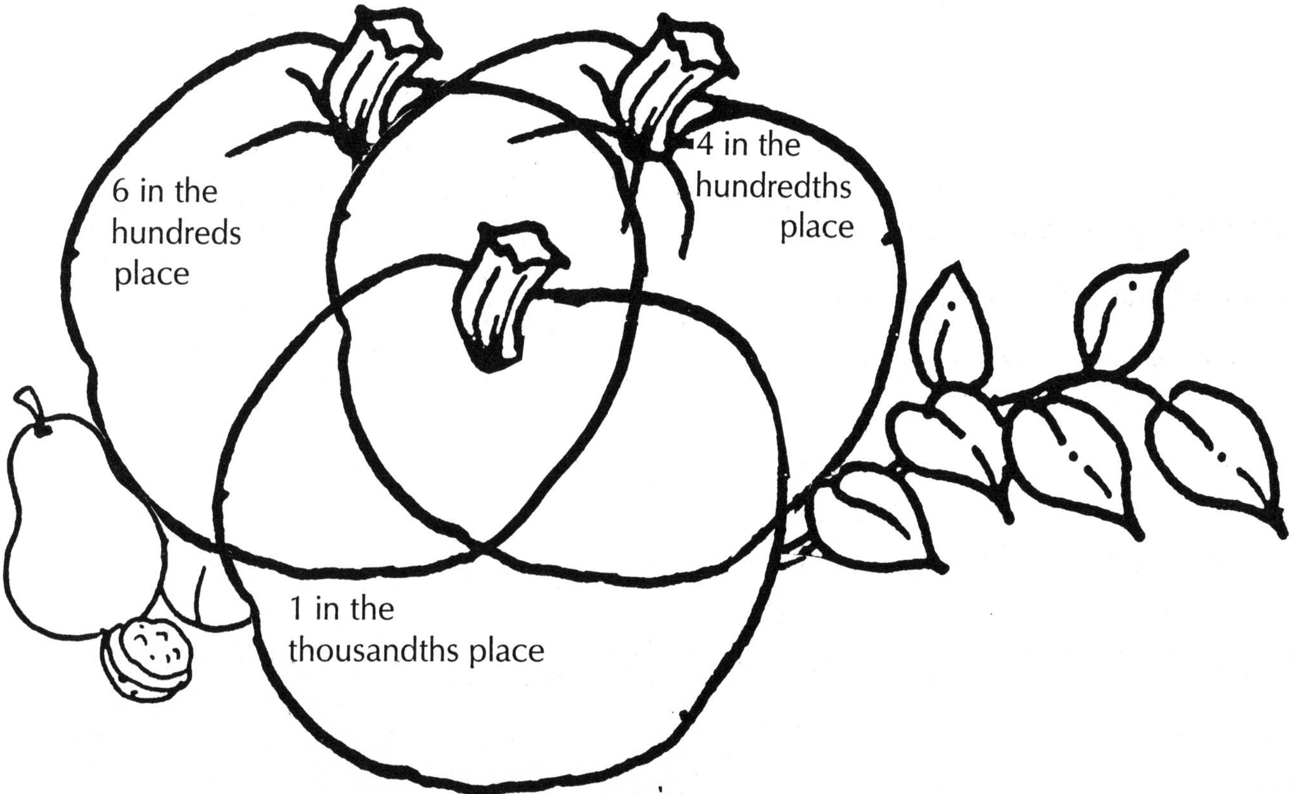

Fill That Basket

Name ____________________

Harvest Time

Solve each problem and shade each answer in the produce baskets to determine who has the largest amount of produce.

1. $6\overline{)13.86}$
2. $8\overline{)370.4}$
3. $4\overline{)21.264}$
4. $24\overline{)8.4}$
5. $36\overline{)60.48}$
6. $87\overline{)405.42}$
7. $49\overline{)17.64}$
8. $.3\overline{)20.772}$
9. $.8\overline{)6.152}$
10. $.04\overline{)13.684}$
11. $.52\overline{)3.8116}$
12. $.86\overline{)2.7735}$
13. $6.2\overline{)380.68}$
14. $3.4\overline{)3.468}$
15. $.06\overline{)1.9206}$
16. $2.1\overline{)118.02}$
17. $4.2\overline{)261.66}$
18. $.14\overline{)1.932}$
19. $2.9\overline{)21.315}$
20. $.013\overline{).37284}$

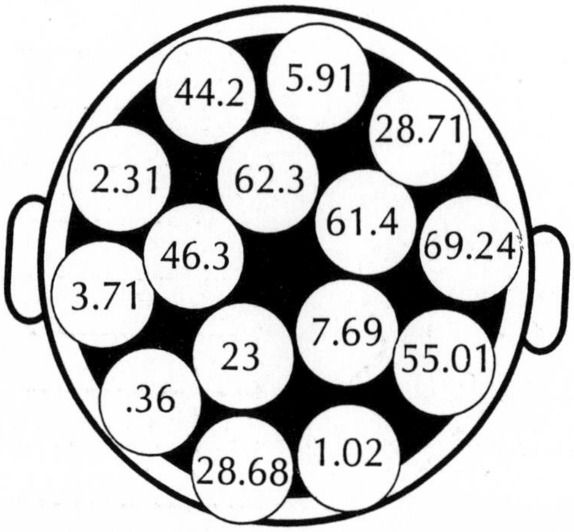

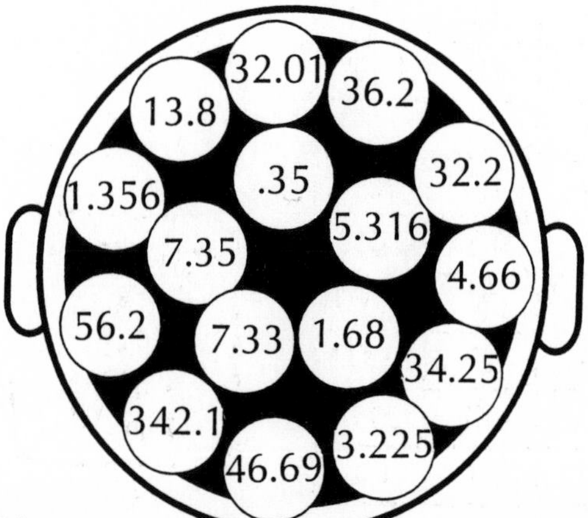

Bases Are Falling

Name ____________________

National Bookkeeper's Day

Complete the base table on the right. Use the tables to answer the problems.

Base 10	Base 8	Base 6	Base 3
1	1	1	1
2	2	2	2
3	3	3	10
4	4	4	11
5	5	5	12
6	6	10	20
7	7	11	21
8	10	12	22
9	11	13	100
10	12	14	101
11	13	15	102
12	14	20	110
13	15	21	111
14	16	22	112
15	17	23	120
16	20	24	121
17	21	25	122
18	22	30	200
19	23	31	201
20	24	32	202
21	25	33	210
22	26	34	211
23	27	35	212
24	30	40	220
25	31	41	221
26	32	42	222
27	33	43	1,000
28	34	44	1,001
29	35	45	1,002
30	36	50	1,010
31	37	51	1,011

1. $132_6 \div 11_6 =$ ________
2. $222_3 + 201_3 =$ ________
3. $15_8 + 35_8 =$ ________
4. $115_6 - 31_6 =$ ________
5. $46_8 - 14_8 =$ ________
6. $112_3 \times 11_3 =$ ________
7. $102_3 + 10_3 =$ ________
8. $25_6 + 40_6 =$ ________
9. $21_8 - 12_8 =$ ________
10. $12_3 \times 12_3 =$ ________
11. $13_8 \times 5_8 =$ ________
12. $120_6 \div 12_6 =$ ________
13. $101_6 - 24_6 =$ ________
14. $11_8 + 23_8 =$ ________
15. $11_3 \times 101_3 =$ ________

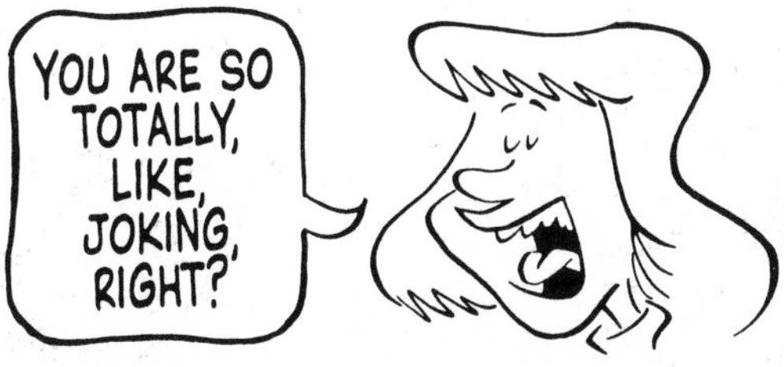
YOU ARE SO TOTALLY, LIKE, JOKING, RIGHT?

Base 10	Base 8	Base 6	Base 3
32			
33			
34			
35			
36			
37		101	
38			
39			
40			
41			
42			
43			
44			
45	55		
46			
47			
48			
49			
50			
51			1,220
52			
53			
54			
55			
56			
57			
58			
59			
60			
61			
62			

The Ships of Columbus

Name ____________________

Columbus requested ships from several kings and queens before getting financing for his trip. On a separate sheet, design a ship for Columbus. Be sure to include the following geometric items, and tally the number of times you used each one.

triangles	________	quadrilaterals	________
circles	________	pentagons	________
ovals	________	open figures	________
hexagons	________	polygons not listed above	________

Use the data you gathered to make a graph in the space below. Once the graph is made, write at least three statements regarding your data. For example: I used twice as many circles as triangles. Some vocabulary you may choose to use includes: more, most, greater than, fewest, less, and compared to.

triangles	circles	ovals	hexagons	quadrilat-erals	penta-gons	open figures	polygons not listed above

CHRISTOPHER COLUMBUS WAS BORN IN 1451!

____

____

____

____

____

Columbus Sails

Name ____________________

Shade all fractions that are equivalent to the eight fractions listed below to find the year Christopher Columbus sailed to the Americas.

$\frac{1}{2}$ $\frac{2}{3}$ $\frac{3}{4}$ $\frac{3}{5}$

$\frac{5}{6}$ $\frac{5}{8}$ $\frac{2}{9}$ $\frac{1}{4}$

5/10	1/6	4/16	2/16	10/16	4/5	30/50	6/9	75/100	6/11	15/20	3/6	8/12
25/30	7/9	9/15	4/5	2/4	3/9	10/45	4/12	15/24	9/10	10/21	4/7	2/8
10/20	10/18	16/24	18/24	7/28	8/29	16/72	30/60	18/30	6/20	3/8	35/42	10/100
20/32	2/6	1/9	6/11	18/27	7/10	21/23	40/50	60/80	70/90	22/88	34/40	90/95
8/36	6/7	4/12	20/50	9/18	17/80	14/16	2/10	6/10	4/9	10/12	6/27	17/34

I WASSA JUST LOOKIN' FOR A DECENT CHEESEBURGER, THASSA ALL!

It's That Time of Year

Name ____________________

Autumn

Find each product. Use the last three digits in each answer to solve the code.
Show all work. No calculators.

1. 32,426 x 63 — **O**
2. 56,841 x 145 — **Y**
3. 241,650 x 21 — **E**
4. 45,186 x 62 — **A**
5. 451,736 x 57 — **U**
6. 35,086 x 83 — **B**
7. 47,214 x 47 — **M**
8. 176,256 x 172 — **H**
9. 316,520 x 33 — **D**
10. 160,544 x 72 — **N**
11. 59,186 x 112 — **R**
12. 862,411 x 40 — **T**
13. 72,443 x 231 — **L**
14. 650,333 x 29 — **G**
15. 59,627 x 301 — **S**

What are students saying this time of year?

I'M OUTTA HERE!!

___ ___ ___ ___ — ___ ___ ___ ___ ___ ___ ___ ___ ___ . . .
657 838 838 160 — 138 945 650 727 952 58 58 650 832 . . .

___ ___ ___ ___ ___ ___ ___ ___ ___ ___ ___
32 650 333 333 838 532 952 440 952 58 168

Fall Festival

name ______________________

Solve each problem. Use the answers in any order to fill in the blanks so the stories make sense.

$326x = 1,304$	$\frac{900}{p} = 6$	$45t = 585$	$\frac{h}{30} = 20$
x = ______	p = ______	t = ______	h = ______

______ students each collected ______ dollars for the fall festival decorations. The committee used the ______ dollars to buy ______ rolls of crepe paper and other supplies.

$12y = 540$	$\frac{m}{25} = 9$	$\frac{z}{5} = 13$	$2s = 720$
y = ______	m = ______	z = ______	s = ______

The food committee spent ______ dollars on ______ pies which could be cut into eight pieces each. They decided to charge ______ cents for each of the ______ pieces of pie in order not to lose any money.

$\frac{306}{r} = 34$	$84g = 672$	$7f = 504$	$\frac{1,152}{v} = 18$
r = ______	g = ______	f = ______	v = ______

Square activity booths were set up along one wall of the gymnasium. ______ feet of wall space was divided into equal spaces for ______ booths. Each booth had ______ feet along the wall. The area of each booth was ______ square feet.

$23p = 690$	$90 \times 7 = n$	$\frac{i}{5} = 127$	$\frac{882}{w} = 42$
p = ______	n = ______	i = ______	w = ______

______ students enjoyed the activities planned for the fall festival. Planning for the festival required ______ students, ten from each grade level. A total of ______ hours went into the planning, with each student contributing ______ hours.

Fall Fruits

Name ____________________

Change each fraction to a decimal. Then find the decimal answers in the tic-tac-toe games. Draw an apple over answers of odd-numbered problems and an orange over answers of even-numbered problems.

1. $\frac{7}{20} =$

2. $\frac{12}{25} =$

3. $\frac{1}{4} =$

4. $\frac{3}{4} =$

5. $\frac{5}{8} =$

6. $\frac{2}{5} =$

7. $\frac{3}{10} =$

8. $\frac{11}{16} =$

9. $\frac{9}{10} =$

10. $\frac{3}{8} =$

11. $\frac{4}{5} =$

12. $\frac{3}{25} =$

13. $\frac{1}{8} =$

14. $\frac{1}{2} =$

15. $\frac{9}{20} =$

16. $\frac{7}{40} =$

17. $\frac{3}{5} =$

18. $\frac{7}{8} =$

19. $\frac{1}{5} =$

20. $\frac{17}{20} =$

21. $\frac{11}{50} =$

22. $\frac{19}{40} =$

.25	.4	.625
.33	.35	.48
.3	.13	.75

.12	.5	.6875
.7	.125	.8
.9	.642	.375

.2	.45	.85
.01	.875	.22
.475	.6	.175

End 1st Marking Period

First Report Card

Name ____________________

Find the mean, or average, of each student's scores. Round to the nearest whole number and record the scores in the last column. Answer the questions below based on this table.

Asia	93	88	97	100	100	97	100	
Dunn	55	60	56	72	43	52	60	
Jorge	88	90	95	100	85	90	90	
Meg	100	100	92	80	100	100	95	
Payne	78	83	79	99	87	92	99	
Shae	97	95	88	100	91	93	98	
Zia	95	100	100	98	95	100	100	

THAT'S ONE MEAN REPORT CARD, DUDE!

Use the students' cumulative scores to answer the following questions.

1. What is the mean of these cumulative scores? ____________________
2. What is the range of these scores? ____________________
3. What is the mode of these scores? ____________________
4. What is the median of these scores? ____________________
5. Who had the median score? ____________________

Use individual student's scores to answer the following questions.

6. What is the range of Dunn's scores? ____________________
7. What is the mode of Payne's scores? ____________________
8. What is the median of Meg's scores? ____________________

Ghosts and Bats

Name ____________________

Solve each problem and find the answers in the tic-tac-toe games. Draw a ghost over the answers for the odd-numbered problems and a bat over the answers for the even-numbered problems.

1. $56\overline{)27{,}384}$
2. $36\overline{)23{,}472}$
3. $15\overline{)9{,}450}$
4. $33\overline{)14{,}619}$
5. $57\overline{)10{,}203}$
6. $23\overline{)12{,}489}$
7. $47\overline{)12{,}549}$
8. $61\overline{)16{,}043}$
9. $82\overline{)12{,}218}$
10. $76\overline{)25{,}156}$
11. $42\overline{)33{,}264}$
12. $59\overline{)37{,}937}$
13. $27\overline{)16{,}146}$
14. $80\overline{)34{,}240}$

THAT ABOUT WRAPS IT UP!

____
winner

179	543	489
267	443	180
630	642	652

____
winner

643	331	428
640	263	149
546	792	598

Pumpkins

Name ________________________

Organize the addends provided in the pumpkins below. Then solve for each sum. Order the sums from greatest to least by placing a number in the box inside each pumpkin.

Work Space

Pumpkin A

45.236
2.8947
571.4 ☐
.0498
9.5046

Pumpkin B

106.753
98.5812
209.0049 ☐
158.601
66.145

Pumpkin C

25.8815
41.6888
138.4076 ☐
6.485
421.5963

Pumpkin D

316.6118
.9842
64.0215 ☐
254.168
3.2145

Pumpkin E

75.6431
66.03403
.60287 ☐
6.5842
490.25

Pumpkin F

39.1804
308.6666
41.0648 ☐
234.942
5.4862

Pumpkin G

59.8276
64.721
105.2047 ☐
3.6487
400.661

Pumpkin H

311.814
71.3541
.0489 ☐
34.2105
213.5621

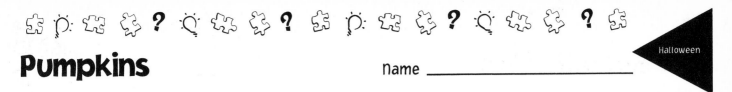

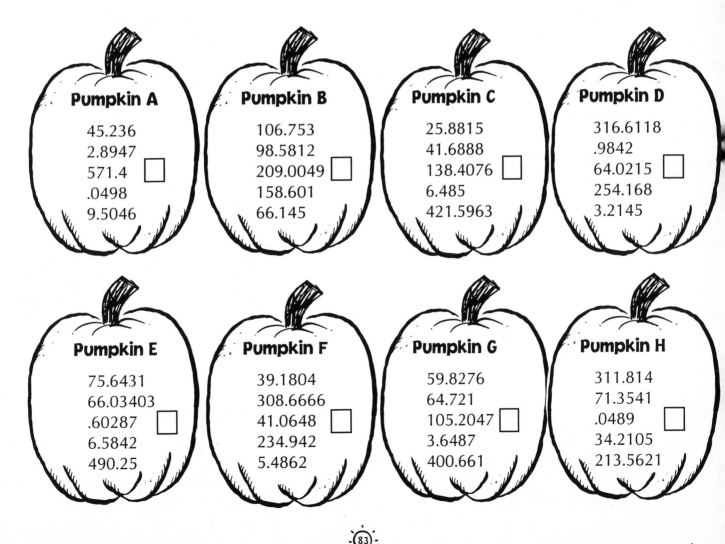

Let's Get Costumed

Name ______________________

Use the data given on this page to answer the questions.

1. Make tree diagrams to show all of the possible combinations for the clown costume.

Hair	Suit
purple	polka dots
red	large stripes
blue	swirls
green	solid
orange	

2. How many combinations are there? __________
3. What is the probability that Yancy will have red hair and a suit with large stripes? __________
4. What is the probability that Pearl will have a suit that is a solid color? __________
5. What is the probability that Wolfe will have blue hair and a suit with polka dots or blue hair and a suit with swirls? __________
6. What is the probability that Barrie will have purple or green hair? __________

Pearl has a candy bag to go with her clown suit. In the bag are mini candy bars. There are 7 solid milk-chocolate bars, 5 bars with almonds, and 3 candy bars with caramel. With the bag full, what is the probability of . . .

- choosing a solid milk-chocolate bar? __________
- choosing a candy bar with caramel? __________
- choosing a piece of gum? __________
- choosing a candy bar with almonds? __________

If Pearl returns the candy bars to the bag each time, what is the probability of . . .

- choosing a candy bar with caramel if she makes 30 picks ?__________
- choosing a solid milk-chocolate bar if she makes 75 picks? __________

Costume Party

Name ______________________

These seven friends went to a costume party dressed as seven different book characters. Use the clues and matrix to determine who was dressed as which character.

1. Sig's character sailed the seas.
2. Jean went as the spider in E.B. White's book, and Tia went as the spider's pig friend.
3. Jay's character lived while the West was being settled.
4. Bob's character tried to catch Moby Dick.
5. Tom's character had a blue ox.

MOBY DICK WAS FIRST PUBLISHED IN 1851, MATEY!

	Captain Ahab	Paul Bunyan	Charlotte	Blackbeard	Laura Ingalls	Tinkerbell	Wilbur
Bob							
Jay							
Jean							
Mae							
Sig							
Tia							
Tom							

Bob was ______________________ Jay was ______________________

Jean was ______________________ Mae was ______________________

Sig was ______________________ Tia was ______________________

Tom was ______________________

Capture the Ghost

Name ______________________

Halloween

Brunhilda and Gwendolyn are playing a game similar to Battleship in which each tries to capture the other's ghost. Brunhilda uses the answers to the odd problems and calls positions on Gwendolyn's board. Gwendolyn uses the answers to the even problems and calls positions on Brunhilda's board. Use the answers to locate the squares called. Place an **X** on each coordinate as it is called. The first to capture the other's ghost wins.

1. −2 + −6 =
2. +10 + -4 =
3. +1 − −8 =
4. −13 − −10 =
5. +3 − +8 =
6. +1 + +9 =
7. −14 − −8 =
8. +4 + +4 =
9. −4 + −7 =
10. +13 + -6 =
11. −5 − −8 =
12. −1 + +3 =
13. −5 + +4 =
14. +10 − +5 =
15. −4 + −3 =
16. +14 + −2 =
17. +2 + −4=
18. −4 − +5 =
19. +8 − +4 =
20. −1 + −9 =

Coordinates

−11	D−4	+2	E−4
−10	E−6	+3	A−3
−9	E−5	+4	D−3
−8	F−1	+5	E−2
−7	B−3	+6	C−1
−6	E−6	+7	D−4
−5	B−5	+8	D−3
−3	D−2	+9	C−2
−2	C−3	+10	E−3
−1	A−2	+12	E−1

Brunhilda

	1	2	3	4	5	6
A						
B						
C						
D						
E						
F						

Gwendolyn

	1	2	3	4	5	6
A						
B						
C						
D						
E						
F						

____
Winner

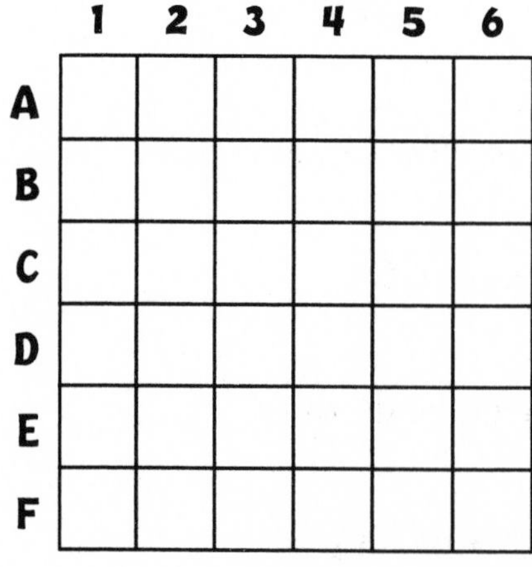

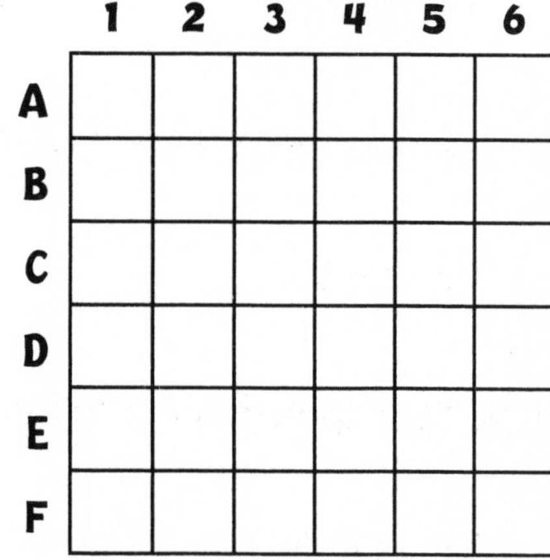

Ghouls and Goblins

Name ______________________________

Ghouls and Goblins are trying desperately to figure out mathematics that involve letters, but can't seem to do so. They want to work with numerals only. Read the directions and help them solve each request.

Write the algebraic expression for each word expression.

1. eight less than p
2. q decreased by five
3. fifteen divided by c
4. m and seven
5. nine more than j
6. f times three

Write the word expression for each algebraic expression.

7. 10r
8. s ÷ 2
9. v + 6
10. 19 – h
11. 24 ÷ d
12. y – 9

Solve the expression *7r* for each given value of *r*.

13. r = 10
14. r = .08
15. r = 3,645

Solve the expression *s – 11* for each given value of *s*.

16. s = 8
17. s = 27.42
18. s = 1,400

Solve the expression *g ÷ 2* for each given value of *g*.

19. g = 65
20. g = .6
21. g = 42.361

Solve the expression *6 + m* for each given value of *m*.

22. m = .3
23. m = –12
24. m = 99,999

Happy Halloween

name ____________________

Solve for each letter. Then use the code to find out when the Halloween festivities begin.

OCTOBER 31 WAS THE LAST DAY OF THE CELTIC YEAR! BOO!

1. n – 6.97 = 5.59

   n = __________

2. 35.15 – c = 15.85

   c = __________

3. 3.46 + s = 14.04

   s = __________

4. 234,567 + w = 833,108

   w = __________

5. l – 98,674 = 157,640

   l = __________

6. 6.012 – r = 2.024

   r = __________

7. 1.645 + m + 29.403 = 47.647

   m = __________

8. 64.008 – d = 25.767

   d = __________

9. 364,825 + k = 857,531

   k = __________

10. 3.041 – 1.183 = e

    e = __________

11. .042 + h + .566 = 1.257

    h = __________

12. g – 8,734 = 5,891

    g = __________

13. t + 57.68 = 84.62

    t = __________

14. 5.203 – i = 2.536

    i = __________

15. 23,546 + o = 53,392

    o = __________

___ 598,541 ___ .649 ___ 1.858 ___ 12.56   ___ 26.94 ___ .649 ___ 1.858

___ 19.3 ___ 256,314 ___ 29,846 ___ 19.3 ___ 492,706

___ 10.58 ___ 26.94 ___ 3.988 ___ 2.667 ___ 492,706 ___ 1.858 ___ 10.58

___ 16.599 ___ 2.667 ___ 38.241 ___ 12.56 ___ 2.667 ___ 14,625 ___ .649 ___ 26.94

Food Drive

Name ____________________

During "No-one-Hungry-on-Thanksgiving Week," Marion Middle School students held a food drive to compliment the turkeys donated by a local grocery store. Use the graph to answer the questions.

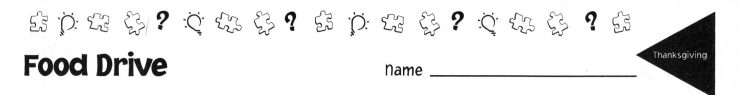

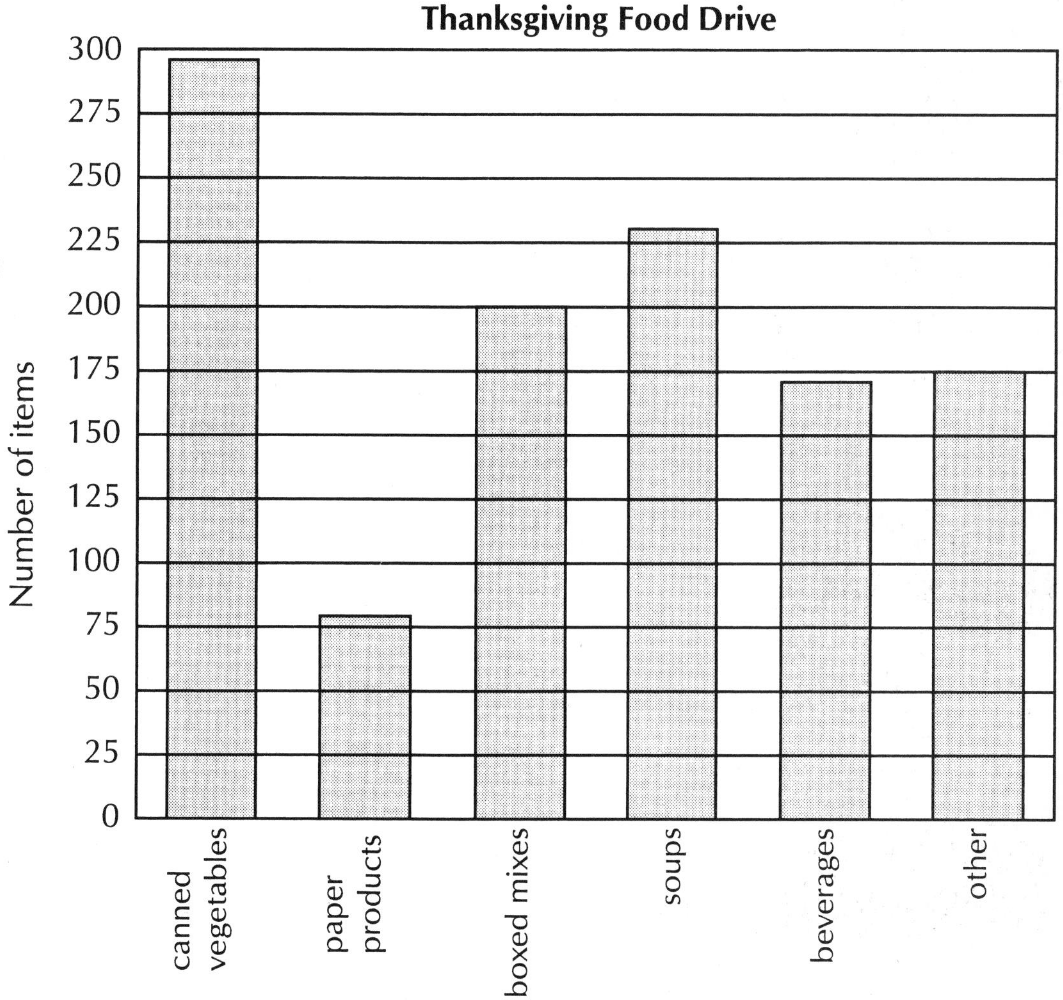

1. Which item did the students collect the greatest number of? ____________________
2. Of which item did the students collect 230 pieces? ____________________
3. Were more beverages or mixes collected? ____________________
4. Write a statement comparing the paper products and soups. ____________________

   ____
5. About how many items were collected all together? ____________

On with the Feast

Name ______________________

Use the data given on this page to answer the questions.

Beverage	Dessert
milk	pumpkin pie
water	mince pie
cola	brownie
	apple crumble

1. On a separate sheet of paper, draw tree diagrams to show all of the possible combinations at Thanksgiving dinner.
2. How many combinations are there? ________
3. What is the probability that June will have milk and pumpkin pie? ____________
4. What is the probability that Mick will have milk with his dessert? ____________
5. What is the probability that Tory will have water and apple crumble or water and mince pie?

   ____

6. What is the probability that Rafe will have a brownie? ____________

Use the frequency table for desserts ordered with school lunch the day before Thanksgiving break to answer the questions. Use the data to make a bar graph.

Frequency Table

Dessert Chosen	Frequency
pumpkin pie	155
apple pie	75
chocolate-chip cookie	60
pumpkin bars	95

Desserts

7. What is the greatest number in the frequency table? _________
8. What is the least number in the frequency table? __________
9. Which numerical scale will be easiest to read, one with intervals of 2, 5, or 10? _________

Baskets of Produce

Name ____________________

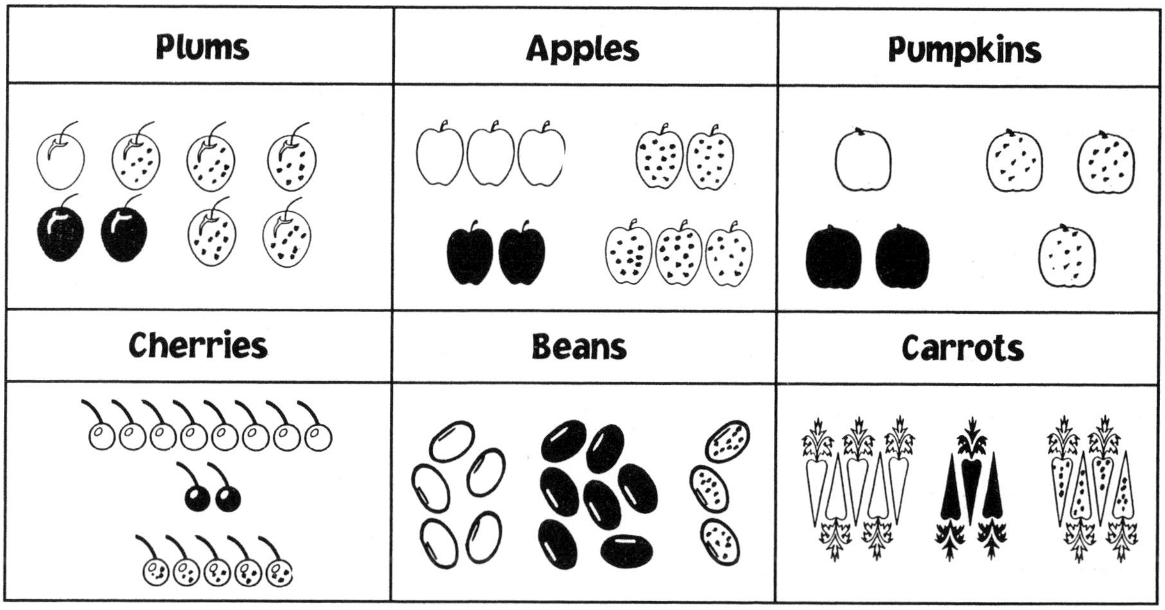

Plums	Apples	Pumpkins
Cherries	Beans	Carrots

Write the fraction for the white portion of the produce. Simplify to lowest terms.

plums	______	apples	______	pumpkins	______
cherries	______	beans	______	carrots	______

Write the fraction for the black portion of the produce. Simplify to lowest terms.

plums	______	apples	______	pumpkins	______
cherries	______	beans	______	carrots	______

Write the fraction for the dotted portion of the produce. Simplify to lowest terms.

plums	______	apples	______	pumpkins	______
cherries	______	beans	______	carrots	______

Write a fraction addition sentence for each and solve. Simplify to lowest terms.

white and dotted plums ____________________

white and black apples ____________________

white and black pumpkins ____________________

dotted and black cherries ____________________

black and dotted beans ____________________

Fabulous Feast

Name ______________________

Thanksgiving

Ms. Kelly's cooking classs decided to put together a Thanksgiving feast for the school's early childhood center. Each student prepared a different dish to complete the meal. Use the clues and matrix to determine what dish each of the seven students made.

1. Sage made a pie.
2. Mia's contribution was a vegetable.
3. Mac used Granny Smiths to make his product.
4. Greer mashed a tuber.
5. Nat did not make a pie but did make a fruit-based dish.
6. Brit made a green vegetable.
7. Abia picked the small fruit for her dish from a tree.

THE FIRST AUTO RACE IN THE UNITED STATES WAS HELD ON THANKSGIVING DAY IN 1895!

	Pumpkin Pie	Apple Pie	Cherry Pie	Corn	Potatoes	Apple-sauce	Beans
Abia							
Brit							
Greer							
Mac							
Mia							
Nat							
Sage							

Abia made ______________________

Brit made ______________________

Greer made ______________________

Mac made ______________________

Mia made ______________________

Nat made ______________________

Sage made ______________________

Pick a Pie

Name ______________________

Change the unlike fractions in each pie to like fractions. Then number them from least to greatest.

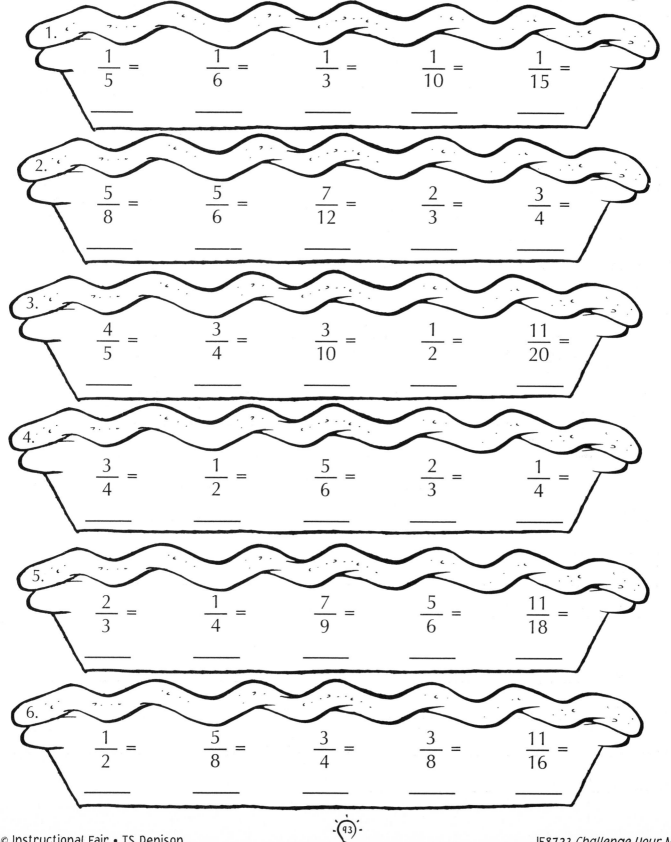

1. $\frac{1}{5} =$ ____ $\frac{1}{6} =$ ____ $\frac{1}{3} =$ ____ $\frac{1}{10} =$ ____ $\frac{1}{15} =$ ____

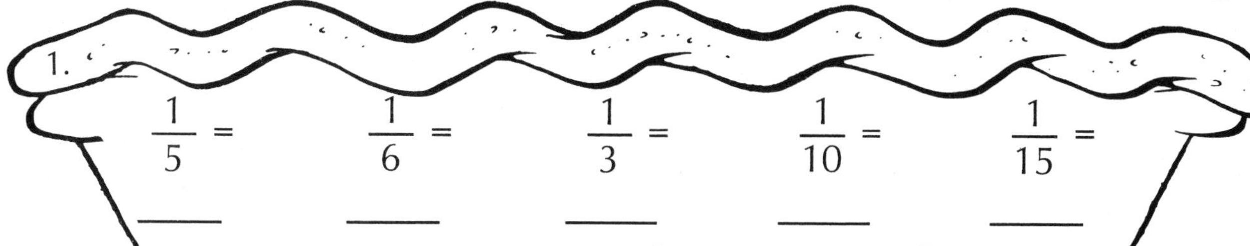

2. $\frac{5}{8} =$ ____ $\frac{5}{6} =$ ____ $\frac{7}{12} =$ ____ $\frac{2}{3} =$ ____ $\frac{3}{4} =$ ____

3. $\frac{4}{5} =$ ____ $\frac{3}{4} =$ ____ $\frac{3}{10} =$ ____ $\frac{1}{2} =$ ____ $\frac{11}{20} =$ ____

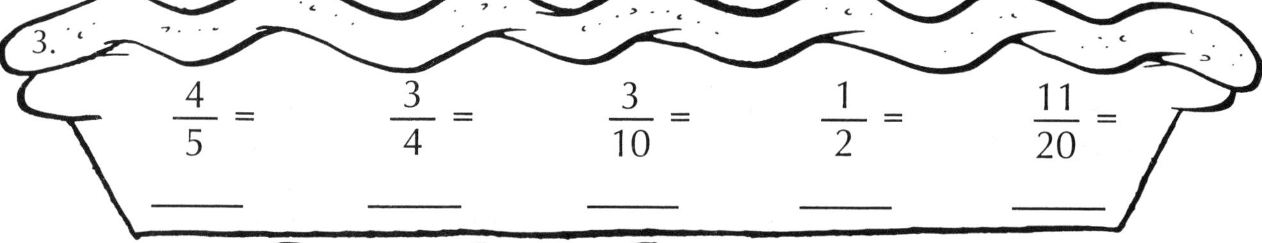

4. $\frac{3}{4} =$ ____ $\frac{1}{2} =$ ____ $\frac{5}{6} =$ ____ $\frac{2}{3} =$ ____ $\frac{1}{4} =$ ____

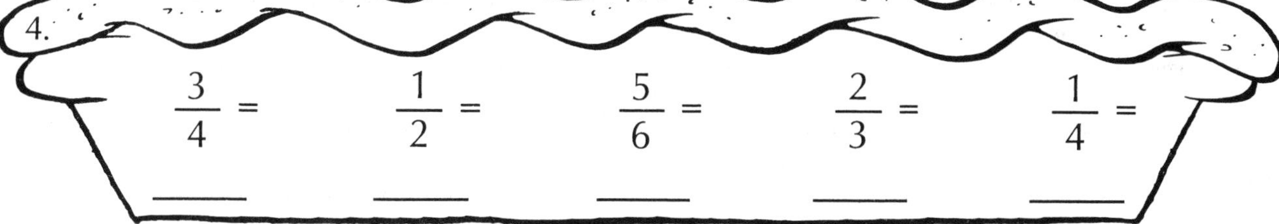

5. $\frac{2}{3} =$ ____ $\frac{1}{4} =$ ____ $\frac{7}{9} =$ ____ $\frac{5}{6} =$ ____ $\frac{11}{18} =$ ____

6. $\frac{1}{2} =$ ____ $\frac{5}{8} =$ ____ $\frac{3}{4} =$ ____ $\frac{3}{8} =$ ____ $\frac{11}{16} =$ ____

In the Air

name ______________________

Famous Firsts

What important event occurred December 17, 1903? Solve each problem. Circle the word by each corresponding answer to determine this event.

Problem			
1. 6,846,733 − 5,923,788	Alexander 1,123,055	The 922,945	transcontinental 1,922,985
2. 2,811,249 − 96,322	railroad 2,885,127	Graham 2,814,927	Wright 2,714,927
3. 9,269,812 − 4,674,266	connects 4,595,544	brothers 4,595,546	Bell 5,215,654
4. 3,641,823 − 2,327,446	flew 1,314,377	invents 1,314,423	the 1,326,423
5. 5,916,734 − 3,625,922	east 2,311,212	the 2,290,812	a 2,290,242
6. 6,381,400 − 576,031	first 5,805,369	and 3,105,369	second 6,215,431
7. 8,926,923 − 6,400,697	wireless 2,526,276	west 2,526,374	powered 2,526,226
8. 1,869,187 − 67,728	at 1,701,459	telephone 1,802,661	aircraft 1,801,459
9. 5,196,801 − 1,961,352	at 3,235,449	Promontory 4,235,449	in 4,825,449
10. 7,410,369 − 815,072	Point 7,595,217	Kitty 6,595,297	the 7,405,297
11. 4,443,924 − 4,358,056	Utah 185,932	United States 185,868	Hawk 85,868

Christmas Shopping

name ____________________

Calculator allowed.

As an early Christmas gift your parents gave you a checkbook and $100. Mom and Dad have decided that you will purchase all of your Christmas gifts to give this year. Balance the checkbook by adding deposits and subtracting debits. Keep a running total.

Date	Check #	Transaction and Reason	Debit	Deposit	Balance
12/1		Deposit—gift from Mom and Dad		$100.00	
12/4		Deposit—babysitting at Smiths'		$16.00	
12/5	101	Clothes House—jacket	$84.32		
12/7	102	Pizza Palace—lunch	$6.46		
12/8	103	Toys and More—craft set for Sammi	$16.89		
12/8		Deposit—shoveling at Cruz's		$15.00	
12/8		Deposit—shoveling at our house and at Grandma T's		$20.00	
12/9		Deposit—shoveling at Cruz's, Vinns', Sniches', Van Dons'		$50.00	
12/10	104	Bath Stuff—gifts for Grandmas T and M	$19.87		
12/10	105	Men's Den—gifts for Dad, Grandpa T, and Grandpa M	$56.82		
12/12		Deposit—babysitting at Smiths'		$24.00	
12/13		Deposit—shoveling at Cruz's, Vinns', Sniches', Van Dons'		$50.00	
12/14	106	Rich's Jewelry Store—gift for Mom	$26.89		
12/14	107	Hamburger Hut—lunch	$4.77		
12/14	108	Toys and More—art set for Randi	$15.73		
12/15		Deposit—babysitting at Cruz's		$17.50	
12/16		Deposit—shoveling at our house and at Grandma T's		$20.00	
12/17		Deposit—shoveling at Cruz's, Vinns', Sniches', Van Dons'		$50.00	
12/19	109	Steele's Steaks—gift certificate for Mom and Dad	$30.00		
12/19	110	Pizza Palace—slumber party with friends	$23.88		

In the Package

name ____________________

Fill up the package by writing the multiples for each number in the table.

1												
2												
3												
4												
5												
6												
7												
8												
9												

Use the table to write common multiples for the following number pairs. Circle the Least Common Multiple (LCM).

1. 8 and 6 ____________________
2. 5 and 3 ____________________
3. 2 and 3 ____________________
4. 7 and 2 ____________________
5. 4 and 6 ____________________
6. 9 and 6 ____________________

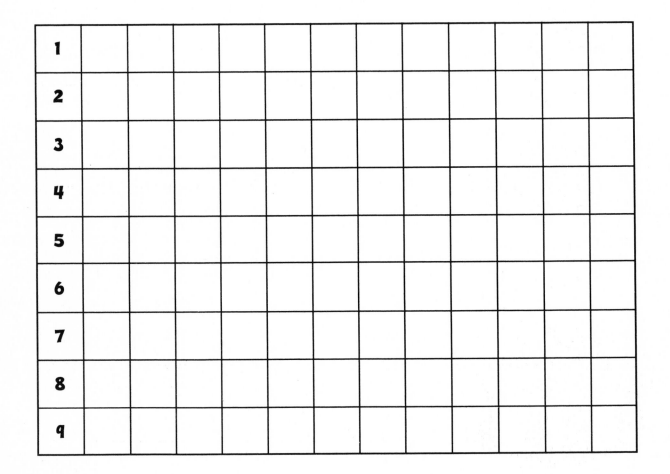

Fill It and Wrap It

Name ______________________________

Find the volume of each gift box listed below. Also find the surface area to help with wrapping paper purchases. The unit of measurement is inches. Hint: determine the area of all 6 sides, then add up the square units.

6x2x4

Determine the volume: __________________________

What is the surface area? __________________________

7.5x2.5x12

Determine the volume: __________________________

What is the surface area? __________________________

8x8x8

Determine the volume: __________________________

What is the surface area? __________________________

4x6x11

Determine the volume: __________________________

What is the surface area? __________________________

Greetings

Name ______________________

Find the common denominators for each of the fractions listed. Write them on the lines below.

$\frac{15}{24}$ $\frac{1}{6}$ $\frac{3}{4}$ $\frac{1}{4}$ $\frac{1}{2}$ $\frac{11}{12}$ $\frac{5}{6}$

$\frac{3}{8}$ $\frac{2}{3}$ $\frac{7}{12}$ $\frac{1}{8}$ $\frac{5}{12}$ $\frac{1}{3}$

Order the fractions using like denominators:

___ ___ ___ ___ ___ ___ ___ ___ ___ ___ ___ ___ ___

Now, order the fractions with unlike denominators and use the Message Key to write a holiday greeting.

___ ___ ___ ___ ___ ___ ___ ___ ___ ___ ___ ___ ___

THE ANCIENT ROMANS CELEBRATED THE FEAST OF THE INVINCIBLE SUN ON DECEMBER 25!

Message Key

A	$\frac{1}{6}$, $\frac{3}{4}$	O	$\frac{1}{2}$
D	$\frac{2}{3}$	P	$\frac{1}{4}$, $\frac{1}{3}$
H	$\frac{1}{8}$, $\frac{5}{12}$	S	$\frac{11}{12}$
I	$\frac{15}{24}$	Y	$\frac{3}{8}$, $\frac{5}{6}$
L	$\frac{7}{12}$		

Write the message:

___ ___ ___ ___ ___   ___ ___ ___ ___ ___ ___ ___ ___

Christmas

Holiday Message

Name ______________________

Write each fraction in the simplest form. Then shade each answer in the puzzle to find a holiday message.

1. $\frac{9}{27} =$
2. $\frac{24}{32} =$
3. $\frac{24}{28} =$
4. $\frac{31}{62} =$
5. $\frac{28}{35} =$
6. $\frac{15}{39} =$
7. $\frac{24}{54} =$
8. $\frac{12}{30} =$
9. $\frac{28}{48} =$
10. $\frac{24}{27} =$
11. $\frac{9}{45} =$
12. $\frac{12}{21} =$
13. $\frac{7}{28} =$
14. $\frac{15}{33} =$
15. $\frac{12}{54} =$
16. $\frac{6}{36} =$
17. $\frac{9}{15} =$
18. $\frac{16}{24} =$
19. $\frac{20}{24} =$
20. $\frac{36}{56} =$
21. $\frac{22}{30} =$
22. $\frac{18}{48} =$
23. $\frac{28}{52} =$
24. $\frac{27}{60} =$
25. $\frac{8}{56} =$
26. $\frac{18}{60} =$
27. $\frac{45}{55} =$
28. $\frac{12}{45} =$
29. $\frac{33}{48} =$
30. $\frac{37}{51} =$
31. $\frac{20}{32} =$
32. $\frac{20}{36} =$
33. $\frac{20}{48} =$
34. $\frac{14}{32} =$
35. $\frac{14}{20} =$
36. $\frac{26}{44} =$
37. $\frac{78}{120} =$
38. $\frac{4}{40} =$
39. $\frac{12}{66} =$

$\frac{1}{7}$	$\frac{5}{3}$	$\frac{2}{15}$	$\frac{9}{11}$	$\frac{3}{2}$	$\frac{7}{8}$	$\frac{9}{17}$	$\frac{13}{22}$	$\frac{9}{10}$	$\frac{7}{6}$	$\frac{5}{9}$	$\frac{2}{3}$	$\frac{2}{5}$	$\frac{5}{4}$	$\frac{7}{16}$	$\frac{2}{7}$	$\frac{6}{11}$
$\frac{9}{14}$	$\frac{13}{20}$	$\frac{2}{13}$	$\frac{1}{6}$	$\frac{8}{11}$	$\frac{3}{10}$	$\frac{1}{9}$	$\frac{3}{3}$	$\frac{1}{4}$	$\frac{1}{11}$	$\frac{2}{9}$	$\frac{3}{16}$	$\frac{4}{13}$	$\frac{1}{33}$	$\frac{1}{2}$	$\frac{5}{7}$	$\frac{2}{15}$
$\frac{5}{13}$	$\frac{1}{16}$	$\frac{4}{5}$	$\frac{5}{12}$	$\frac{2}{17}$	$\frac{9}{20}$	$\frac{11}{6}$	$\frac{1}{19}$	$\frac{6}{7}$	$\frac{1}{9}$	$\frac{7}{10}$	$\frac{3}{8}$	$\frac{10}{9}$	$\frac{6}{5}$	$\frac{4}{15}$	$\frac{1}{32}$	$\frac{2}{61}$
$\frac{5}{11}$	$\frac{5}{4}$	$\frac{1}{21}$	$\frac{11}{16}$	$\frac{1}{8}$	$\frac{3}{4}$	$\frac{3}{13}$	$\frac{5}{16}$	$\frac{7}{12}$	$\frac{1}{22}$	$\frac{8}{9}$	$\frac{3}{23}$	$\frac{1}{43}$	$\frac{5}{2}$	$\frac{7}{13}$	$\frac{8}{11}$	$\frac{1}{13}$
$\frac{1}{10}$	$\frac{3}{2}$	$\frac{1}{12}$	$\frac{3}{5}$	$\frac{6}{5}$	$\frac{1}{17}$	$\frac{4}{7}$	$\frac{1}{3}$	$\frac{4}{25}$	$\frac{5}{21}$	$\frac{11}{15}$	$\frac{1}{5}$	$\frac{5}{6}$	$\frac{1}{9}$	$\frac{4}{9}$	$\frac{5}{8}$	$\frac{2}{11}$

Hang the Stockings with Care

Name ____________________

Christmas

Each stocking is filled with a different function machine. Determine the missing functions and fill the stockings with number goodies.

Rule add $2\frac{1}{4}$

$4\frac{3}{4}$	7
$6\frac{1}{4}$	
$7\frac{3}{8}$	
$3\frac{1}{3}$	
$5\frac{5}{12}$	
$1\frac{5}{8}$	
$2\frac{1}{5}$	
$10\frac{1}{2}$	
$8\frac{5}{6}$	
$3\frac{7}{10}$	

Rule $+1 \div 3$

8	3
5	
29	
17	
14	
11	
20	
23	
26	
32	

Rule ________

6	3
25	12.5
18	9
15	
15.2	
40	
96	
2	
.75	
10	

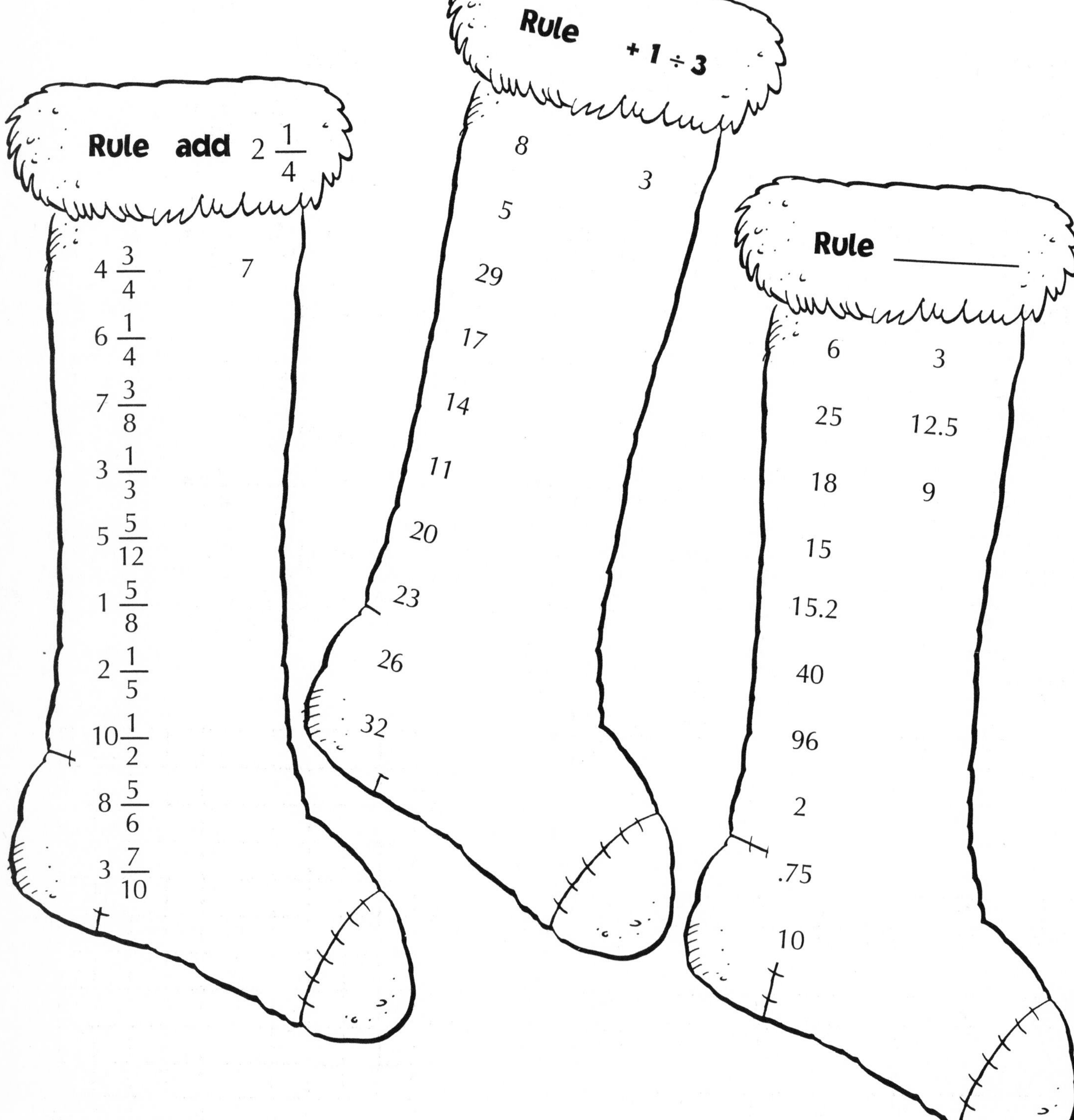

Christmas Symbol

Name ______________________________

Solve each problem. Find the answers below and write the corresponding grid coordinates.

(2, 4)
1. $\frac{5}{6} - \frac{1}{6} =$

(6, 0)
2. $\frac{5}{9} - \frac{2}{9} =$

(6, 8)
3. $\frac{9}{15} - \frac{6}{15} =$

(9, 4)
4. $\frac{7}{8} - \frac{5}{8} =$

(5, 10)
5. $\frac{15}{16} - \frac{3}{16} =$

(7, 6)
6. $\frac{19}{20} - \frac{3}{20} =$

(10, 2)
7. $\frac{11}{16} - \frac{5}{16} =$

(0, 2)
8. $\frac{14}{21} - \frac{8}{21} =$

(1, 4)
9. $\frac{17}{18} - \frac{7}{18} =$

(2, 6)
10. $\frac{1}{2} - \frac{1}{10} =$

(6, 2)
11. $\frac{3}{4} - \frac{2}{3} =$

(0, 2)
12. $\frac{1}{5} - \frac{1}{6} =$

(8, 6)
13. $\frac{2}{3} - \frac{1}{2} =$

(4, 0)
14. $\frac{5}{6} - \frac{5}{8} =$

(4, 8)
15. $\frac{7}{10} - \frac{3}{5} =$

(8, 6)
16. $\frac{2}{3} - \frac{2}{5} =$

(8, 4)
17. $\frac{5}{6} - \frac{7}{9} =$

(7, 8)
18. $\frac{7}{8} - \frac{2}{3} =$

(4, 2)
19. $\frac{8}{11} - \frac{5}{22} =$

(3, 8)
20. $\frac{3}{4} - \frac{2}{5} =$

____ $\frac{2}{7}$	____ $\frac{1}{12}$	____ $\frac{1}{3}$	____ $\frac{5}{24}$	____ $\frac{1}{2}$	____ $\frac{3}{8}$	____ $\frac{1}{18}$
____ $\frac{1}{4}$	____ $\frac{4}{5}$	____ $\frac{1}{6}$	____ $\frac{1}{5}$	____ $\frac{5}{24}$	____ $\frac{3}{4}$	____ $\frac{7}{20}$
____ $\frac{1}{10}$	____ $\frac{2}{5}$	____ $\frac{4}{15}$	____ $\frac{5}{9}$	____ $\frac{2}{3}$	____ $\frac{1}{30}$	

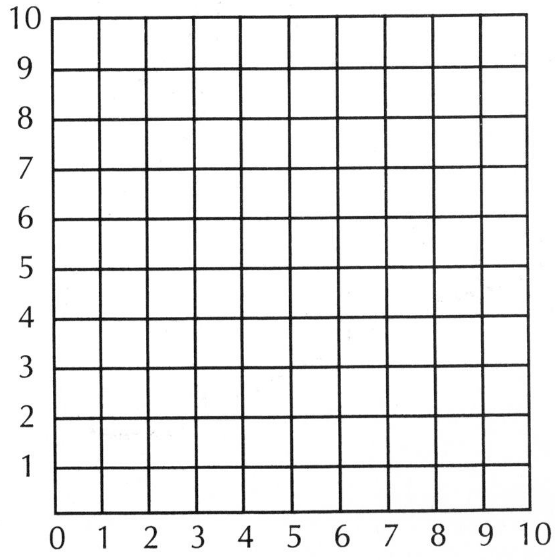

Factor Trees

Name ____________________

Develop a factor tree for each of the composite numbers listed below. Any factor tree with 5 or more factors is large enough to be cut as a Christmas tree. Outline the trees ready for cutting.

210	128	324	68
132	253	66	432
394	87	235	168
252	420	45	376

Holiday Traditions

Name ______________________

Kwanzaa honors African American people and their past. It begins on December 26 and lasts until January 1. It was first celebrated in 1966 by Dr. Maulana Karenga so African American people could learn about their history and customs. Following are some words associated with Kwanzaa. Use the matrix and clues to determine the definition of each word.

1. Ted explained that the Mkeka is not flown or eaten.
2. Jala used Mazao to make a wonderful fruit salad as part of the Karamu.
3. Theo wore his Dashiki.
4. Ashanta lit the Mishumaa Saba, the seven candles of Kwanzaa, that were in the Kinara.
5. Zawadi are more meaningful when they are ceated or made with the giver's own hands or mind.
6. The green, black, and red Bendera was hung for guests to see.

	Bendera	Dashiki	Karamu	Kinara	Mazao	Mkeka	Zawadi
place mat for table							
African American flag							
candle holder							
gifts given on the last day of Kwanzaa							
fruits and vegetables of the harvest							
special feast							
piece of clothing							

Bendera ______________________

Dashiki ______________________

Karamu ______________________

Kinara ______________________

Mazao ______________________

Mkeka ______________________

Zawadi ______________________

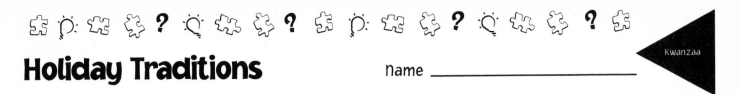

Common Factors Through Time

Name ____________

New Year's

As the year is completed and a new one begun, it is time to consider the history of numbers. Erathosthenes, an ancient Greek mathematician, developed a method to determine prime numbers. His method for finding the 25 prime numbers between 1 and 100 is explained below. A prime number is a number with only two factors. Circle all prime numbers. Then cross out all composite numbers (those with more than two factors).

X	(2)	(3)	X	(5)	X	(7)	X	X	X
(11)	X	(13)	X	X	X	(17)	X	(19)	X
X	X	(23)	X	X	X	X	X	(29)	X
(31)	X	X	X	X	X	(37)	X	X	X
(41)	X	(43)	X	X	X	(47)	X	X	X
X	X	(53)	X	X	X	X	X	(59)	X
(61)	X	X	X	X	X	(67)	X	X	X
(71)	X	(73)	X	X	X	X	X	(79)	X
X	X	(83)	X	X	X	X	X	(89)	X
X	X	X	X	X	X	(97)	X	X	X

1. Cross out 1.
2. Circle the smallest prime number. What is it? 2
3. Cross out all multiples of this number.
4. Circle the next prime number. What is it? 3
5. Cross out all multiples of this number.
6. Circle the next prime number. What is it? 5
7. Cross out all multiples of this number.
8. Circle the next prime number. What is it? 7
9. Cross out all multiples of this number.
10. Circle the prime numbers.

THIS METHOD OF FINDING PRIME NUMBERS IS CALLED THE SIEVE OF ERATHOSTHENES!

Page 4

After-Holiday Sale!

Name ____________

New Year's

After the holidays, everything at Big Buys is discounted. From 9 A.M. to 9 P.M. nothing is full price! Calculate the discounts and subtract from the regular prices. Write the pre-tax prices on the sale tags.

- $129.95 — 33% Off — portable sound system — $87.07
- $46.97 — 33% Off — telephone — $31.47
- $99.99 — 33% Off — camera — $66.99
- $85.29 — 55% Off — winter jacket — $38.38
- $25.14 — 55% Off — holiday craft kit — $11.31
- $99.99 — 55% Off — large stuffed bear — $45.00
- $37.89 — 25% Off — watch — $28.42
- $67.99 — 25% Off — hand-held game — $50.99
- $19.95 — 25% Off — latest VCR movie — $14.96

Page 5

Holiday Cash

Name ____________

New Years

You received a total of $164.00 as gift money during the holiday season. Read each of the following situations and keep a running balance. Notice that each situation begins with the remaining balance of the previous situation; you do not begin with $164.00 each time. Show your work.

Beginning balance: $164.00

1. Your parents have decided that you must put 30% of your gift money into your savings account.
   remaining balance: $114.80
   $164. × .30 = $49.20; $164.00 − 49.20 = $114.80
2. You lost your ski boots and you must replace them. They are normally $87.95, but are 35% off with the post-holiday sales.
   remaining balance: $57.63
   $87.95 − 30.78 = $57.17; $114.80 − 57.17 = $57.63
3. You promised your brother you would buy him an action figure for helping you shovel the driveway. You can buy 3 for $7.00, but you only need to buy one.
   remaining balance: $55.30
   7.00 ÷ 3 = 2.33; $57.63 − 2.33 = $55.30
4. Mom and Dad pay you $6.50 each time you shovel the driveway. You shoveled 4 times this week.
   new balance: $81.30
   $6.50 × 4 = $26.00; $55.30 + 26.00 = $81.30
5. You went out for pizza with 7 friends. You split the cost of two pizzas with all of your friends. The pizzas, without beverages, cost $16.50. You also paid for two large drinks at $1.09 each.
   remaining balance: $77.06
   $16.50 ÷ 8 = 2.0625; $2.06 + 2.18 = $4.24; $81.30 − 4.24 = $77.06

Page 6

Let It Snow

Name ____________

Winter

Solve each problem. Use the corresponding letters in the code below to determine some words used for various types of snow. These words come from the Inuit Indians and the Lapps.

K 1. $\frac{2}{3} \times 1\frac{1}{8} = \frac{3}{4}$

O 2. $4\frac{1}{2} \times 2\frac{2}{3} = 12$

I 3. $1\frac{2}{3} \times \frac{4}{5} = 1\frac{1}{3}$

A 4. $\frac{3}{4} \times 5\frac{1}{3} = 4$

T 5. $5\frac{1}{4} \times 4\frac{2}{3} = 24\frac{1}{2}$

S 6. $\frac{1}{3} \times 3\frac{1}{2} = 1\frac{1}{6}$

Q 7. $4\frac{2}{5} \times 1\frac{3}{7} = 6\frac{2}{7}$

P 8. $4\frac{1}{12} \times 1\frac{3}{7} = 5\frac{5}{6}$

L 9. $2\frac{1}{5} \times 6\frac{1}{9} = 13\frac{4}{9}$

U 10. $5\frac{1}{3} \times 4\frac{1}{2} = 24$

A 11. $3\frac{3}{5} \times 7\frac{1}{6} = 25\frac{4}{5}$

I 12. $2\frac{1}{6} \times 3\frac{1}{3} = 7\frac{2}{9}$

A P I ($25\frac{4}{5}$, $5\frac{5}{6}$, $1\frac{1}{3}$): The blanket of snow that insulates and covers the ground.

P U K A K ($5\frac{5}{6}$, 24, $\frac{3}{4}$, 4, $\frac{3}{4}$): The bottom layer of snow that is melted by the earth and creates tunnels for mice and other small animals.

Q A L I ($6\frac{2}{7}$, $25\frac{4}{5}$, $13\frac{4}{9}$, $7\frac{2}{9}$): Snow that blankets tree and bush branches; helps winter animals hide and pushes food into their reach.

U P S I K (24, $5\frac{5}{6}$, $1\frac{1}{6}$, $1\frac{1}{3}$, $\frac{3}{4}$): Snow that is wind-packed and hard; used to make igloos.

S I Q O Q T O A Q ($1\frac{1}{6}$, $7\frac{2}{9}$, $6\frac{2}{7}$, 12, $6\frac{2}{7}$, $24\frac{1}{2}$, 12, 4, $6\frac{2}{7}$): Snow with a crust on top, formed when melted snow refreezes.

Page 7

Winter Fences

Name ____________

Write the factors of each composite number below it on the fence post. Write the Greatest Common Factors (GCF) in the rungs between the posts. The first one is done for you.

26	GCF	4	GCF	16	GCF	12	GCF	18	GCF	27
1, 2, 13, 26	2	1, 2, 4	4	1, 2, 4, 8, 16	4	1, 2, 3, 4, 6, 12	6	1, 2, 3, 6, 9, 18	9	1, 3, 9, 27

21	GCF	14	GCF	42	GCF	15	GCF	20	GCF	30
1, 3, 7, 21	7	1, 2, 7, 14	14	1, 2, 3, 6, 7, 14, 21, 42	3	1, 3, 5, 15	5	1, 2, 4, 5, 10, 20	10	1, 2, 3, 5, 6, 10, 15, 30

6	GCF	48	GCF	8	GCF	28	GCF	22	GCF	55
1, 2, 3, 6	6	1, 2, 3, 4, 6, 8, 12, 16, 24, 48	8	1, 2, 4, 8	4	1, 2, 4, 7, 14, 28	2	1, 2, 11, 22	11	1, 5, 11, 55

63	GCF	45	GCF	36	GCF	24	GCF	50	GCF	10
1, 3, 7, 9, 21, 63	9	1, 3, 5, 9, 15, 45	9	1, 2, 3, 4, 6, 9, 12, 18, 36	12	1, 2, 3, 4, 6, 8, 12, 24	2	1, 2, 5, 10, 25, 50	10	1, 2, 5, 10

Page 8

Through the Blizzard

Name ____________

Wade through the blizzard of multiples. One number in each row of the chart is not a multiple of the given number. Circle it in each line. Arrange the circled numbers and follow the rules for order of operations to arrive at the given answer.

Number	Multiples									
2	10	4	2	(7)	8	26	32	12	14	16
3	15	3	24	6	12	21	9	(26)	30	18
6	(46)	18	36	12	48	6	24	42	54	30
9	36	72	9	63	18	45	(15)	27	54	81

List the incorrect multiples: 7 26 46 15 Arrange these numbers to make the following equation true: (46 - 26) x (15 - 7) = 160

Number	Multiples									
4	20	16	36	8	24	4	32	12	(18)	28
5	10	50	15	(9)	5	40	30	20	35	25
7	35	7	63	28	42	(24)	14	56	21	49
8	56	24	48	72	16	(20)	32	64	8	40

List the incorrect multiples: 18 9 24 20 Arrange these numbers to make the following equation true: (24 - 20) x 9 - 18 = 18

Page 9

Build a Snowman

Name ____________

Solve each addition problem.

1. 4.571 + 24.85 + 360.521 + .0391 = 389.9811
2. 981.1 + 89.342 + 2.013 + 10.906 = 1083.361
3. 108.61 + 3.386 + 51.105 + .009 = 163.11
4. 31.61 + 111.364 + 8.008 + 942.1 = 1093.082
5. .4632 + 50.11 + 9.0501 + 8.76 = 68.3833
6. 833.3 + 68.89 + 361.275 + 5.687 = 1269.152
7. 69.125 + 152.96 + 3.892 + 2,115.6 = 2341.577
8. .785 + 432.1 + 41.52 + 962.38 = 1436.785
9. 36.54 + 147.02 + 6,205.6 + 8.699 = 6397.859
10. 85.36 + 397.6 + 5,900.369 + 77.1205 = 6460.4495
11. 52.141 + 9.511 + 214.9 + 69.341 = 345.893
12. 27.99 + 713.24 + 58.378 + 464.8 = 1264.408
13. 64.12 + 408.4 + 5.99 + 709.577 = 1188.087

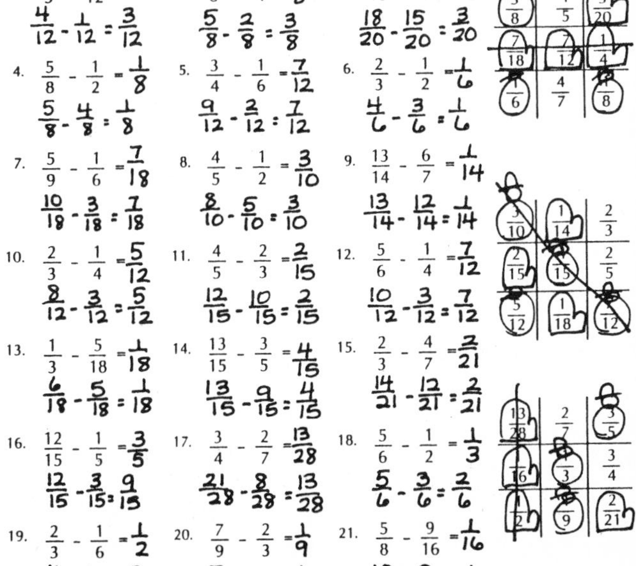

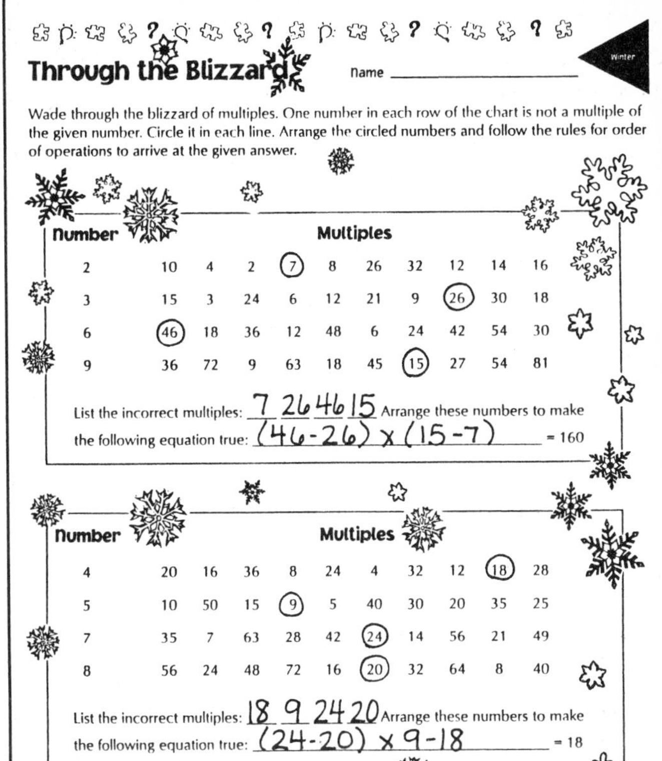

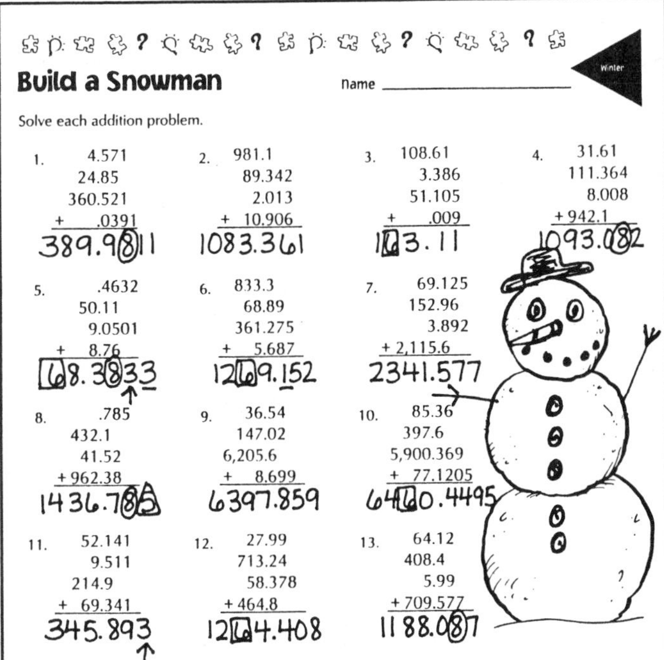

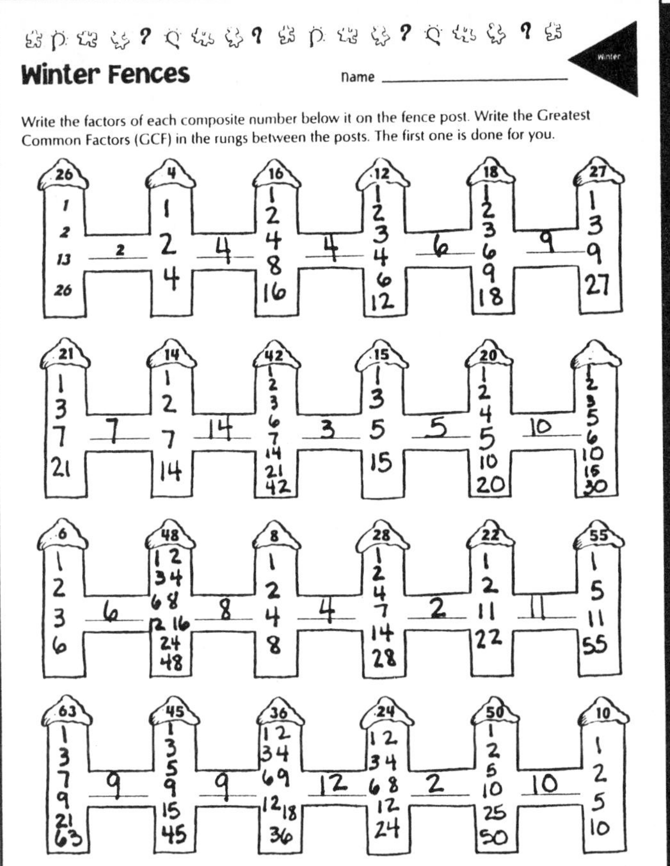

Look at each sum. Follow the directions.

1. Circle all 8s in the hundredths place. Draw one piece of coal for the mouth for each. 5
2. Underline all 1s in the tenths place. Draw one eye for each. 2
3. Put a triangle around each 5 in the ten thousandths place. Draw one carrot nose for each. 1
4. Draw an arrow beneath each 3 in the thousandths place. Draw one stick arm for each. 2
5. Put a box around each 6 in the tens place. Draw one charcoal button for each. 5
6. Underline each 3 in the ten thousandths place. Draw one hat for each. 1

Page 10

Tic-Tac-Toe Is Cool

Name ____________

Solve each subtraction problem. Then locate each answer in the tic-tac-toe games. Replace the traditional Xs and Os with snowment and mittens. Draw a snowman over the answer of each even-numbered difference and a mitten over the odd-numbered differences.

1. $\frac{1}{3} - \frac{1}{12} = \frac{1}{4}$; $\frac{4}{12} - \frac{1}{12} = \frac{3}{12}$
2. $\frac{5}{8} - \frac{1}{4} = \frac{3}{8}$; $\frac{5}{8} - \frac{2}{8} = \frac{3}{8}$
3. $\frac{9}{10} - \frac{3}{4} = \frac{3}{20}$; $\frac{18}{20} - \frac{15}{20} = \frac{3}{20}$
4. $\frac{5}{8} - \frac{1}{2} = \frac{1}{8}$; $\frac{5}{8} - \frac{4}{8} = \frac{1}{8}$
5. $\frac{3}{4} - \frac{1}{6} = \frac{7}{12}$; $\frac{9}{12} - \frac{2}{12} = \frac{7}{12}$
6. $\frac{2}{3} - \frac{1}{2} = \frac{1}{6}$; $\frac{4}{6} - \frac{3}{6} = \frac{1}{6}$
7. $\frac{5}{9} - \frac{1}{6} = \frac{7}{18}$; $\frac{10}{18} - \frac{3}{18} = \frac{7}{18}$
8. $\frac{4}{5} - \frac{1}{2} = \frac{3}{10}$; $\frac{8}{10} - \frac{5}{10} = \frac{3}{10}$
9. $\frac{13}{14} - \frac{6}{7} = \frac{1}{14}$; $\frac{13}{14} - \frac{12}{14} = \frac{1}{14}$
10. $\frac{2}{3} - \frac{1}{4} = \frac{5}{12}$; $\frac{8}{12} - \frac{3}{12} = \frac{5}{12}$
11. $\frac{4}{5} - \frac{2}{3} = \frac{2}{15}$; $\frac{12}{15} - \frac{10}{15} = \frac{2}{15}$
12. $\frac{5}{6} - \frac{1}{4} = \frac{7}{12}$; $\frac{10}{12} - \frac{3}{12} = \frac{7}{12}$
13. $\frac{1}{3} - \frac{5}{18} = \frac{1}{18}$; $\frac{6}{18} - \frac{5}{18} = \frac{1}{18}$
14. $\frac{13}{15} - \frac{3}{5} = \frac{4}{15}$; $\frac{13}{15} - \frac{9}{15} = \frac{4}{15}$
15. $\frac{2}{3} - \frac{4}{7} = \frac{2}{21}$; $\frac{14}{21} - \frac{12}{21} = \frac{2}{21}$
16. $\frac{12}{15} - \frac{1}{5} = \frac{3}{5}$; $\frac{12}{15} - \frac{3}{15} = \frac{9}{15}$
17. $\frac{3}{4} - \frac{2}{7} = \frac{13}{28}$; $\frac{21}{28} - \frac{8}{28} = \frac{13}{28}$
18. $\frac{5}{6} - \frac{1}{2} = \frac{1}{3}$; $\frac{5}{6} - \frac{3}{6} = \frac{2}{6}$
19. $\frac{2}{3} - \frac{1}{6} = \frac{1}{2}$; $\frac{4}{6} - \frac{1}{6} = \frac{3}{6}$
20. $\frac{7}{9} - \frac{2}{3} = \frac{1}{9}$; $\frac{7}{9} - \frac{6}{9} = \frac{1}{9}$
21. $\frac{5}{8} - \frac{9}{16} = \frac{1}{16}$; $\frac{10}{16} - \frac{9}{16} = \frac{1}{16}$

3/8	1/5	3/20
7/18	7/12	1/4
1/6	4/7	1/8

3/10	1/14	2/3
2/15	1/15	2/5
5/12	1/18	7/12

13/28	2/7	3/5
1/6	1/3	3/4
1/2	1/9	2/21

Page 11

Let it Snow . . .

Name ________________

Bryan and Mikaela collected data regarding snow types that fell during January. They collected a snow sample on a 2" by 2" piece of black cloth from 3:00 to 3:15 P.M. each time it snowed on school days. Use the frequency table to answer the questions. Use the data to make a graph.

Bryan and Mikaela's Frequency Table

Snow Crystals	Frequency
hexagonal plate	456
stellar dendrite	364
column	203
needle	289
tsuzumi	0

1. What is the greatest number in the frequency table? 456
2. What is the least number in the frequency table? 0
3. Name a numerical scale with equal intervals that you believe is appropriate for graphing the given data. 25

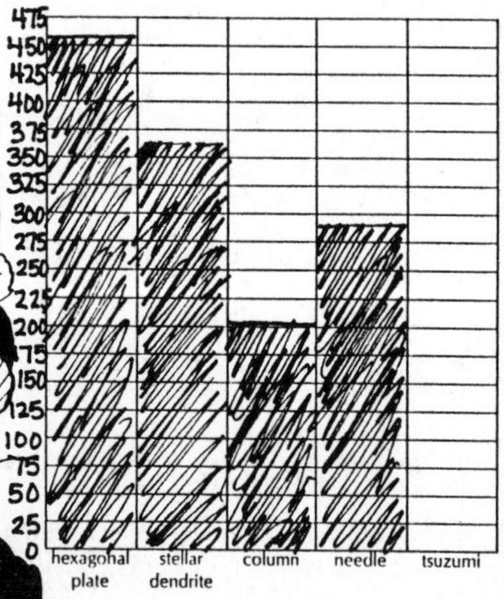

It's Freezing Out There!

Name ________________

Solve each temperature problem.

1. It was 5°C degrees outside at noon. Four hours later, the temperature had dropped 8 degrees. What was the temperature outside at 4:00? -3°

   +5 + -8 = -3 degrees

2. It was -6°F outside at Kevin's house. His friend Jan called to say it was 32°F outside at his house. How much colder is it at Kevin's house than at Jan's? -38°

   -6 - +32 = -38 degrees

3. At 3:00, it was -6°F outside. The windchill made it feel like -10°F. How much colder did the windchill make the temperature? -4°

   -6 + □ = -10 -10 - -6 = -4 degrees

4. The air temperature was -7°C. The water temperature was 4°C. How much warmer is the water temperature? +11°

   +4 - -7 = +11 degrees

5. Solve the equations below. Write the sums and differences in order from least to greatest. Write the corresponding letters in the same order. The letters will spell the answer to the following question: What measurement tool is used with temperature?

A T H E R M O M E T E R
-12 -7 -4 -2 0 +1 +2 +5 +6 +7 +8 +10

-4 – +3 = T -7	+6 + -10 = H -4	+8 – -2 = R +10
-5 – -7 = O +2	-9 + -3 = A -12	+6 + -6 = R 0
+2 + +5 = T +7	-1 + +9 = E +8	+13 + -7 = E +6
+4 + -6 = E -2	-3 – -8 = M +5	-8 + +9 = M +1

Snowball Buildings

Name ________________

Build the snow pyramids. Some blocks are missing. Use your addition skills to fill them in. Each pyramid adds to the top.

1.

$10\frac{1}{3}$

$\frac{61}{12}$ $\frac{63}{12}$

$\frac{15}{6}$ $\frac{31}{12}$ $\frac{32}{12}$

$\frac{7}{6}$ $\frac{8}{6}$ $\frac{5}{4}$ $\frac{17}{12}$

$\frac{1}{3}$ $\frac{5}{6}$ $\frac{1}{2}$ $\frac{3}{4}$ $\frac{2}{3}$

2.

$\frac{192}{24} = 8$

$\frac{113}{24}$ $\frac{79}{24}$

$\frac{20}{8}$ $\frac{53}{24}$ $\frac{13}{12}$

$\frac{9}{8}$ $\frac{11}{8}$ $\frac{10}{12}$ $\frac{3}{12}$

$\frac{1}{2}$ $\frac{5}{8}$ $\frac{3}{4}$ $\frac{1}{12}$ $\frac{1}{6}$

3.

$\frac{221}{36} = 6\frac{5}{36}$

$\frac{51}{18}$ $\frac{119}{36}$

$\frac{26}{18}$ $\frac{25}{18}$ $\frac{69}{36}$

$\frac{13}{18}$ $\frac{13}{18}$ $\frac{12}{18}$ $\frac{5}{4}$

$\frac{1}{6}$ $\frac{5}{9}$ $\frac{3}{18}$ $\frac{1}{2}$ $\frac{3}{4}$

4.

$\frac{110}{12} = 9\frac{1}{6}$

$\frac{63}{12}$ $\frac{47}{12}$

$\frac{17}{6}$ $\frac{29}{12}$ $\frac{18}{12}$

$\frac{8}{6}$ $\frac{9}{6}$ $\frac{11}{12}$ $\frac{7}{12}$

$\frac{1}{2}$ $\frac{5}{6}$ $\frac{2}{3}$ $\frac{1}{4}$ $\frac{1}{3}$

5.

$9\frac{3}{16}$

$\frac{71}{16}$ $\frac{38}{8}$

$\frac{33}{16}$ $\frac{19}{8}$ $\frac{19}{8}$

$\frac{15}{16}$ $\frac{9}{8}$ $\frac{5}{4}$ $\frac{9}{8}$

$\frac{9}{16}$ $\frac{3}{8}$ $\frac{3}{4}$ $\frac{1}{2}$ $\frac{5}{8}$

What's Your Favorite Winter Sport?

Name ________________

Determine the favorite winter sport of each of seven Internet pen pals. Use the clues and matrix to determine who likes each winter sport.

1. Denzel lives in Hawaii and enjoys water sports.
2. Manny loves snow country.
3. Ulf does not like downhill skiing.
4. Judy needs a board to enjoy her water sport.
5. Ione had to wait for the pond to freeze before she could enjoy her sport.
6. Quinn grabs a backpack and heads into the Arizona desert.
7. Whitney had to fix the engine of her sport vehicle last week.

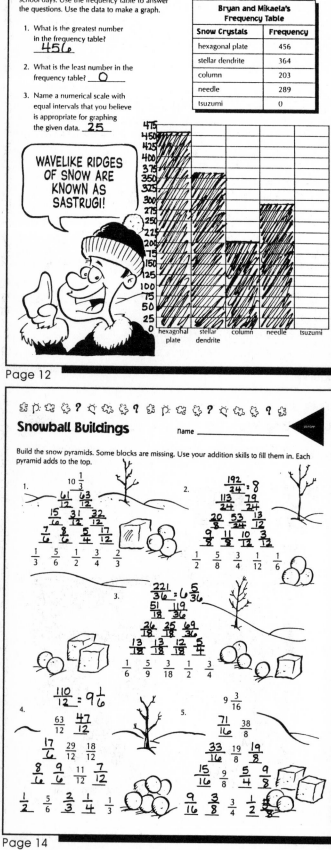

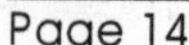

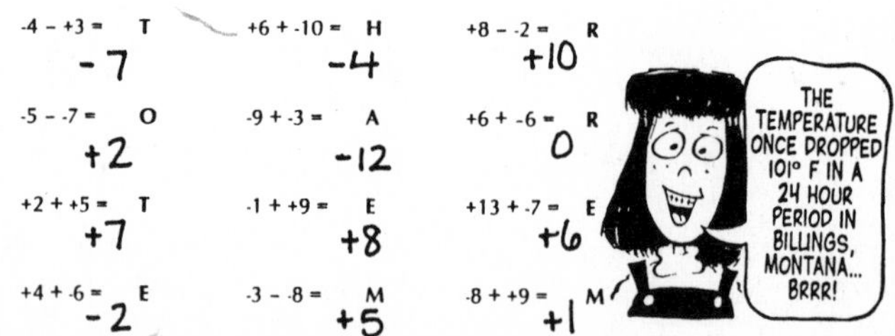

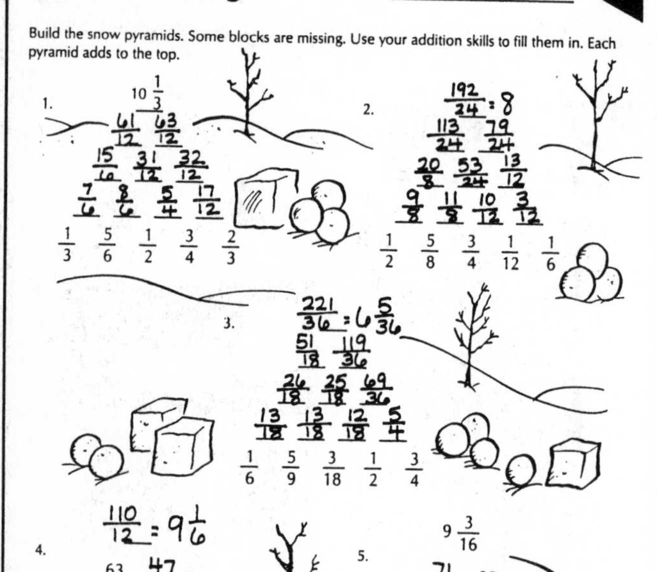

	Cross-country skiing	Down-hill skiing	Hiking	Ice Skating	Snow-mobiling	Surfing	Swim-ming
Denzel	X	X	X	X	X	X	YES
Ione	X	X	X	YES	X	X	X
Judy	X	X	X	X	X	YES	X
Manny	X	YES	X	X	X	X	X
Quinn	X	X	YES	X	X	X	X
Ulf	YES	X	X	X	X	X	X
Whitney	X	X	X	X	YES	X	X

Denzel enjoys SWIMMING

Ione enjoys ICE SKATING

Judy enjoys SURFING

Manny enjoys DOWNHILL SKIING

Quinn enjoys HIKING

Ulf enjoys C.C. SKIING

Whitney enjoys SNOWMOBILING

A Solemn Pledge

Name ____________________

Inauguration Day

Every four years, the president is sworn in on January 20 by the top judge on the U.S. Supreme Court. Solve each problem. Convert any improper fractions. Then use the answers and the key to write "The Presidential Oath of Office." The problem numbers are written below the blanks.

" I (19) DO (9) SOLEMNLY (18) SWEAR (2) THAT (14)
I (19) WILL (13) FAITHFULLY (16) EXECUTE (4) THE (1)
OFFICE (24) OF (12) PRESIDENT (20) OF (12) THE (3)
UNITED (17) STATES, (10) AND (15) WILL (13) TO (8)
THE (7) BEST (12) OF (22) MY (23) ABILITY,
PRESERVE (6) PROTECT, (11) AND (15) DEFEND (21) THE (3)
CONSTITUTION (5) OF (12) THE (1) UNITED (17) STATES (10)."

ability	16/35	do	1 1/3	of	1/5	solemnly	8/15	the	4/5
and	6 1/8	execute	1/11	office	5 1/4	States	5/6	to	1 1/9
best	1 1/7	faithfully	1 4/7	preserve	3/4	swear	1 1/14	United	7/10
Constitution	1/2	I	2/15	President	1	that	3 1/3	will	2/3
defend	1 1/2	my	7/18	protect	1 1/5				

1. $\frac{2}{3}+\frac{5}{6}=\frac{4}{5}$
2. $\frac{6}{7}+\frac{4}{5}=1\frac{1}{14}$
3. $\frac{1}{2}+\frac{5}{8}=\frac{4}{5}$
4. $\frac{1}{4}+\frac{11}{12}=\frac{3}{11}$
5. $\frac{1}{3}+\frac{7}{9}=\frac{3}{7}$
6. $\frac{1}{3}+\frac{4}{9}=\frac{3}{4}$
7. $\frac{6}{7}+\frac{3}{4}=1\frac{1}{7}$
8. $\frac{5}{6}+\frac{3}{4}=1\frac{1}{9}$
9. $\frac{8}{9}+\frac{2}{3}=1\frac{1}{3}$
10. $\frac{5}{8}+\frac{3}{4}=\frac{5}{6}$
11. $\frac{9}{10}+\frac{3}{4}=1\frac{1}{5}$
12. $\frac{1}{5}+\frac{1}{3}=\frac{3}{5}$
13. $\frac{8}{21}+\frac{4}{7}=\frac{2}{3}$
14. $\frac{5}{7}+\frac{3}{14}=3\frac{1}{3}$
15. $\frac{7}{8}+\frac{1}{7}=6\frac{1}{8}$
16. $\frac{6}{7}+\frac{6}{11}=1\frac{4}{7}$
17. $\frac{14}{25}+\frac{4}{5}=\frac{7}{10}$
18. $\frac{2}{9}+\frac{5}{12}=\frac{8}{15}$
19. $\frac{1}{9}+\frac{5}{6}=\frac{2}{15}$
20. $\frac{6}{15}+\frac{2}{5}=1$
21. $\frac{1}{6}+\frac{1}{9}=1\frac{1}{2}$
22. $\frac{1}{3}+\frac{6}{7}=\frac{7}{18}$
23. $\frac{2}{7}+\frac{5}{8}=\frac{16}{35}$
24. $\frac{3}{8}+\frac{1}{14}=5\frac{1}{4}$

Page 16

Famous Black Americans

Name ____________________

Black History Month

Solve each problem. Use the answers to decode the names of famous people who contributed to our history.

1. +5 + -3 = 2
2. -10 – -4 = -6
3. -1 + -7 = -8
4. -4 – -9 = 5
5. -4 + +7 = 3
6. +2 + +9 = ~~18~~ 11
7. +6 – +7 = -1
8. -7 + -5 = -12
9. -14 – -15 = 1
10. +6 + -9 = -3
11. -9 + +15 = 6
12. +5 + -9 = -4
13. -10 – -14 = 4
14. +16 + -6 = 10
15. -2 + -3 = -5
16. -4 – +5 = -9
17. +6 – -3 = 9
18. -10 – -8 = -2
19. -16 – -6 = -10
20. -7 + +14 = 7

A +2	D +9	G +4	J -1	M -5	P +7	T +5
B -4	E +1	H -6	K -8	N +3	R -3	U +11
C -12	F -10	I -9	L +6	O +10	S -2	

First black woman astronaut:
DR MAE JEMISON (17 10 15 1 9 7 9 15 16 18 14 5)

Talented opera singer:
MARIAN ANDERSON (15 1 10 16 14 5 1 5 17 9 10 18 14 5)

First African American baseball player to play for the major leagues:
JACKIE ROBINSON (7 1 8 3 16 9 10 14 12 16 5 18 14 5)

First African American Supreme Court justice:
THURGOOD MARSHALL (4 2 6 10 13 14 14 17 15 1 10 18 2 1 11 11)

Teacher who founded Kwanzaa:
DR MAULANA KARENGA (17 10 15 1 6 11 1 5 1 3 1 10 9 5 13 1)

Woman who refused to give up her seat to a white person on a public bus:
ROSA PARKS (10 14 18 1 20 1 10 3 18)

Page 17

Super Scientist

Name ____________________

Black History Month

In 1946, Congress designated January 5 as a day to honor a famous scientist. This agricultural scientist developed over 200 ways to use the peanut and sweet potato. Who is this scientist? Solve for each letter. Write the letter in caps above each corresponding answer.

GEORGE (2.45 6.2 2.56 .65 .15 .73)
WASHINGTON (.78 .61 .56 .25 .88 .36 .899 .98 .87 .66)
CARVER (.51 .11 .413 2.6 9.45 .47)

1. 350h = 87.5 — h = .25
2. 3.12 + r = 3.77 — r = .65
3. t + .4 = 2.45 — t = .98
4. 1r = .2209 — r = .47
5. 465 + g = 3100 — g = .15
6. e – .578 = 8.872 — e = 9.45
7. 0(.13) = .3328 — o = 2.56
8. 77/a = 700 — a = .11
9. 6.12 – g = 3.67 — g = 2.45
10. .652 + a = 1.262 — a = .61
11. 1.512 + n = 4.2 — n = .36
12. r + 4.87 = 5.283 — r = .413
13. n(.23) = .1518 — n = .66
14. 4.6 – w = 3.82 — w = .78
15. e9 = 55.8 — e = 6.2
16. 4.61 + g = 5.509 — g = .899
17. v – 1.54 = 1.06 — v = 2.6
18. 4.21i = 3.7048 — i = .88
19. o + 5.68 = 6.55 — o = .87
20. .1938/c = .38 — c = .51
21. 6e = 4.38 — e = .73
22. 1.848/3.3 = s — s = .56

Page 18

Groundhog Day

Name ____________________

Groundhog Day

On Groundhog Day, the groundhog looks for its shadow to predict winter's length. Look at the shadows on this page. Determine the shadowed area of each figure.

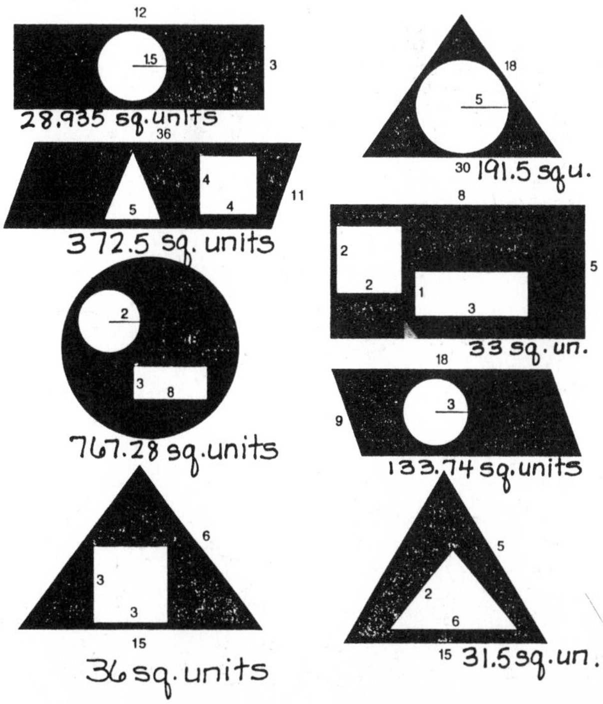

Page 19

Report Card Time

Name ____________________

End of Semester

Ms. Phreye grades on improvement. Before determining semester grades, she eliminates the lowest of the first four test scores. Then she places the highest of the last three scores in the highest score column. Using Ms. Phreye's system, find the mean, or average, of each student's scores. Use the eight unmarked scores, including the one in the highest score column, to find the mean. Round the mean score to the nearest whole number and record it in the last column. The first one is done for you. Answer the questions based on this table.

Weekly Test Scores									Highest Score	Mean Score
Edrea	78	93	X	92	86	89	91	96	96	90
Nevin	75	80	89	X	95	86	90	89	90	86
Philippa	X	87	93	87	87	87	98	94	98	90
Quinn	X	100	100	98	95	96	100	89	100	97
Ramiro	87	94	X	64	50	100	36	50	100	69
Tessa	89	93	X	97	100	100	97	100	100	97
Zedra	X	60	56	72	43	52	60	70	70	59

Use the students' cumulative scores to answer the following questions.

1. What is the mean of all the cumulative scores? 84
2. What is the range of these scores? 38
3. What is the mode of these scores? 97
4. What is the median of these scores? 90

Use individual student's scores to answer the following questions.

5. What is the range of Ramiro's scores? 64
6. What is the mode of Philippa's scores? 87
7. What is the median of Nevin's scores? 89

HUH...?

Page 20

Look at Those Test Grades

Name ____________________

Ms. Prince recorded the folowing grades for the unit test. Each of her tests has bonus points built in and identified. Read the data in the stem-and-leaf plot then answer the questions.

Stem	Leaves
11	1 3 4 4 4 5 6 9
10	0 0 0 1 1 3 4 5 5 8 9
9	3 4 5 5 5 5 5 6 7 7 8 9 9
8	1 1 2 3 4 5 6 6 7 8 9 9
7	1 2 5 7 8 8
6	2 3 3 4 7 9 9
5	0 2 6 9
4	1 6 8

Grading Scale

Grade	Score
A+	105 +
A	96–104
A-	90–95
B	80–89
C	70–79
Retake	< 69

...THINK I'LL MAKE LIKE A TREE AND LEAF...

1. How many students took the test? 64
2. What percentage of the students earned an A- or better? 50%
3. What percentage of the students had to retake the test? 22%
4. What is the range of grades? 78
5. What is the mode? 95
6. Cal took the test. What is the probability that he had to retake the test? 14:64 = 7:32
7. Sasha took the test. What is the probability that she passed the test? 50:64 = 25:32
8. How many students earned the following grades:

   A+ 12 A 13

   A- 7 B 12

   C 6 Retake 14
9. What is the probability that Tony earned a B or a C? 18:64 = 9:32
10. Did more students pass or need to retake the test? PASS

    Explain: 50 passed, 14 had to retake

Page 21

Name That Inventor

Name ____________________

Famous Inventor's Birthday

Solve each problem. Use the code to find out which inventor was born on February 11, 1847. Among this inventor's over 1,300 patents are the carbon telephone transmitter, the phonograph, and the incandescent lamp. Who is this famous inventor?

3,741	197	243	518	268	669	864	635	5,410	725	299	411
A	D	E	H	I	L	M	N	O	S	T	V

1. $66\overline{)246,906}$ = 3741
2. $42\overline{)11,256}$ = 268
3. $97\overline{)524,770}$ = 5410
4. $55\overline{)34,925}$ = 635
5. $38\overline{)15,618}$ = 411
6. $61\overline{)31,598}$ = 518
7. $13\overline{)8,697}$ = 669
8. $94\overline{)18,518}$ = 197
9. $71\overline{)21,229}$ = 299
10. $76\overline{)18,468}$ = 243
11. $18\overline{)15,552}$ = 864
12. $25\overline{)18,125}$ = 725

THIS GUY HAD ONLY THREE MONTHS OF FORMAL SCHOOLING!

THOMAS ALVA EDISON

9 6 3 11 1 12   1 7 5 1   10 8 2 12 3 4

Page 22

Message to a Sweetheart

Name ____________________

Valentine's Day

Solve the problems. Find the answers in the Coordinate Box. Write the grid coordinates in the blanks above the problem numbers, then find them on the grid. Connect the points in order. Complete the grid by connecting the grid coordinates to the right of the grid. You'll discover a Valentine message.

1. $\frac{4}{5} \times \frac{15}{16} = \frac{3}{4}$
2. $\frac{6}{7} \times \frac{7}{12} = \frac{1}{2}$
3. $\frac{2}{3} \times \frac{9}{16} = \frac{3}{8}$
4. $\frac{5}{18} \times \frac{9}{10} = \frac{1}{4}$
5. $\frac{16}{21} \times \frac{7}{8} = \frac{2}{3}$
6. $\frac{12}{25} \times \frac{15}{16} = \frac{9}{20}$
7. $\frac{4}{9} \times \frac{6}{10} = \frac{4}{15}$
8. $\frac{6}{15} \times \frac{5}{6} = \frac{1}{3}$
9. $\frac{8}{9} \times \frac{3}{20} = \frac{2}{15}$
10. $\frac{7}{20} \times \frac{4}{7} = \frac{1}{5}$
11. $\frac{7}{16} \times \frac{6}{21} = \frac{3}{24}$

Coordinate Box

(4, 6)	$\frac{1}{2}$	(7, 8)	$\frac{1}{3}$	(5, 9)	$\frac{1}{5}$	(9, 9)	$\frac{9}{20}$	(7, 4)	$\frac{3}{8}$
(4, 8)	$\frac{3}{4}$, $\frac{3}{24}$	(8, 9)	$\frac{4}{15}$	(6, 9)	$\frac{2}{15}$	(10, 6)	$\frac{1}{4}$	(10, 8)	$\frac{2}{3}$

(4, 8)₁ (4, 6)₂ (7, 4)₃ (10, 6)₄ (10, 8)₅

(9, 9)₆ (8, 9)₇ (7, 8)₈ (6, 9)₉ (5, 9)₁₀ (4, 8)₁₁

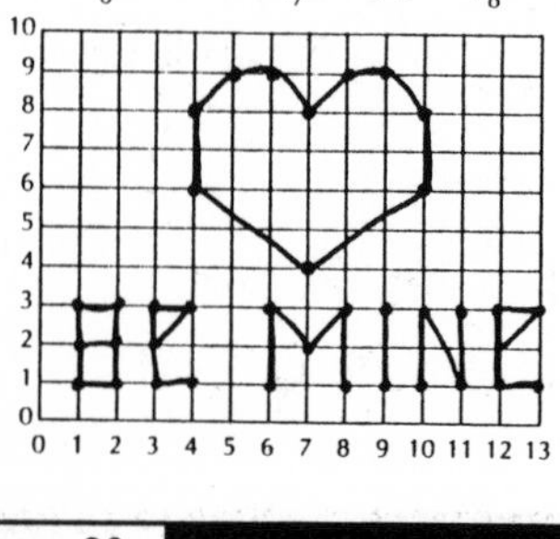

(1, 2), (1, 1), (2, 1), (2, 3), (1, 3), (1, 2), (2, 2) stop

(4, 1), (3, 1), (3, 3), (4, 3), (3, 2) stop

(8, 1), (8, 3), (7, 2), (6, 3), (6, 1) stop

(9, 1), (9, 3) stop

(10, 1), (10, 3), (11, 1), (11, 3) stop

(12, 2), (13, 3), (12, 3), (12, 1), (13, 1) stop

Page 23

Valentine Rhyme

Name ______________________

Valentine's Day

Solve each problem. Circle the word in each row with the corresponding answer. Read the words top to bottom and write the rhyme on the lines below.

Problem	Answer			
1. $6 + 2 \times 3 - 6 + 2 =$	9	3 I	21 Love	(9 Roses)
2. $(5 - 2) + (2 + 1) =$	1	(1 Are)	5 Is	$4\frac{1}{3}$ Am
3. $12 + 4 + 2 \times 5 =$	13	10 In	(13 Red)	$\frac{6}{7}$ A
4. $(4 + 6 + 2) - (10 + 2 - 5) =$	7	5 Many	(7 Violets)	$-2\frac{2}{3}$ Love
5. $2 \times (3 + 4 - 5) - 10 =$	−6	−5 Splendor	−1 With	(−6 Are)
6. $(10 + 2 + 10) + 3 =$	5	$\frac{1}{6}$ Thing	$7\frac{1}{3}$ Blue	(5 White)
7. $2 \times 2 \times 5 \times 4 - 6 =$	74	(74 Mathematics)	−40 Sugar	56 I
8. $(16 + 2 - 6) \times 12 =$	24	−64 Love	(24 Is)	−48 Am
9. $7 \times 6 - 10 \times 8 + 2 =$	2	−112 Sweet	128 You	(2 Fun)
10. $8 \times 8 + 2 + -4 \times 5 =$	12	(12 Both)	−160 Do	$-6\frac{2}{3}$ And
11. $(42 - 20) + 11 + 8 =$	10	$1\frac{1}{19}$ You	$43\frac{1}{19}$ So	(10 Day)
12. $(8 - 2 \times 2) \times 20 + 5 =$	16	(16 And)	12 Are	48 Love
13. $(5 \times 5 - 10) + 5 =$	3	−1 Me?	23 You!	(3 Night!)

FOOTBALLS ARE BROWN, GOLF BALLS ARE WHITE, TO DO THIS PAGE MIGHT TAKE YOU ALL NIGHT!

Valentine Message:
Roses Are Red, Violets Are White
Mathematics Is Fun, Both Day And Night!

Page 24

Presidents

Name ______________________

Presidents' Day

Use the clues to complete the matrix and determine each president's term of office.

1. Lyndon B. Johnson became president when President John Kennedy was shot. He finished Kennedy's term and was elected for an additional four years.
2. John Adams was the second president of the United States.
3. Ulysses S. Grant and Theodore Roosevelt were both elected to two terms.
4. Andew Johnson was the seventeenth president. He was elected just after Abraham Lincoln, the sixteenth president, and just before Ulysses S. Grant, the eighteenth president.
5. Millard Fillmore was the thirteenth president. He resided in the White House when the first bath tub with running water was installed.

	John Adams	Millard Fillmore	Ulysses S. Grant	Andrew Johnson	Lyndon B. Johnson	Theodore Roosevelt	William H. Taft
1797–1801	YES	X	X	X	X	X	X
1850–1853	X	YES	X	X	X	X	X
1865–1869	X	X	X	YES	X	X	X
1869–1877	X	X	YES	X	X	X	X
1901–1909	X	X	X	X	X	YES	X
1909–1913	X	X	X	X	X	X	YES
1963–1969	X	X	X	X	YES	X	X

John Adams: 1797-1801
Millard Fillmore: 1850-1853
Ulysses S. Grant: 1869-1877
Andrew Johnson: 1865-1869
Lyndon B. Johnson: 1963-1969
Theodore Roosevelt: 1901-1909
William Howard Taft: 1909-1913

Page 25

It's Still Winter

Name ______________________

Winter

1. $4\frac{1}{3} + 2\frac{8}{9} = 1\frac{1}{2}$
2. $2\frac{1}{5} + 1\frac{1}{10} = 2$
3. $5\frac{1}{4} + 2\frac{1}{3} = 2\frac{1}{4}$
4. $4\frac{1}{6} + 1\frac{2}{3} = 2\frac{1}{2}$
5. $2\frac{1}{7} + 1\frac{2}{9} = 1\frac{58}{77}$
6. $3\frac{8}{9} + 8\frac{1}{3} = \frac{7}{15}$
7. $4\frac{1}{2} + 2\frac{8}{9} = 1\frac{1}{3}$
8. $2\frac{2}{3} + 4\frac{2}{3} = \frac{4}{7}$
9. $2\frac{3}{4} + 4\frac{1}{8} = \frac{2}{3}$
10. $9\frac{3}{7} + 5\frac{1}{2} = 1\frac{5}{7}$
11. $3\frac{3}{4} + 2\frac{1}{2} = 1\frac{1}{2}$
12. $5\frac{1}{3} + 2\frac{2}{15} = 2\frac{1}{2}$

Code

E	$1\frac{1}{2}$	T	$2\frac{1}{2}$
I	$\frac{4}{7}$	V	$1\frac{58}{77}$
N	$2\frac{1}{4}$	W	$\frac{2}{3}$
O	2	Y	$\frac{7}{15}$
R	$1\frac{1}{3}$		
S	$1\frac{5}{7}$		

SCIENTIFIC FACT NO. 33: IT'S USUALLY COLDER IN THE WINTER!

I (8) S (10) N (3) 'T (4)
W (9) I (8) N (3) T (12) E (11) R (7)
O (2) V (5) E (1) R (7) Y (6) E (11) T (4) !?

Page 26

Leprechaun's Gold

Name ______________________

St. Patrick's Day

Find the products. Then shade the corresponding pieces of gold to find out which leprechaun has the most gold.

1. $\frac{2}{5} \times \frac{3}{8} = \frac{3}{20}$
2. $\frac{4}{7} \times \frac{1}{8} = \frac{1}{14}$
3. $\frac{3}{5} \times \frac{5}{6} = \frac{1}{2}$
4. $\frac{8}{9} \times \frac{3}{10} = \frac{4}{15}$
5. $\frac{2}{9} \times \frac{6}{7} = \frac{4}{21}$
6. $\frac{1}{5} \times \frac{10}{11} = \frac{2}{11}$
7. $\frac{4}{13} \times \frac{1}{8} = \frac{1}{26}$
8. $\frac{14}{15} \times \frac{5}{6} = \frac{7}{9}$
9. $\frac{4}{9} \times \frac{3}{4} = \frac{1}{3}$
10. $\frac{2}{3} \times \frac{9}{10} = \frac{3}{5}$
11. $\frac{4}{5} \times \frac{1}{4} = \frac{1}{5}$
12. $\frac{15}{16} \times \frac{2}{5} = \frac{3}{8}$
13. $\frac{7}{9} \times \frac{9}{28} = \frac{1}{4}$
14. $\frac{3}{8} \times \frac{4}{9} = \frac{1}{6}$
15. $\frac{9}{14} \times \frac{2}{3} = \frac{3}{7}$

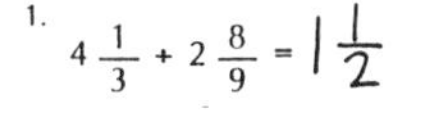

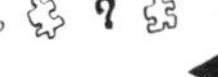

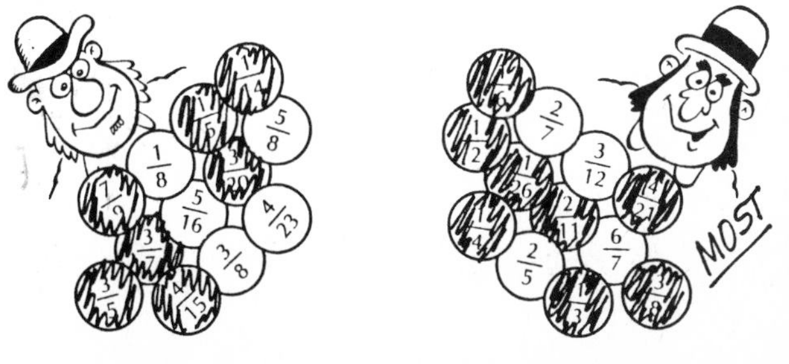
MOST

Page 27

Hide and Seek

Name ____________________

St. Patrick's Day

The leprechauns have hidden more than gold. Find the following mathematical words in the puzzle. If a math term consists of more than one word, it can change direction at the space. Words can be found →, ←, ↗↙, ↕. They can be spelled forward or backward.

addend	liter	mass	quotient
area	ordered pair	mean	range
average	order of operations	median	rate
bar graph	prime number	percent	ratio
factor tree	square root	perimeter	meter
fraction	tree diagram	probability	sum
gram	greatest common factor	product	mode
numerator	least common denominator	proportion	unit rate
integers	least common multiple		

Q	U	O	T	I	E	N	T	O	P	E	R	A	T	I	O	N	S	T	A
M	D	I	A	G	R	A	M	F	N	U	M	E	R	A	T	F	M	E	A
P	R	E	G	R	A	T	I	O	O	R	D	T	N	E	C	R	E	P	R
T	N	E	M	R	V	L	I	R	E	D	R	O	R	D	E	A	R	E	M
Y	N	R	E	P	E	R	I	M	E	T	E	R	A	N	G	C	O	M	M
T	E	T	E	R	R	A	N	N	U	N	U	M	E	R	A	T	O	R	S
I	I	L	E	T	A	R	T	A	N	G	L	E	M	E	D	I	A	N	Q
A	I	T	E	G	U	N	D	E	N	O	M	I	N	A	T	O	R	T	U
I	N	T	E	R	E	Q	O	M	S	E	S	Q	U	A	R	N	I	O	A
B	L	E	A	S	T	R	Q	M	G	T	C	O	M	M	O	N	U	O	R
A	R	M	E	T	C	O	S	N	M	E	D	I	A	S	Q	F	M	R	E
B	A	B	I	O	A	S	A	P	R	O	D	U	C	T	I	A	E	M	T
O	I	N	M	E	E	R	T	R	O	T	C	A	F	L	S	C	E	N	A
R	I	M	R	A	R	Q	L	E	A	S	T	M	U	S	M	T	R	O	R
P	O	A	P	R	I	M	B	A	R	G	R	A	P	H	E	O	Q	C	T
N	U	M	B	E	A	N	O	I	T	R	O	P	O	R	P	R	D	R	[illegible]
M	U	L	T	I	P	L	E	S	R	E	B	M	U	N	U	E	C	E	N
A	D	D	E	N	D	E	R	E	D	R	O	S	Q	E	M	I	R	P	U

Four Leaf Clovers

Name ____________________

St. Patrick's Day

Multiply the number in each cloverleaf by the number in the center of the clover. Shade each piece of clover whose four products add up to a number > 4,000. These are the genuine four-leaf clovers.

How Could It Be True?

Name ____________________

April Fool's Day

Don't be fooled by these challenging problems! Complete the base table which is continued at the bottom of the page. Then use both tables to find the correct base to make each problem true.

base 10	1	2	3	4	5	6	7	8	9	10	11	12	13	14	15	16	17
base 7	1	2	3	4	5	6	10	11	12	13	14	15	16	20	21	22	23
base 5	1	2	3	4	10	11	12	13	14	20	21	22	23	24	30	31	32
base 4	1	2	3	10	11	12	13	20	21	22	23	30	31	32	33	100	101
base 3	1	2	10	11	12	20	21	22	100	101	102	110	112	112	120	121	122

1. $10_3 + 21_3 = 101_3$
2. $101_4 - 20_4 = 21_4$
3. $5_7 \times 3_7 = 21_7$
4. $11_4 + 23_4 = 100_4$
5. $1{,}022_3 + 21_3 = 12_3$
6. $111_5 - 24_5 = 32_5$
7. $2_7 \times 14_7 = 31_7$
8. $41_5 + 3_5 = 12_5$
9. $1{,}020_3 - 221_3 = 22_3$
10. $20_5 \times 3_5 = 110_5$
11. $23_4 + 102_4 = 131_4$
12. $13_5 \times 2_5 = 31_5$
13. $102_5 + 3_5 = 14_5$
14. $40_7 - 33_7 = 4_7$
15. $1{,}002_3 - 21_3 = 211_3$

base 10	18	19	20	21	22	23	24	25	26	27	28	29	30	31	32	33	34
base 7	24	25	26	30	31	32	33	34	35	36	40	41	42	43	44	45	46
base 5	33	34	40	41	42	43	44	100	101	102	103	104	110	111	112	113	114
base 4	102	103	110	111	112	113	120	121	122	123	130	131	132	133	200	201	202
base 3	200	201	202	210	211	212	220	221	222	1000	1001	1002	1010	1011	1012	1020	1021

Spring's Upon Us

Name ____________________

Springtime

Color the squares as indicated. Use the grid coordinates to discover a sign of spring.

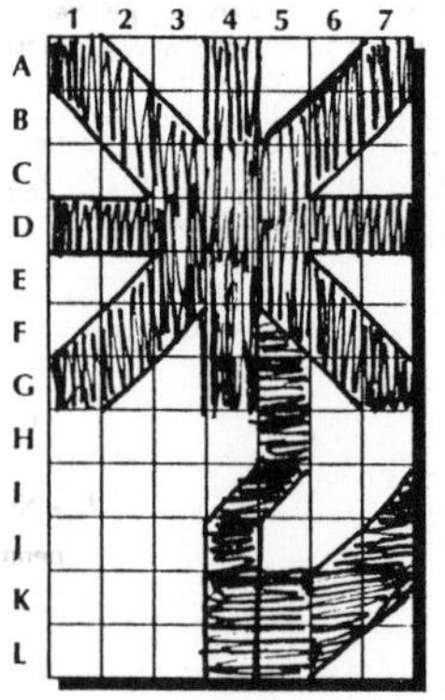

Color Key

B = color blue

O = color orange

G = color green

Coordinates

B: A-3, A-5, B-1, B-7, D-4, E-1, E-7, G-3, H-1, H-2, H-3, H-4, H-6, H–7, I-1, I-2, I-3, I-6, J-1, J-2, J-3, J-5, K-1, K-2, K-3, L-1, L-2, L-3, L-7

B/O: B-1, C-2, G-6

O/B: A-2, B-3, E-6, F-7

O/B: B-7, C-6, F-3, G-2

B/O: A-6, B -5, E-2, F-1

O: A-1, A-4, A-7, B-2, B-4, B-6, C-3, C-4, C-5, D-1, D-2, D-3, D-5, D-6, D-7, E-3, E-4, E-5, F-2, F-4, F-6, G-1, G-4, G-7

G/O: F-5

G: G-5, H-5, J-4, J-7, K-4, K-5, K-6, L-4, L-5

G/B: T-5, K-7, L-6

B/G: I-4, 1-7, J-6

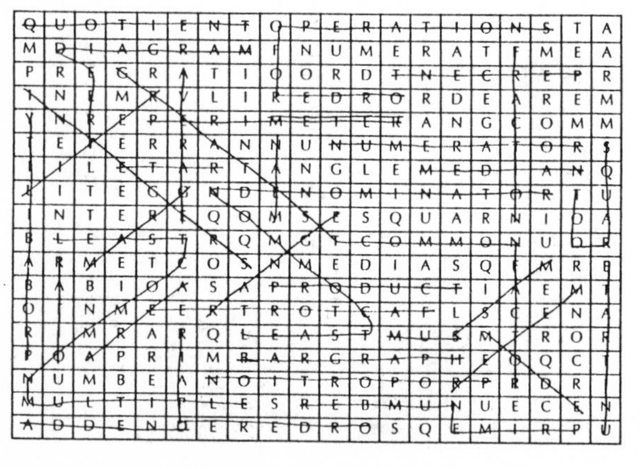

SCIENTIFIC FACT NO. 1372: SPRING IS A GREAT TIME TO START A BASEBALL SEASON!

April Showers

Name ____________

April showers bring May flowers. Put the numbers on the petals into the raindrops in order to arrive at the answer in the center of the flower. Use order of operations.

6 - 5 + 4 x 8 - 22 + 2 - 11

36 + 6 + 10 + 5 - 7 + 2 x 9

24 + 6 + 9 + 21 + 3 - 10 x 2

5 x 2 + 10 + 7 x 8 + 4 - 9

81 + 9 x 4 + 6 + 1 - 5 + 2

Page 32

Water the Flowers

Name ____________

Solve each problem. Find the answers in the tic-tac-toe boards. Place a raindrop on the answers of the odd-numbered problems and a flower on the even-numbered problems. Who won each game?

1. $2\frac{1}{3} + 7\frac{1}{6}$ = $9\frac{1}{2}$
2. $8\frac{4}{5} + 1\frac{4}{15}$ = $10\frac{1}{15}$
3. $7\frac{3}{4} - 2\frac{1}{6}$ = $5\frac{7}{12}$
4. $1\frac{6}{7} + 5\frac{1}{2}$ = $7\frac{5}{14}$
5. $8\frac{3}{8} - 5\frac{3}{4}$ = $2\frac{5}{8}$
6. $4\frac{1}{4} - 1\frac{2}{3}$ = $2\frac{7}{12}$
7. $1\frac{5}{6} + 1\frac{8}{9}$ = $3\frac{13}{18}$
8. $10\frac{1}{2} - 6\frac{2}{3}$ = $3\frac{5}{6}$
9. $2\frac{5}{6} + 4\frac{1}{3}$ = $7\frac{1}{6}$
10. $1\frac{3}{8} + 1\frac{3}{4}$ = $3\frac{1}{8}$
11. $5\frac{1}{8} - 3\frac{3}{4}$ = $1\frac{3}{8}$
12. $3\frac{5}{16} + 2\frac{5}{8}$ = $5\frac{15}{16}$
13. $2\frac{3}{5} + 3\frac{2}{3}$ = $6\frac{4}{15}$
14. $6\frac{1}{4} - 1\frac{4}{5}$ = $4\frac{9}{20}$
15. $11\frac{13}{15} - 9\frac{1}{5}$ = $2\frac{2}{3}$

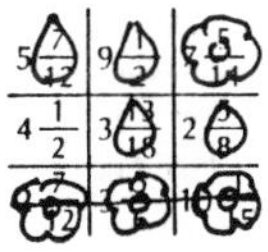

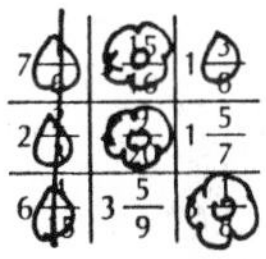

Page 33

Gardens

Name ____________

Hy plans gardens. He needs to know the area and perimeter of each plot to determine the number of plants he needs and the amount of edging or fencing needed. Help him calculate the perimeter and area of the following plots.

1. area 72 ft.
   perimeter 36 ft.

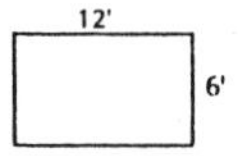

2. area 58 ft.
   perimeter 34 ft.

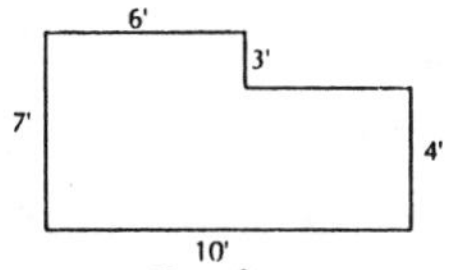

3. area 54 ft.
   perimeter 36 ft.

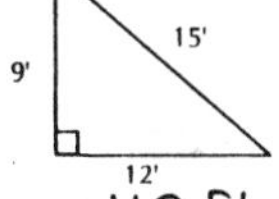

4. area 95 ft.
   perimeter 48 ft.

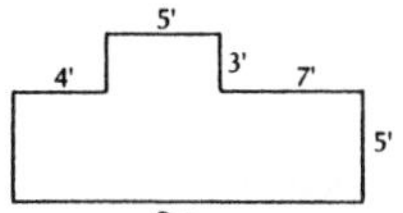

5. area 49 ft.
   perimeter 36 ft.

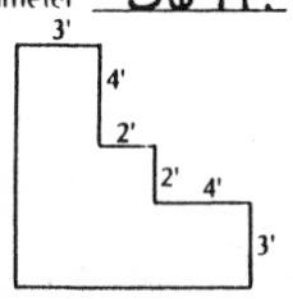

6. area 60 ft.
   perimeter 32 ft.

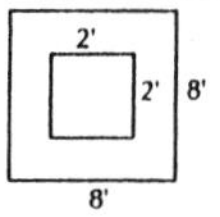

Do all figures with the same area have the same perimeter? NO
Prove your answer here:

Do all figures with the same perimeter have the same area? NO
Give evidence to support your answer:

Page 34

Gardening

Name ____________

Each of seven students was in charge of planting and caring for a different plant in the greenhouse. Use the matrix to determine who grew each item.

1. Alix planted a root vegetable.
2. The edible part of Zora's plant is green.
3. Paz's plant grew to be a leaf you can eat on a sandwich or in a salad.
4. Hal planted neither an edible root nor an edible flower.
5. The mature plant Isla tends is a seed you can eat.
6. Lev's plant is not a carrot, but it is a root vegetable.

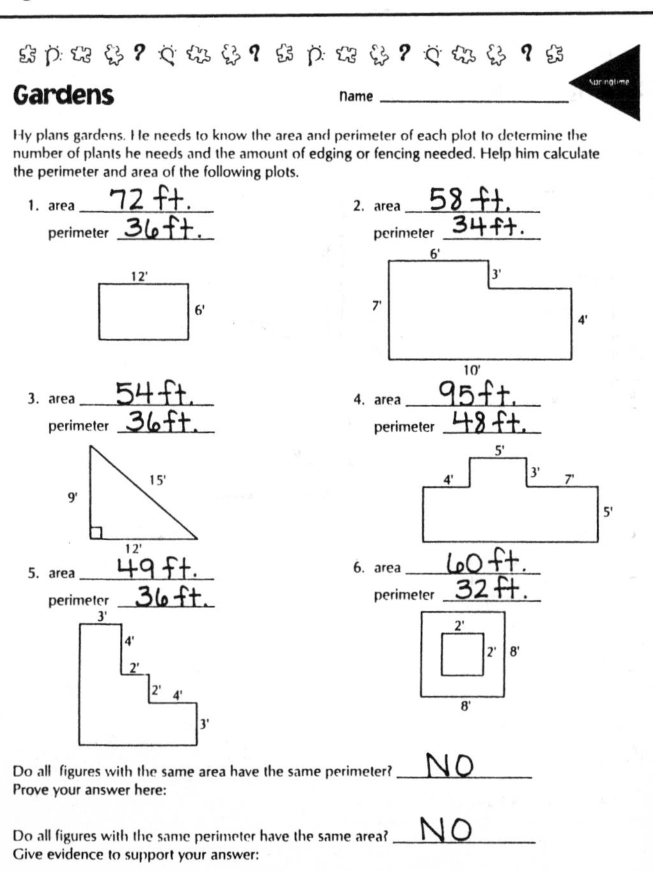

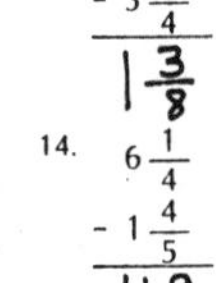

	broccoli	carrots	cauliflower	celery	corn	lettuce	radishes
Alix	X	YES	X	X	X	X	X
Ean	X	X	YES	X	X	X	X
Hal	X	X	X	YES	X	X	X
Isla	X	X	X	X	YES	X	X
Lev	X	X	X	X	X	X	YES
Paz	X	X	X	X	X	YES	X
Zora	YES	X	X	X	X	X	X

Alix grew CARROTS
Ean grew CAULIFLOWER
Hal grew CELERY
Isla grew CORN
Lev grew RADISHES
Paz grew LETTUCE
Zora grew BROCCOLI

Page 35

Tree Planting

Name ____________________ Arbor Day

The three grades at High Marks Middle School planted trees for Arbor Day. Below is a table with the data regarding the trees. Use the table to answer the probability questions.

Trees Planted on Arbor Day by High Marks Middle School

Grade	Spruce	Maple	Dogwood	Total
6	67	46	97	210
7	87	62	41	190
8	50	74	86	210
Totals	204	182	224	610

SCIENTIFIC FACT NO. 2173: SOME TREES GROW REALLY BIG!

1. What is the probability that a sixth grader planted a spruce tree? 67:210
2. What is the probability that a seventh grader planted a maple or dogwood tree? 103:190
3. Terry is in eighth grade. What is the probability that she planted a dogwood tree? 86:210
4. Ashur is a sixth grade student. What is the probability that he planted a spruce or maple? 113:210
5. What is the probability that a sixth, seventh or eighth grade student planted a dogwood tree? 224:610
   a maple tree? 182:610

The sixth graders were each able to take a tree home in a pot. Make a tree diagram to find out the choices.

clay pot	spruce
plastic pot	maple
cardboard pot	dogwood

clay pot — spruce, maple, dogwood
plastic pot — spruce, maple, dogwood
cardboard pot — spruce, maple, dogwood

What is the probability that a sixth grader . . .

- took home a spruce in a clay pot? 1:9
- took home a plastic pot? 3:9
- took home a maple or dogwood? 6:9
- took home a maple or a spruce in a clay pot? 2:9

Page 36

Who Planted More?

Name ____________________ Arbor Day

On Arbor Day, two classes planted trees. Shade the answers on the trees to find out which class planted the most. TIE

Mr. Larson's Homeroom — Ms. Young's Homeroom

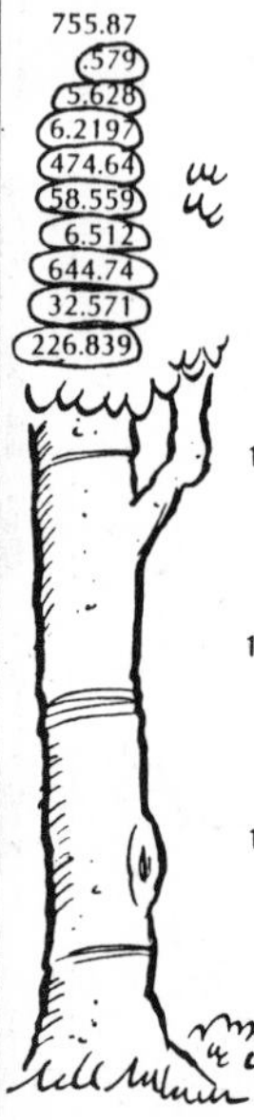

1. 276.2 − 49.361 = 226.839
2. 84.66 − 52.089 = 32.571
3. 653.64 − 8.9 = 644.74
4. 2.3004 − .6856 = 1.6148
5. 375.4 − 72.86 = 302.54
6. 351.3 − .562 = 350.738
7. 8.26 − 1.748 = 6.512
8. 65.018 − 6.459 = 58.559
9. 942.06 − 186.19 = 755.87
10. 427.21 − 98.151 = 329.059
11. 1.738 − .6232 = 1.1148
12. 548.3 − 73.66 = 474.64
13. 12.647 − 6.4273 = 6.2197
14. 24.663 − 7.218 = 17.445
15. 6.8022 − 1.899 = 4.9032
16. 333.2 − 42.721 = 290.479
17. 12.111 − 6.483 = 5.628
18. 2.055 − 1.476 = .579

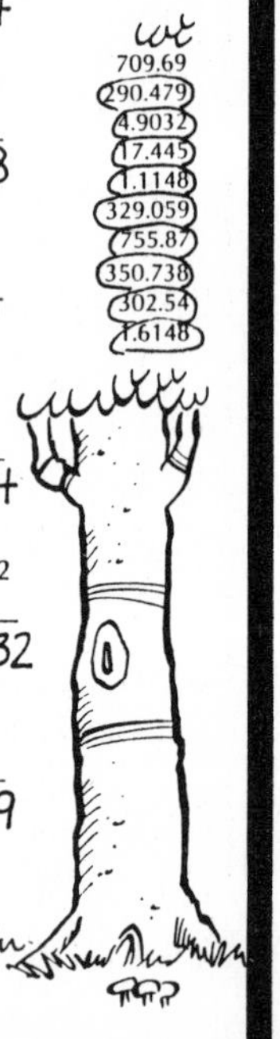

Page 37

Trees in the Ground

Name ____________________ Arbor Day

These seven friends each planted a different tree for Arbor Day. Use the matrix to determine who planted which tree.

1. Brier planted an evergreen.
2. Flint planted a fruit tree.
3. Guy planted a deciduous tree that does not bear edible fruit.
4. Jackie planted a fruit tree that grows in the northern United States.
5. Pam will be able to make pancake syrup from the sap of the tree she planted.
6. Ranee planted a tree brought across the United States by John Chapman.
7. Tyrone did not plant a spruce.

	Apple	Ash	Hemlock	Maple	Orange	Plum	Spruce
Brier	X	X	X	X	X	X	YES
Flint	X	X	X	X	YES	X	X
Guy	X	YES	X	X	X	X	X
Jackie	X	X	X	X	X	YES	
Pam	X	X	X	YES	X	X	
Ranee	YES	X	X	X	X	X	
Tyrone	X	X	YES	X	X	X	

Brier planted SPRUCE
Guy planted ASH
Pam planted MAPLE
Tyrone planted HEMLOCK
Flint planted ORANGE
Jackie planted PLUM
Ranee planted APPLE

Page 38

Through the Mud and Ooze

Name ____________________ Springtime

Find the missing term in each proportion. Use cross products to make the ratios equivalent.

1. $\frac{6}{8} = \frac{d}{12}$ d = 9
2. $\frac{1}{c} = \frac{3}{6}$ c = 2
3. $\frac{p}{7.2} = \frac{5}{12}$ p = 3
4. $\frac{3}{9} = \frac{y}{21}$ y = 7
5. $\frac{3}{h} = \frac{4}{6}$ h = 4.5
6. $\frac{12}{4} = \frac{r}{12}$ r = 36
7. $\frac{2}{k} = \frac{10}{25}$ k = 5
8. $\frac{2}{7} = \frac{6}{m}$ m = 21
9. $\frac{4}{9} = \frac{r}{27}$ r = 12
10. $\frac{3}{8} = \frac{9}{z}$ z = 24
11. $\frac{6}{2} = \frac{12}{w}$ w = 4
12. $\frac{5}{3} = \frac{r}{6}$ r = 10
13. $\frac{8}{4} = \frac{7}{2}$ g = 14
14. $\frac{6}{4} = \frac{12}{s}$ s = 8
15. $\frac{25}{a} = \frac{5}{3}$ a = 15
16. $\frac{7}{p} = \frac{6}{36}$ p = 42
17. $\frac{5}{16} = \frac{10}{k}$ k = 32
18. $\frac{n}{4} = \frac{22}{8}$ n = 11
19. $\frac{2}{h} = \frac{4}{26}$ h = 13
20. $\frac{57}{u} = \frac{19}{2}$ u = 6
21. $\frac{8}{3} = \frac{j}{6}$ j = 16
22. $\frac{26}{y} = \frac{40}{8}$ y = 5.2
23. $\frac{4}{8.5} = \frac{8}{f}$ f = 17
24. $\frac{4}{6} = \frac{r}{5.85}$ r = 3.9
25. $\frac{s}{6} = \frac{9}{3}$ s = 18
26. $\frac{5}{4} = \frac{25}{g}$ g = 20
27. $\frac{2}{m} = \frac{6}{69}$ m = 23
28. $\frac{4}{3} = \frac{h}{21}$ h = 28

It's a muddy May. Use the answers to find the coordinates of the stepping stones in the mud and ooze. Using one color for the answers to the odd problems and another color for the even problems, shade each stone. Four stones in a row; horizontally, vertically, or diagonally; is one point. How many points do even and odd each get?

2	(2,4)	13	(4,3)
3	(4,5)	14	(5,3)
3.9	(0,3)	15	(5,6)
4	(5,5)	16	(6,5)
4.5	(3,6)	17	(2,5)
5	(5,4)	18	(4,2)
5.2	(2,3)	20	(1,2)
6	(0,2)	21	(1,2)
7	(4,4)	23	(3,1)
8	(3,3)	24	(2,6)
9	(4,6)	28	(0,1)
10	(3,5)	32	(3,2)
11	(1,3)	36	(3,4)
12	(6,3)	42	(6,6)

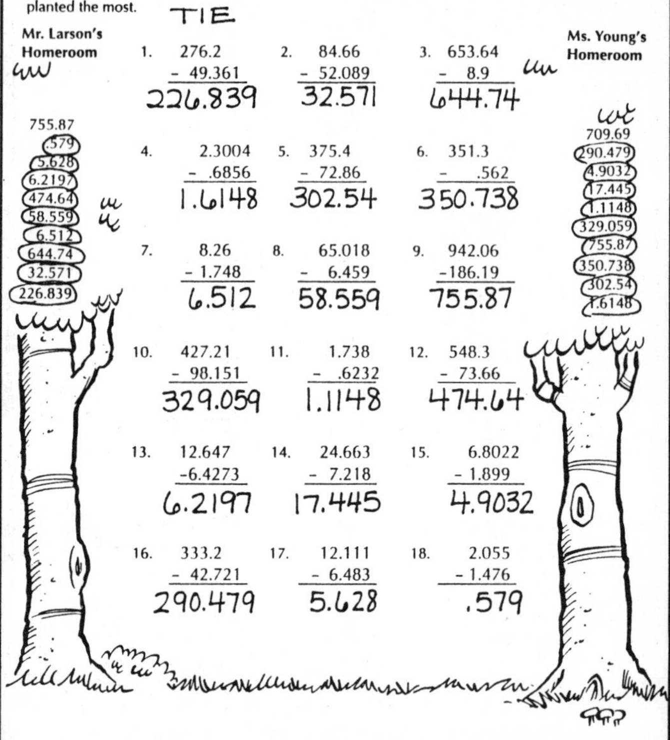

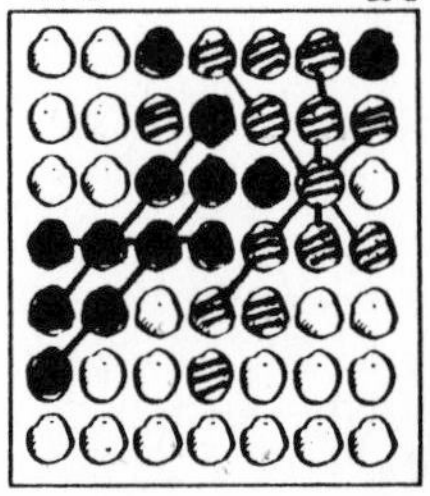

Page 39

To Market, to Market

Name ____________________

At the store, you noticed that prices vary greatly, and most items come in a variety of package sizes. A wise shopper finds the unit rate or unit price, then bases purchasing decisions on the best prices. Find the unit rate of each item. Circle the best deal.

Potato Chips—14-oz. package of Brand A for $2.66 $0.19 per oz.	14-oz. package of store brand for $1.96 ($0.14 per oz.)
8-oz. package of cream cheese for $1.84 $0.23 per oz.	8-oz. package of store brand for $1.36 ($0.17 per oz.)
Ice cream—2 quarts of Brand B for $5.00 $1.25 per pint	2 quarts of Brand C for $3.20 ($0.80 per pint)
Apple Juice—64 ounces of Brand M for $2.56 $0.04 per oz.	64 ounces of Brand T for $1.92 ($0.03 per oz.)
32 ounces of taco chips for $1.76 .055 or $0.06 per oz.	32 ounces of Brand T for $1.12 (.035 or $0.04 per oz.)
Microwave Popcorn—3 packages of Brand P for $3.36 $1.12 per package	4 packages of Brand S for $1.47 ($0.37 per package)
3 packages of snack crackers for $2.07 ($0.69 per package)	6 packages of Brand P crackers for $5.76 $0.96 per package

SCIENTIFIC FACT NO. 8167:
POPCORN AND SODA POP GO WELL
WITH LATE NIGHT MONSTER MOVIES!

Page 40

Phone Bill

Name ____________________

Mom and Dad were quite upset by the last phone bill and all the calls you made during the month of May. After a family discussion, it was decided that you would begin paying for your own calls. Your parents have decided to charge 6¢ for each local call (includes each time you hook up to the Internet) and 15¢ a minute for long-distance calls. Complete the phone record to determine how much you owe the "phone bank" after one week.

Date	Call Placed to	Local	Long Distance	Start	Stop	Total Time
5/6	Geena	/				
5/6	Tyler		/	5:05	5:15	10 MIN
5/6	Internet	/				
5/6	Jill	/				
5/6	Geena	/				
5/6	Casilda		/	7:21	7:57	36 MIN
5/6	Geena	/				
5/7	Taisha	/				
5/7	Internet	/				
5/7	Dane	/				
5/7	Fred	/				
5/7	Casilda		/	9:12	9:23	11 MIN.
5/8	Internet	/				
5/8	Tyler		/	6:03	6:14	11 MIN.
5/8	Geena	/				
5/8	Robyn		/	7:32	7:48	16 MIN.
5/9	Internet	/				
5/9	Grandma	/				
5/9	Casilda			6:44	6:58	14 MIN
5/9	Internet	/				
5/9	Robyn		/	8:03	8:24	21 MIN
5/10	Geena	/				
5/10	Jill	/				
5/10	Internet	/				
5/10	Taisha	/				
5/10	Fred	/				
5/11	Internet	/				
5/11	Tyler		/	5:36	5:55	19 MIN
5/11	Robyn		/	6:12	6:19	7 MIN
5/11	Internet	/				
5/12	Ty	/				
5/12	Casilda		/	7:38	7:44	6 MIN
5/12	Geena	/				
5/12	Jill	/				
5/12	Internet	/				

THE INTERNET STARTED AS A MILITARY PROJECT!

OWE $24.15

How much would you owe if your parents charged 10¢ a local call and 10¢ per minute for long- distance calls? $2.50 + $15.10 = $17.60

Page 41

Measurements

Name ____________________

Use the metric units to answer the following spring gardening questions.

thousands	hundreds	tens	ones	tenths	hundredths	thousandths
kilo-	hecto-	deka-	base unit	deci-	centi-	milli-

1. a kilogram = 1000 grams
2. a milliliter = .001 OR 1/1000 liters
3. a centimeter = .01 OR 1/100 meters
4. a hectoliter = 100 liters
5. a decigram = .1 OR 1/10 grams
6. a dekameter = 10 meters
7. Antonio needs a plant stake that is 1 meter high. The store measures them by the centimeter. How many centimeters long is the plant stake that Antonio needs to buy?

   1 meter = 100 cm
8. Jenna wants to buy 2.36 kilograms of seed. The seed comes in 20-gram packages. How many packages does she need to buy?

   118 packages
9. Tangie planted 100 grams of seed. Tell how many of each she planted:

   100,000 mg   10,000 cg   1 hg   .01 kg

10. The plants grew an average of 25 centimeters in 2 weeks. Convert to the following:

    2500 mm   2.5 dm   .25 m   .0025 km
11. Each plant needs 2.5 liters of water. Sulu has a deciliter container. How many deciliter containers does he need to fill for each plant?

    25 containers
12. Each row has 8 plants. Each plant needs 2.5 liters of water. How many dekaliters of water are needed per row?

    2 per row

Page 42

Coordinate Planes

Name ____________________

Use the coordinate planes to answer questions about and give ordered pairs.

Always start at (0, 0). Give directions to each location and name the ordered pair.

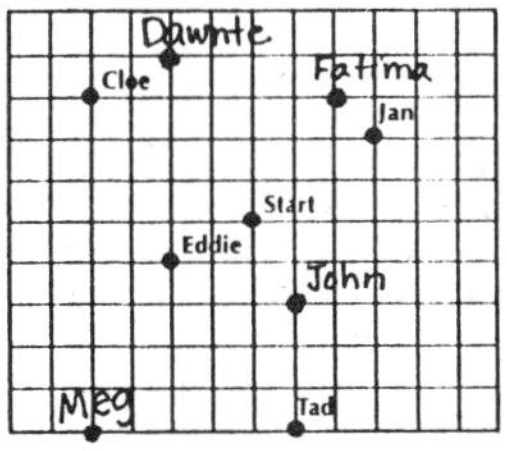
Dawnte
Cloe
Fatima
Jan
Start
Eddie
John
Meg
Tad

1. Jan's house:
   3 blocks east, 2 blocks north (3, 2)
2. Tad's house:
   1 block E, 5 blocks S (1, -5)
3. Cloe's house:
   4 blocks W, 3 blocks N (-4, 3)
4. Eddie's house:
   2 blocks W, 1 block S (-2, -1)

Plot each house (point) and name the ordered pair.

5. Meg's house: 4 blocks west, 5 blocks south (-4, -5)
6. John's house: 1 block east, 2 blocks south (1, -2)
7. Fatima's house: 2 blocks east, 3 blocks north (2, 3)
8. Dawnte's house: 2 blocks west, 4 blocks north (-2, 4)

Plot each set of points. Connect them in order. Label each shape.

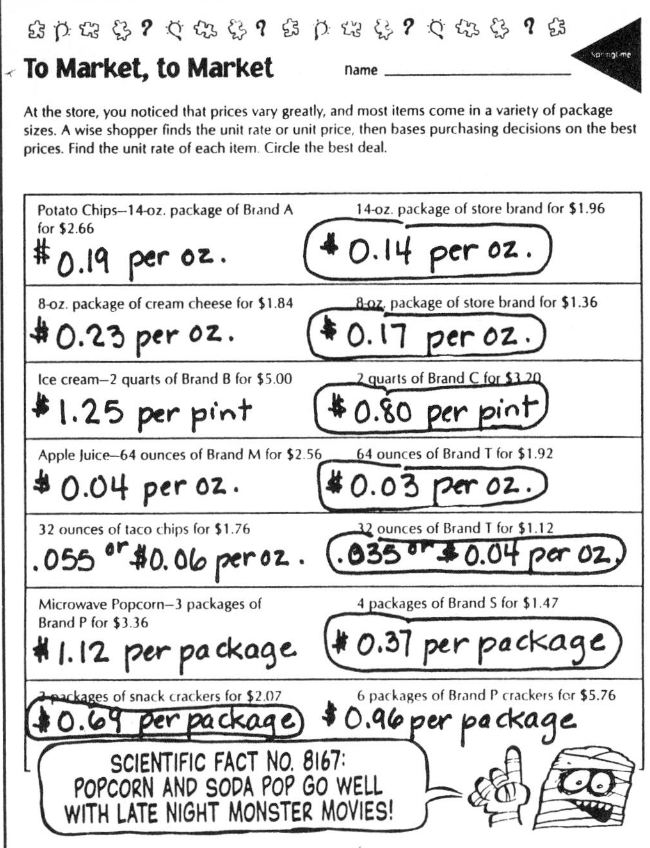

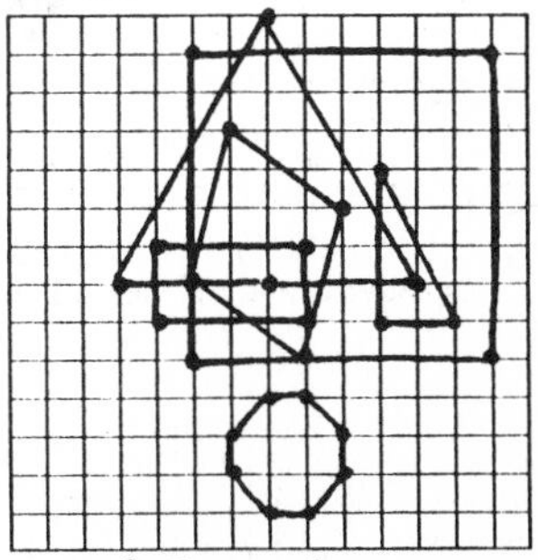

9. (3, 3) (3, -1) (5, -1)
   RIGHT TRIANGLE
10. (4, 0) (-4, 0) (0, 7)
    EQUILATERAL TRIANGLE
11. (2, 2) (-1, 4) (-2, 0) (1, -2)
    QUADRILATERAL or PARALLELOGRAM
12. (1, 1) (-3, 1) (-3, -1) (1, -1)
    RECTANGLE
13. (-2, -2) (6, -2) (6, 6) (-2, 6)
    SQUARE
14. (1, -3) (2, -4) (2, -5) (1, -6) (0, -6) (-1, -5) (-1, -4) (0, -3) OCTAGON

Page 43

Science Grades

Third Marking Period

Name ______________________

Mrs. Wall's grading scale uses points based on effort and quality. All assignments have built-in extra-credit points, so a student can earn more points than required. Use Mrs. Wall's scoring system to determine Jayde's grade for science this marking period. Her individual scores are printed below.

Science—Seeds and Plants
Teacher Mrs. Wall
Seeds and Plants Unit Grade A

Grade #1—Vocabulary and Questions Assignments . Score: 103

___ NHI* ___ F (0–49) ___ D (50–59) ___ C (60–69) ✓ B (70–79) ✓ A (80 +

Grade #2—Projects and Assignments Total Score: 323

___ F (0–190) ___ D (191–224) ___ C (225–260) ___ B (261–280) ✓ A (281 +)

a) Edible Plant Parts homework (36 pts.**) ✓ NHI* score 0
b) Plant Cycle (60 pts.**) ___ NHI* score 75
c) Leaf Rubbings and Information (60 pts.**) ___ NHI* score 84
d) Plants Parts drawing (25 pts.**) ___ NHI* score 28
e) Farmers' Market homework (50 pts.**) ✓ NHI* score 0
f) Bean Parts poster (30 pts.**) ___ NHI* score 36
h) Bonus Work ___ NHI* score 100

SCIENCE FACT NO. 342: IF YOU PLANT SEEDS, STUFF WILL GROW OUT OF THE GROUND!

Grade #3—Final Test (103 pts.) Score 127 Grade A
___ F (<59) ___ D (60-79) ___ C (80-94)
___ B (90-105) ✓ A (106+)

*NHI—not handed in (0 points)
**If minimum requirements were met

1. Jayde completed her vocabulary and questions assignments with a total of 35 points for vocabulary and 68 points for the questions.
2. Jayde did not hand in her Farmers' Market or her Edible Plant Parts homework assignments.
3. She did extra leaf rubbings with information about each tree type and growing needs. She received 84 points for this assignment.
4. Jayde earned 36 points on her Bean Parts poster and 28 points on her Plant Parts assignment.
5. The Plant Cycle was top quality work for which Jayde earned 75 points.
6. Jayde designed and executed a scientific plan to determine the fertilizer preferences of green beans. When complete, she reported to the class and received 100 points for this.
7. Her final test was 127 points.

Page 44

Let's Go Bowling

Springtime Fun

Name ______________________

Who won the bowling match? Use the following information to fill out the scoring sheet. The first two frames have been done for you.

- A *frame* consists of two consecutive balls thrown at the same 10 pins.
- Add both balls to the score of the previous frame to arrive at the total for that frame. The first ball in a frame is recorded to the left of the small top square, and the second ball is recorded in the small square. The accumulated score is recorded in the lower portion of the frame.
- Draw an **X** in the small square to record a strike. Add 10 points plus the score for the next two balls to that frame.
- Draw a / to record a spare. Add 10 points to that frame plus the score of the next ball.

Family Bowling Center
111 Main Street
Anywhere, Michigan
616-400-1234

	Name	1	2	3	4	5	6	7	8	9	10	Total
1	Hye	5 4 9	7 1 17	3 / 32	5 0 37	X 56	8 1 65	4 / 85	X 103	6 2 111	3 5 119	119
2	Theddy	3 / 16	6 1 23	9 / 41	8 1 50	7 / 70	X 99	X 118	9 0 127	8 / 147	X 8 1 166	166

Hye			Theddy		
Frame	**Ball 1**	**Ball 2**	**Frame**	**Ball 1**	**Ball 2**
1	5 pins down	4 pins down	1	3 pins down	7 pins down
2	7 pins down	1 pin down	2	6 pins down	1 pin down
3	3 pins down	7 pins down	3	9 pins down	1 pin down
4	5 pins down	0 pins down	4	8 pins down	1 pin down
5	10 pins down		5	7 pins down	3 pins down
6	8 pins down	1 pin down	6	10 pins down	
7	4 pins down	6 pins down	7	10 pins down	
8	10 pins down		8	9 pins down	0 pins down
9	6 pins down	2 pins down	9	8 pins down	2 pins down
10	3 pins down	5 pins down	10	10 pins down	
11			11	8 pins down	1 pin down

Page 45

Golfing

Springtime Fun

Name ______________________

Who won the 9 holes of golf? The person with the lowest score wins. Use the following golf information to fill out the scorecard and determine the winner.

Triple Bogey	par + 3	Birdie	par -1
Double Bogey	par +2	Eagle	par -2
Bogey	par + 1	Double Eagle	par -3
Par	expected score for the hole		

DID SOMEONE SAY BOGEY?

Scorecard for Golf Meadows

Hole Par	1 4	2 4	3 5	4 4	5 3	6 5	7 4	8 3	9 4	Out 36	Over/ Under Par
Rick	6	7	6	4	4	4	4	5	5	45	+9
Ernie	5	5	5	6	3	8	5	3	3	43	+7
Willie	4	4	3	5	5	5	3	4	4	37	+1
Ian	3	4	6	3	5	6	5	3	3	38	+2

Rick:
hole 1 = double bogey
hole 2 = triple bogey
hole 3 = bogey
hole 4 = par
hole 5 = bogey
hole 6 = birdie
hole 7 = par
hole 8 = double bogey
hole 9 = bogey

Ernie:
hole 1 = bogey
hole 2 = bogey
hole 3 = par
hole 4 = double bogey
hole 5 = par
hole 6 = triple bogey
hole 7 = bogey
hole 8 = par
hole 9 = birdie

Willie:
hole 1 = par
hole 2 = par
hole 3 = eagle
hole 4 = bogey
hole 5 = double bogey
hole 6 = par
hole 7 = birdie
hole 8 = bogey
hole 9 = par

Ian:
hole 1 = birdie
hole 2 = par
hole 3 = bogey
hole 4 = birdie
hole 5 = double bogey
hole 6 = bogey
hole 7 = bogey
hole 8 = par
hole 9 = birdie

Page 46

Outdoor Fun

Spring Sports

Name ______________________

Solve each problem. Refer to the Coordinate Key to complete the code and make the diagram. Find out what the plans are for this weekend. Complete the problems at the bottom of the page to solve the letter code.

1. $\frac{1}{2} \times \frac{4}{5} = \frac{2}{5}$
2. $4\frac{1}{5} \times 3\frac{4}{7} = 15$
3. $2\frac{2}{3} + 2\frac{2}{9} = 1\frac{1}{5}$
4. $2\frac{5}{8} + 4\frac{1}{2} = 7\frac{1}{8}$
5. $6\frac{1}{3} - 4\frac{2}{3} = 1\frac{2}{3}$
6. $\frac{6}{7} - \frac{1}{3} = \frac{11}{21}$
7. $\frac{1}{5} + \frac{2}{3} = 1\frac{5}{9}$
8. $6\frac{2}{3} \times 2\frac{7}{10} = 18$

___ ___ ___ ___ ___ ___ ___ ___
3 6 1 8 2 5 7 4

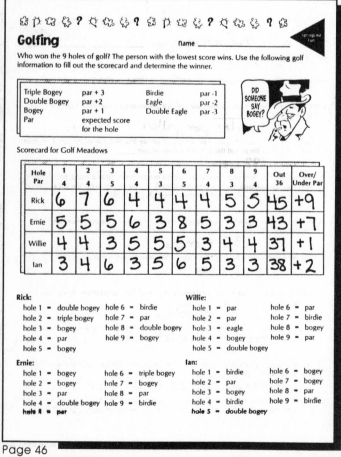

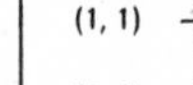

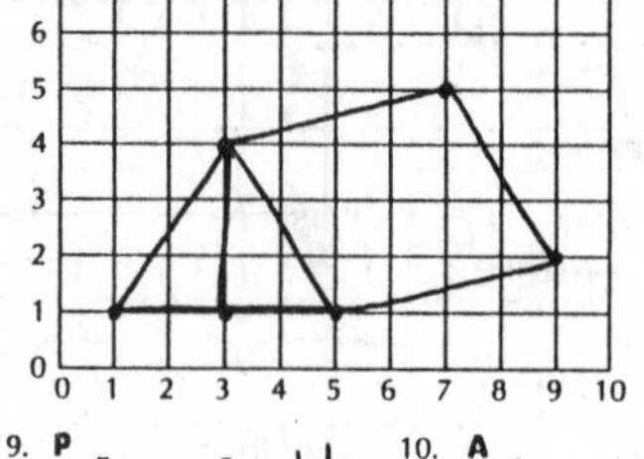

Coordinate Key

(1, 1)	$\frac{2}{5}$
(3, 1)	$1\frac{1}{5}$
(3, 4)	$\frac{11}{21}$ and 15
(5, 1)	$7\frac{1}{8}$ and 18
(7, 5)	$1\frac{2}{3}$
(9, 2)	$1\frac{5}{9}$

9. **P** $5\frac{5}{8} + 3\frac{3}{4} = 1\frac{1}{2}$
10. **A** $9\frac{1}{4} - 3\frac{7}{8} = 5\frac{3}{8}$
11. **N** $2\frac{5}{6} + 1\frac{11}{12} = 4\frac{3}{4}$
12. **M** $3\frac{5}{6} + 1\frac{1}{3} = 2\frac{7}{8}$
13. **I** $6\frac{3}{4} - 1\frac{7}{8} = 4\frac{7}{8}$
14. **G** $2\frac{2}{9} + 6\frac{2}{3} = \frac{1}{3}$
15. **C** $2\frac{2}{7} + 2\frac{1}{2} = 8\frac{11}{14}$

C	A	M	P	I	N	G
$8\frac{11}{16}$	$5\frac{3}{8}$	$2\frac{7}{8}$	$1\frac{1}{2}$	$4\frac{7}{8}$	$4\frac{3}{4}$	$\frac{1}{3}$

Page 47

Springtime Fun
Fishing
name
Multiply the numbers in the small fish and circle each correct answer in the largest fish to determine the "keepers."
634.82 x 2.93 =
1860.0226
31.547 x .68 =
21.45196
8.6291 x 77.9 =
672.20689
57.81 x 6.74 =
389.6394
1860.0226
672.20689
6272.06
18600.226
386.9394
21.45196
389.6394
Divide the numbers in each small fish and circle the correct answers in the large fish.
.948315 ÷ .015 =
63.221
1.42298 ÷ 26 =
0.05473
33.2648 ÷ 4.3 =
7.736
218.688 ÷ 6.7 =
32.64
5.473
326.4
32.64
0.05473
7.736
63.221

Page 48

Springtime Fun
Jump into the Pool
name
Solve the problems and place each answer in the appropriate "pool" of the Venn diagram. Remember, Venn diagrams have an outside set. Place a star next to each problem whose answer goes in the outside set.
1. 3,467,931 + 4,813,566 = 8281497
2. 2,791,342 x 27 = 75,366,234
3. 6,943,782 - 2,395,824 = 4,547,958
4. 3,890,688 ÷ 68 = 57,216 ☆
5. 8,206,512 ÷ 34 = 241,368
6. 28 x 358,491 = 10,037,748
7. 3,695,842 + 1,783,395 = 5,479,237
8. 8,213,234 - 3,846,709 = 4,366,525 ☆
9. 6,054,001 - 1,968,157 = 4,085,844 ☆
10. 1,972,501 x 36 = 71,010,036
11. 8,100,569 + 1,939,854 = 10,040,423
12. 10,442,813 ÷ 29 = 360,097
57,216
thousands digit is < or = to 4
4,547,958
10,037,748
the number is > 5,000,000
75,366,234
241,368
360,097
8281497
5,479,237
71,010,036
10,040,423
ones digit is > or = to 7
4,085,844
4,366,525

Page 49

Springtime Fun
Amusement Park Map
name
Before leaving on the class trip, each student was required to make a map of the amusement park using the coordinates given. Locate, label, and outline each item on the map.
Entrance A
A-11, A-12
Tilt-A-Whirl
G-15, G-16, H-15, H-16
Log Jam
D-1, E-1, F-1, F-2, F-3
Spiral Coaster
P-19, P-20, Q-19, R-16, R-19, R-20, S-16, S-17, S-20, T-17, T-18, T-19, T-20
Ferris Wheel
I-6, I-7, I-8, I-9, J-6, J-7, J-8, J-9
Wave Runner
N-1, N-2, N-5, N-6, O-2, O-3, O-4, O-5
Submarine
H-1, H-2, I-1, J-1, K-1, L-1
Drop Off
D-17, E-16, E-17
Rest Rooms
T-1, T-2; A-14, A-15; G-5, G-6; N-14, N-15
Entrance B
Q-1, R-1
Water Ride
B-1, B-2, B-3, C-3
Roller Coaster
R-9, S-5, S-7, S-8, S-9, T-5, T-6, T-7
Cliff Drop
A-19, A-20, B-19, B-20, C-19
Fun House
A-5, A-6, A-7, A-8, A-9, B-9, C-9, D-9, E-9, F-9
Arcade
E-19, E-20, F-20, G-20, H-20, I-20, J-19, J-20
Whip-A-Round
E-12, E-13, F-12, F-13
Bumper Cars
I-12, I-13, J-12, J-13, K-12, K-13
Food
A-16, A-17, B-15, B-16; E-5, E-6, F-5, F-6; N-10, N-11, N-12, N-13, O-10, O-11, O-12, O-13, O-14, O-15
SCIENCE FACT NO. 1742: COTTON CANDY AND CORN DOGS AND ROLLERCOASTERS ARE A BAD COMBINATION!
FUN
HOUSE
EA
RR
FOOD
CLIFF
DROP
WATER
LOG JAM
FOOD
WHIP
DROP
RR
TILT
ARCADE
FERRIS WHEEL
BUMPER
SUB
WAVER.
FOOD
RR
E.
B
C.
RR
ROLLER
SPIRAL

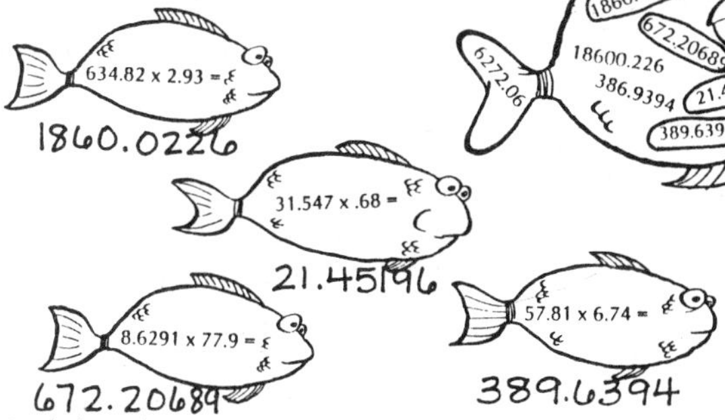

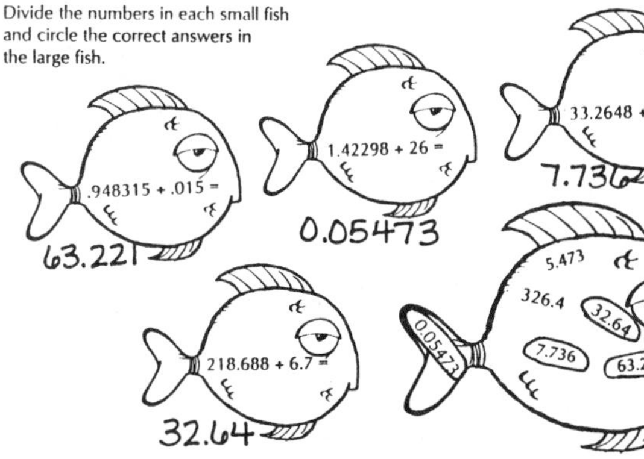

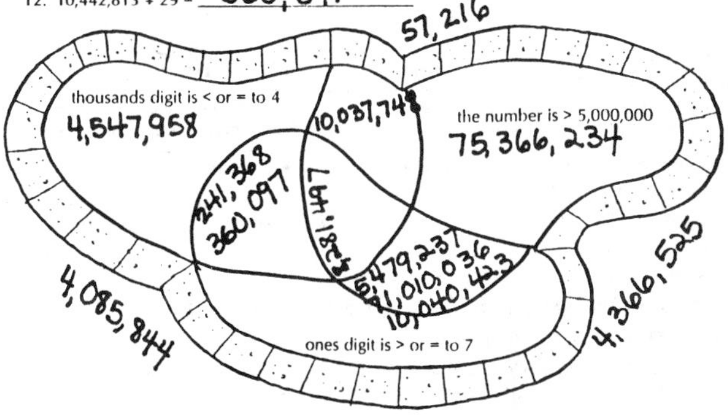

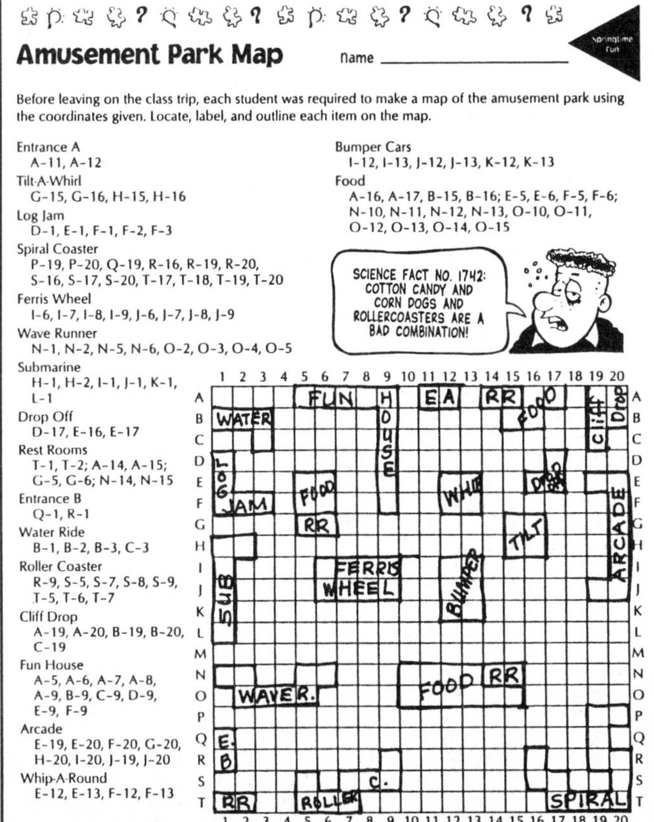

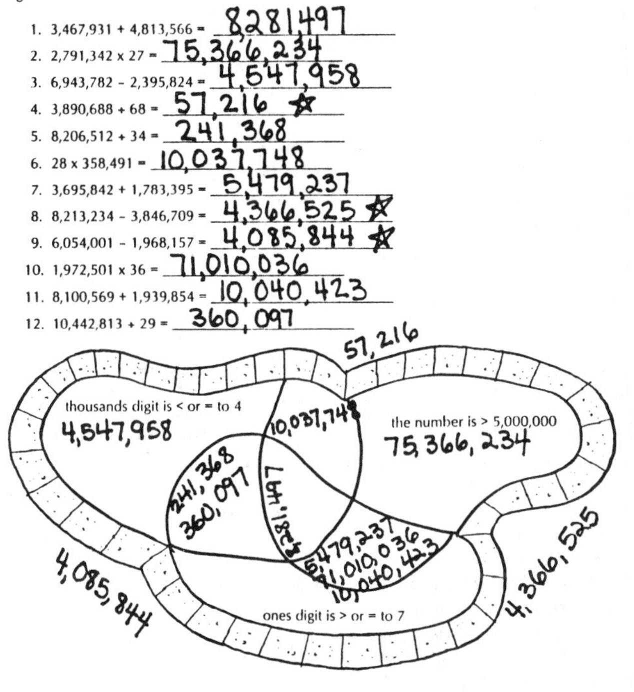

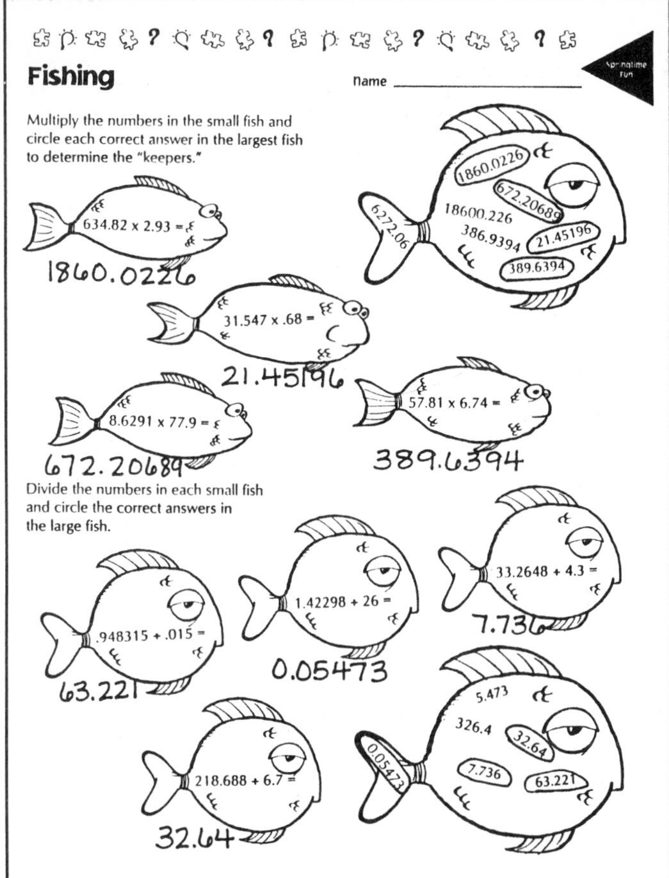

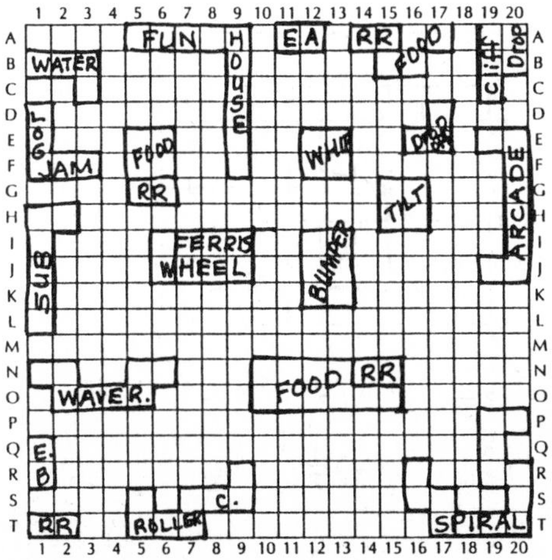

Page 50

Amusement Park Ratios and Proportions

name ______________

Springtime Fun

Use ratios and proportions to answer each question about the amusement park field trip.

1. One of the buses traveled 133 miles and used 19 gallons of gas. How many miles per gallon did the bus get? 7 miles per gallon
2. Each turnstile can admit 36 people per minute. There are 8 turnstiles at entrance A. How many people can enter the park at this entrance in one minute? 288 people per minute
3. Each student was given an amusement park drink cup for attending as a group. Each time it is filled, the beverage costs 6¢ per ounce. You filled this 16-ounce cup to the top. How much did you pay? .96 How much to fill it 4 times? $3.84
4. The Whip-A-Round spins five times every 3 seconds. If you go on the minute-and-a-half ride (besides feeling like you are going to vomit) how many times will you have spun around? 150 times
5. One vendor sells fruit salad for $4.16 a pound. You want 6 ounces. How much will you pay? $ 1.56
6. The Cliff Drop can accommodate 720 people each hour. There are 444 people in front of you. How long until you get to ride? 37 minutes
7. The Wave Runner cycles 240 gallons of water per minute. How many gallons does it cycle each second? 4gal. Each hour? 14,400 gallons
8. One gear on the Spiral Coaster turns 7 revolutions each second. How many revolutions on each minute and a half ride? 630 revolutions on each ride
9. You are in line for the Submarine. A sign says 15 minutes and there are 330 people in front of you. How many people per minute does this ride accommodate? 22 people

Page 51

Class Trip

Spring Vacation

Name ____________________

After a class trip to an amusement park, the following data was collected. Use the data from each table to find the range, mean, median, and mode.

Students on buses

bus number	*number of students*
251	75
216	73
172	74
135	73
228	72

range: 3 median: 73
mean: 73 mode: 73

Money spent to nearest dollar

name	*amount*
Petra	$5.00
Torrie	$25.00
Clark	$16.00
Yates	$2.00
Xenia	$5.00

range: $23. median: $5.00
mean: $11. mode: $5.00

Number of photographs taken

name	*number of photos*
Zale	0
Maisie	15
Hyatt	7
Irma	32
Kyle	24
Larkin	0
Willie	16

range: 32 median: 15
mean: 13 mode: 0

Number of rides

name	*number of rides*
Aisla	16
Armani	22
Calvin	22
Ernie	25
Judy	15

range: 10 median: 22
mean: 20 mode: 22

Page 52

Take a Class

Summer School

Name ____________________

Use the data given on this page to answer the questions about summer school experiences.

1. Make a tree diagram to show all of the possible combinations for advanced summer classes.

Health	Academic	Application
swimming	adv. mathematics	internship
hiking	adv. science	lab
golf	adv. writing	computer
		partnership

2. How many choices are there? 36
3. What is the probability that Julie will take golf and lab? 3:36
4. What is the probability that August will take advanced science? 12:36
5. What is the probability that May will take hiking and internship or hiking and computer? 6:36
6. What is the probability that June will take advanced mathematics? 12:36

The advanced science class measured trees in a lot. They make the following stem-and-leaf plot. Answer the questions regarding this data.

Tree Height in Feet

4	0 3 3 5 6 7 7 8
3	1 1 1 2 2 4 5 5 5 7 9 9 9 9
2	0 0 2 2 6 8 8 9
1	1 2 5 5 5 6 8
0	2 2 2 3 3 4 5 5 6 7 7 8 9

7. How many trees grew in the lot? 50
8. What is the range of tree heights? 46 ft. The mode? 39 ft.
9. What percent of trees are over 34 feet tall? 32%
10. What is the probability that a tree was less than or equal to 12 feet? 15:50
11. How many trees were greater than or equal to 49 feet? 0
12. What percent of trees were 20 to 25 feet tall? 8%

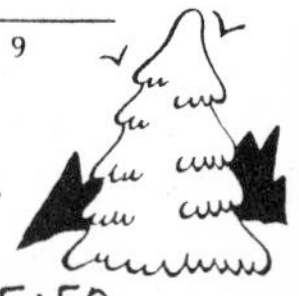

Page 53

Cross-Number Puzzle

Summer School

Name ____________________

Solve each problem. Then write each sum in the cross-number puzzle. Each decimal will take a box.

1. 146.4 x .3 = 43.92
2. .827 x .61 = .50447
3. 265.05 x .07 = 18.5535
4. 93.02 x 413 = 38,417.26
5. 50.07 x .68 = 34.0476
6. 60.82 x .6 = 36.492
7. .342 x 528 = 180.576
8. 505.05 x 97 = 48989.85
9. 46.941 x .8 = 37.5528
10. 56.3 x .004 = .2252
11. 49.9 x .65 = 32.435
12. 4.475 x .32 = 1.432
13. 21.41 x 3 = 64.23
14. 78.1 x .07 = 5.467

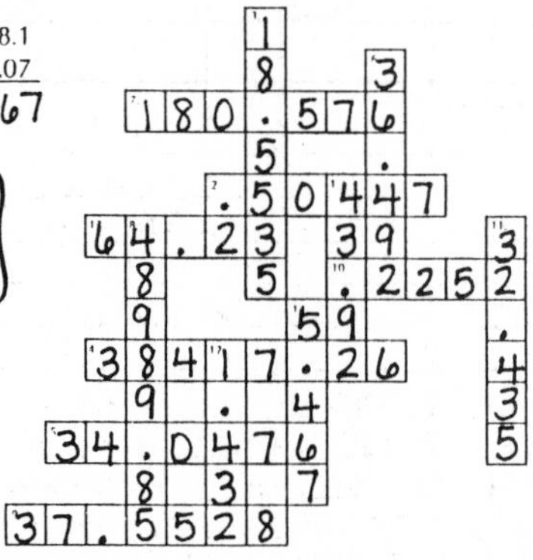

SCIENCE FACT NO. 342: TOO MUCH MATH WILL TURN YOUR HAIR BLUE!

						1						
						8			3			
			1	8	0	.	5	7	6			
						5			.			
					.	5	0	4	4	7		
		6	4	.	2	3		3	9			3
			8			5		.	2	2	5	2
			9				5	9				.
		3	8	4	1	7	.	2	6			4
			9		.		4					3
	3	4	.	0	4	7	6					5
			8		3		7					
3	7	.	5	5	2	8						

Page 54

Let's Visit

Summer School

Name ____________________

These eight students each chose a different national park or national monument on which to research and report. Use the clues and matrix to determine who researched each location.

1. Dan chose a location east of the Mississippi River.
2. Fay and Joe chose parks without manmade monuments.
3. Neither Abi nor Joe chose the Grand Canyon.
4. Eli studied an active glacier in this Alaska Park.
5. Fay's report did not include a geyser, but Moe's report did.
6. Ian reported that panthers, crocodiles, snakes, and pelicans lived in this park.
7. Lee reported that his is the tallest manmade monument in the U.S.

THE GATEWAY ARCH IN ST. LOUIS IS ON THE ORIGINAL RIVERFRONT TOWN SITE!

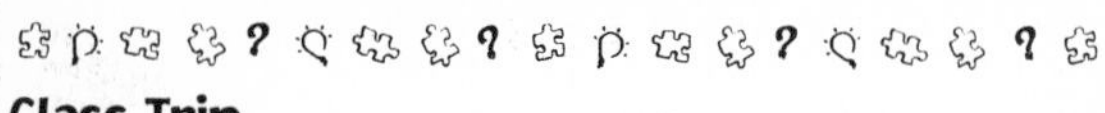

	Abi	Dan	Eli	Fay	Ian	Joe	Lee	Moe
Everglades	X	X	X	X	YES	X	X	X
Gateway Arch	X	X	X	X	X	X	YES	X
Grand Canyon	X	X	X	YES	X	X	X	X
Kenai Fjords	X	X	YES	X	X	X	X	X
Mt. Rushmore	YES	X	X	X	X	X	X	X
Sequoia	X	X	X	X	X	YES	X	X
Yellowstone	X	X	X	X	X	X	X	YES
Washington Monument	X	YES	X	X	X	X	X	X

Abi studied Mt. Rushmore
Dan studied Washington Mon.
Eli studied Kanai Fjords
Fay studied Grand Canyon
Ian studied Everglades
Joe studied Sequoia
Lee studied Gateway Arch
Moe studied Yellowstone

Page 55

What Am I?

U.S. Independence Day

Name ____________

I was a gift from France for America's 100th birthday. My crown has seven spikes, which represent the world's seven continents.

Solve each equation. Locate the answer to the problem in the code below. Write the correct letter above the answer.

Letter Key	1	2	3	4	5	6	7	8	9	10	11	12
	A	B	E	F	I	L	O	R	S	T	U	Y

1. $\frac{3}{5} + \frac{1}{3} + \frac{8}{15} = 1\frac{7}{15}$
2. $\frac{1}{2} + \frac{3}{4} \times \frac{2}{3} = 1$
3. $3\frac{2}{3} - \frac{5}{6} + \frac{5}{8} = 2\frac{1}{3}$
4. $(\frac{1}{2} - \frac{1}{3}) \times \frac{2}{3} = \frac{1}{9}$
5. $\frac{2}{9} + (\frac{5}{6} + \frac{4}{9}) = \frac{4}{23}$
6. $\frac{1}{5} + (\frac{1}{5} + \frac{3}{4}) = \frac{4}{19}$
7. $(\frac{2}{3} + \frac{2}{5}) + 1\frac{3}{5} = \frac{2}{3}$
8. $\frac{1}{2} + \frac{3}{4} \times \frac{9}{10} = \frac{3}{5}$
9. $2\frac{7}{10} + \frac{1}{4} + \frac{5}{6} = 3$
10. $2\frac{2}{9} \times \frac{3}{8} - \frac{1}{3} = \frac{1}{2}$
11. $6 + \frac{2}{3} \times \frac{5}{18} = 2\frac{1}{2}$
12. $6\frac{1}{3} - 3\frac{1}{3} + 1\frac{1}{4} = 3\frac{2}{3}$

S	T	A	T	U	E	O	F
3	$\frac{1}{2}$	$1\frac{7}{15}$	$\frac{1}{2}$	$2\frac{1}{2}$	$2\frac{1}{3}$	$\frac{2}{3}$	$\frac{1}{9}$

L	I	B	E	R	T	Y
$\frac{4}{19}$	$\frac{4}{23}$	1	$2\frac{1}{3}$	$\frac{3}{5}$	$\frac{1}{2}$	$3\frac{2}{3}$

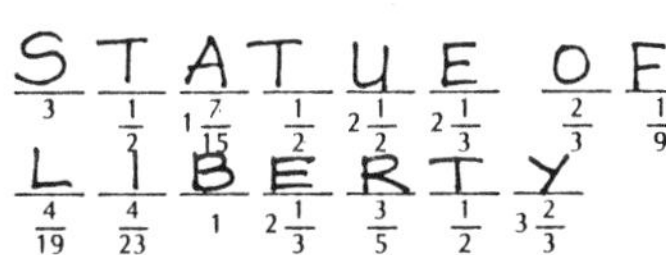

THIS FAMOUS MONUMENT IS 150.9 FEET HIGH!

Page 56

First Flight

Special Days

Name ____________

Find each sum. Then follow the directions below.

1. 762,489 + 5,628 + 6,562,899 + 2,258,364 = 9,589,380 R
2. 7,986,140 + 628,309 + 1,421,602 + 26,876 = 10,062,927 A
3. 62,927 + 6,291,673 + 982,735 + 468,098 = 7,805,433 A
4. 4,634,923 + 848,577 + 2,698 + 1,249,864 = 6,736,062 R
5. 1,840,294 + 728,166 + 5,050,671 + 3,615,800 = 11,234,931 E
6. 1,650,205 + 95,364 + 1,079,643 + 346,725 = 3,171,937 T
7. 34,925,635 + 55,869,722 + 9,182,528 = 99,977,885 A
8. 86,624,690 + 6,518,315 + 4,003,189 = 97,146,194 M
9. 44,649,417 + 8,155,627 + 24,318,243 = 77,123,287 L
10. 2,612,536 + 905,428 + 4,183,620 + 1,009,087 = 8,710,671 H
11. 13,421,673 + 2,730,948 + 457,831 + 41,173,996 = 57,784,448 I
12. 997,173 + 26,321,730 + 84,651 + 1,256,788 = 28,660,342 A
13. 53,601,717 + 4,183,552 + 8,234,606 + 13,976,378 = 79,996,253 E

Who tried to fly around the world at the equator?

Order the sums from greatest to least and write the letters of the problems in that order below to learn the pilot's name. One sum is the date the flight began. Can you find it? Write the date here. 3-17-1937

A M E L I A
E A R H A R T

Page 57

Scientific Find

Special Days

Name ____________

In November 1996, scientists in China found something very special that may prove dinosaurs were the ancestors of birds. Solve each problem. Circle the word by each corresponding answer to determine this event.

Problem	Answer			
1. 6,428,921 − 619,563	5,809,358	**The 5,809,358**	Cave 6,211,442	65 5,819,441
2. 234,896 − 159,347	75,549	paintings 125,551	trillion 75,551	**150 75,549**
3. 7,640,358 − 3,732,947	3,907,411	**million 3,907,411**	year 4,112,611	depicting 4,907,511
4. 9,631,400 − 6,298,261	3,333,139	old 3,433,239	**year 3,333,139**	feathered 3,467,261
5. 4,125,634 − 943,573	3,182,061	DNA 4,822,141	**old 3,182,061**	dinosaurs 3,882,161
6. 8,341,087 − 2,915,149	5,425,938	**fossil 5,425,938**	flying 6,634,142	with 5,434,942
7. 1,842,573 − 1,296,499	546,074	and 554,074	**of 546,074**	gene 654,426
8. 3,664,715 − 2,579,806	1,084,909	gliding 1,125,111	strands 1,085,119	**feathered 1,084,909**
9. 2,671,482 − 843,594	1,827,888	for 1,832,882	**Sinosauropteryx 1,827,888**	through 2,232,112
10. 5,963,117 − 2,695,528	3,267,589	space 3,332,411	**Prima 3,267,589**	feathers 3,267,411

Page 58

Wild Animals in Our World

Special Days

Name ____________

These ten students each chose a different wild animal to research. Use the matrix to determine who researched each animal.

1. Roe, Van, and Web studied water animals.
2. Lou and Zoe studied birds.
3. Nat and Lou saw their black and white animals at a zoo.
4. Bud studied the only extinct animal listed. It once lived on the island of Mauritius.
5. Kay studied one of the larger mammals on earth.
6. Pam said her water mammal was a slow moving herbivore, often referred to as a sea cow.
7. Roe did not study a reptile.
8. Van studied the largest marine mammal listed.

	Bud	Kay	Lou	Nat	Pam	Roe	Tye	Van	Web	Zoe
dodo	YES									
dolphin						YES				
elephant		YES								
humpback whale								YES		
leatherback turtle									YES	
manatee					YES					
panda				YES						
parrot										YES
penguin			YES							
tiger							YES			

Bud studied DODO

Kay studied ELEPHANT

Lou studied PENGUIN

Nat studied PANDA

Pam studied MANATEE

Roe studied DOLPHIN

Tye studied TIGER

Van studied HUMPBACK WHALE

Web studied LEATHERBACK TURTLE

Zoe studied PARROT

Page 59

In The Stars

Name ____________________

During the time of slavery in the United States, those escaping through the Underground Railroad used stars and directional songs to help them travel north to safety. Find the sums. Match the problem number to the coordinates given and draw the constellation in the grid.

1. $\frac{3}{4} + \frac{3}{4} = 1\frac{1}{2}$
2. $\frac{5}{8} + \frac{1}{8} = \frac{6}{8}$
3. $\frac{4}{7} + \frac{6}{7} = 1\frac{3}{7}$
4. $\frac{5}{9} + \frac{8}{9} = 1\frac{4}{9}$
5. $\frac{1}{5} + \frac{2}{5} = \frac{3}{5}$
6. $\frac{1}{2} + \frac{5}{8} = 1\frac{1}{8}$
7. $\frac{2}{3} + \frac{4}{9} = 1\frac{1}{9}$
8. $\frac{1}{6} + \frac{2}{3} = \frac{5}{6}$

Connect the (x, y) coordinates in the order of the answers.

VINCENT VAN GOGH PAINTED "THE STARRY NIGHT" IN JUNE, 1889!

Use the (x, y) coordinates in the order of the answers given.

$\frac{3}{5}$ (9, 2)	$\frac{6}{8}$ (3, 4)	$1\frac{3}{7}$ (5, 3)	$1\frac{1}{9}$ (12, 6)
$\frac{5}{6}$ (8, 4)	$1\frac{1}{2}$ (1, 3)	$1\frac{1}{8}$ (12, 3)	$1\frac{4}{9}$ (8, 4)

Page 60

New Planet

Name ____________________

In 1996, scientists discovered a new planet larger than Jupiter and 17 times larger than Earth. It was discovered 600 trillion miles away from Earth, outside of our solar system in the constellation Cygnus. Something is very unusual about this planet. Solve each problem and use the Letter Bank and code to determine what is so unusual about this planet.

Letter Bank

A. $1\frac{1}{2}$	H. $1\frac{9}{14}$	N. $1\frac{11}{18}$	S. $1\frac{11}{24}$
B. $1\frac{5}{8}$	I. $1\frac{7}{15}$	O. $1\frac{7}{20}$	T. 2
G. $1\frac{11}{12}$	L. $1\frac{13}{16}$	R. $1\frac{11}{21}$	

SCIENCE FACT NO. 675: 600 TRILLION MILES IS PRETTY FAR!

1. $\frac{1}{3} + \frac{3}{4} + \frac{5}{6} = 1\frac{11}{12}$
2. $\frac{1}{2} + \frac{6}{7} + \frac{2}{7} = 1\frac{9}{14}$
3. $\frac{5}{8} + \frac{3}{4} + \frac{1}{8} = 1\frac{1}{2}$
4. $\frac{3}{8} + \frac{1}{4} + \frac{5}{6} = 1\frac{11}{24}$
5. $\frac{5}{7} + \frac{2}{3} + \frac{1}{7} = 1\frac{11}{21}$
6. $\frac{2}{3} + \frac{1}{2} + \frac{5}{6} = 2$
7. $\frac{4}{9} + \frac{5}{6} + \frac{1}{3} = 1\frac{11}{18}$
8. $\frac{3}{5} + \frac{1}{3} + \frac{8}{15} = 1\frac{7}{15}$
9. $\frac{5}{8} + \frac{1}{4} + \frac{15}{16} = 1\frac{13}{16}$
10. $\frac{3}{4} + \frac{3}{8} + \frac{1}{2} = 1\frac{5}{8}$
11. $\frac{1}{4} + \frac{1}{2} + \frac{3}{5} = 1\frac{7}{20}$

I T (8 6) H A S (2 3 4) A N (3 7)
O B L O N G (11 10 9 11 7 1) O R B I T (11 5 10 8 6)

Page 61

Nine Planets?

Name ____________________

Subtract the mixed numbers. Use the answers in the code to name eight planets in our solar system. **Bonus:** Which planet is missing? mercury

1. $5\frac{1}{3} - 1\frac{2}{3} = 3\frac{2}{3}$
2. $7\frac{1}{5} - 4\frac{4}{5} = 2\frac{2}{5}$
3. $11\frac{2}{7} - 8\frac{5}{7} = 2\frac{4}{7}$
4. $6\frac{4}{9} - 5\frac{5}{9} = \frac{8}{9}$
5. $15\frac{5}{8} - 10\frac{7}{8} = 4\frac{3}{4}$
6. $9\frac{1}{4} - 2\frac{3}{4} = 6\frac{1}{2}$
7. $12\frac{7}{12} - 6\frac{9}{12} = 5\frac{5}{6}$
8. $14\frac{1}{2} - 11\frac{5}{6} = 2\frac{2}{3}$
9. $3\frac{2}{5} - 1\frac{3}{5} = 1\frac{4}{5}$
10. $2\frac{1}{3} - 1\frac{7}{12} = \frac{3}{4}$
11. $9\frac{3}{5} - 4\frac{7}{10} = 4\frac{9}{10}$
12. $8\frac{1}{3} - 5\frac{5}{6} = 2\frac{1}{2}$
13. $16\frac{5}{7} - 13\frac{18}{21} = 2\frac{6}{7}$
14. $11\frac{2}{3} - 7\frac{7}{9} = 3\frac{8}{9}$
15. $6\frac{1}{8} - 1\frac{3}{4} = 4\frac{3}{8}$

Find the letter for each answer and write it on the corresponding line below.

Letter Box

$1\frac{4}{5}$	$\frac{8}{9}$	$3\frac{2}{3}$	$6\frac{1}{2}$	$2\frac{1}{2}$	$2\frac{4}{7}$	$3\frac{8}{9}$	$2\frac{2}{3}$
A	E	H	I	J	L	M	N
$2\frac{6}{7}$	$2\frac{2}{5}$	$\frac{3}{4}$	$4\frac{3}{8}$	$4\frac{3}{4}$	$5\frac{5}{6}$	$4\frac{9}{10}$	
O	P	R	S	T	U	V	

EARTH (4 9 10 5 1)
JUPITER (12 7 2 6 5 4 10)
MARS (14 9 10 15) NEPTUNE (8 4 2 5 7 8 4)
PLUTO (2 3 7 5 13) SATURN (15 9 5 7 10 8)
URANUS (7 10 9 8 7 15) VENUS (11 4 8 7 15)

Page 62

How Will You Labor?

Name ____________________

Students were given a Labor Day assignment to poll 100 classmates to learn what they "wanted to be when they grew up." The results were to be shown in a pie graph.

Tallie polled 100 students, grouped the responses, and made this information chart. Answer the questions and design a pie graph to display her data.

Category	Number of Students
business	20
health	15
science	10
education	5
government	5
entertainment	30
other	15

1. What category did the greatest number of students choose? ENTERTAINMENT
2. What is the range for these categories? 30-5=25
3. If you were one of the students polled by Tallie, what is the probability that you told her you wanted to have a job in the field of science? 10:100 or 1:10

Jennie polled another 100 students. She made the following information chart. Answer the questions and design a pie graph to display her data.

Category	Number of Students
business	15 +20=35
health	25 +15=40
science	25+10=35
education	5 +5=10
government	15 +5=20
entertainment	10 +30=40
other	5 +15=20

4. If you were one of the students polled by Jenny, what is the probability that you told her you wanted to have a job in the field of science? 25:100 or 1:4
5. Whose information is more valid? Equally valid Explain: Both polled 100 students. Demonstrates one cross-section of data may not be exactly accurate for 100% of population.
6. Combine Tallie and Jenny's data. Make a pie graph on the back of this sheet showing the information regarding the 200 students.

Page 63

Back to Order

Name ____________________

Start of School

As school begins, procedures and schedules start again. These math problems each have their own procedure. Use the order of operations rules to solve each number sentence.

1. 6 + 7 x 2 - 5 = 15
2. 4 - 3 + 10 + 2 = 6
3. (4 - 1) x 5 - 10 = 5
4. 6 x 6 - 5 x 4 = 16
5. 9 + 3 + (8 - 2 x 3) = 5
6. 14 + 2 - 6 + 10 = 11
7. (3 + 1) x (2 + 8) = 40
8. (4 + 5) x 6 + 3 = 18
9. (5 + 4 x 4) + 7 = 3
10. 8 + 27 + 3 = 17
11. (12 + 4 + 5) x 6 = 48
12. 4 x (5 + 1) + 2 = 12

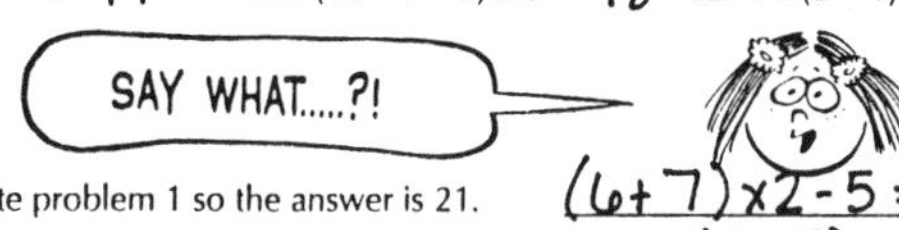

SAY WHAT.....?!

13. Rewrite problem 1 so the answer is 21. (6+7)x2-5 = 21
14. Rewrite problem 4 so the answer is 24. 6 x (6-5)x4 = 24
15. Rewrite problem 7 so the answer is 13. 3+(1x2)+8 = 13
16. Rewrite problem 11 so the answer is 33. 12 ÷ 4 + (5x6) = 33

Use the number 3 four times for numbers 17–20. Use the order of operations to organize the threes to get the given answers.

17. (3+3)x(3+3) = 36
18. 3+3 ÷ 3+3 = 7
19. (3-3) x 3+3 = 3
20. (3+3+3) x3 = 27

Page 64

Where's that Locker?

Name ____________________

Start of School

Solve to find each difference. Then add the digits in each answer and shade the sums in the grid to find the route from the classroom to the lockers. The first one is done for you.

1. 9,522,519 - 2,893,026 = 6,629,493 = 39
2. 5,050,671 - 321,263 = 4,729,408 = 34
3. 6,291,673 - 3,186,849 = 3,104,824 = 22
4. 6,291,673 - 826,496 = 5,465,177 = 35
5. 7,986,140 - 92,685 = 7,893,455 = 41
6. 4,634,923 - 2,468,537 = 2,166,386 = 32
7. 3,947,621 - 52,366 = 3,895,255 = 37
8. 5,281,923 - 1,165,737 = 4,116,186 = 27
9. 6,562,899 - 648,920 = 5,913,979 = 43
10. 9,747,507 - 9,269,628 = 477,879 = 42
11. 4,235,403 - 536,926 = 3,698,477 = 44
12. 8,485,577 - 6,499,038 = 1,986,539 = 41
13. 4,634,923 - 9,355 = 4,625,568 = 36
14. 7,934,846 - 2,689,572 = 5,245,274 = 29
15. 4,053,803 - 2,144,735 = 1,909,068 = 33

35	23	19	45	31	50
42	17	56	48	34	41
29	37	41	21	36	12
49	52	43	30	32	25
28	53	33	46	27	16
51	49	22	44	39	40

DOES IT GET ANY BETTER THAN THIS? HOO-BOY!

Page 65

Schedules

Name ____________________

Start of School

1. Make tree diagrams on the back of this sheet to show all of the possible combinations for first and second hour. Use them to answer the questions.

First Hour	Second Hour
general math English I social studies band	physical education study hall music general science

THE SCIENCE OF DATING EVENTS AND STRUCTURES USING TREE RINGS IS KNOWN AS DENDOCHRONOLOGY!

2. How many combinations are there? 16
3. What is the probability that Abbey will have band first hour and physical education second hour? 1:16
4. What is the probability that Chessa will have general math first hour? 4:16
5. What is the probability that Beck will have study hall first hour? 0:16
6. What is the probability that Darnell will have English I first hour and music or general science second hour? 2:16

Use the data below to answer the following questions about sixth graders at Open Middle School.

Sixth Grade Course Selections at Open Middle School					
Mathematics		Science		Fine Arts	
general	*advanced*	*chemistry*	*earth*	*music*	*drama*
175	*25*	*66*	*134*	*98*	*102*

7. Which math class is Tait most likely in? General Math
   Why did you choose your answer? More people are in general math
8. Which science class is Ingrid least likely to be enrolled in? Chemistry
   How did you come up with this conclusion? Less people are taking chemistry
9. Which three classes is Juan probably taking? General Math, Earth Science, Drama
   What evidence do you have to support this? All three have more students enrolled than the other classes

Page 66

Jesse Owens

Name ____________________

Jesse Owen's Birthday

Jesse Owens, born on September 12, 1915, won four gold medals in the 1936 Olympics. To find out his winning events, solve each problem for the missing digits. Then tally the number of times you filled in a given digit. The event with the most tallies is the one in which Jesse Owens won his gold medals. Circle the event.

1. 62,153,648 + 3,461,890 + 10,357,677 = 75,973,215
2. 31,045,387 + ,982,490 + 53,004,831 = 85,032,708
3. 9,475,086 + 25,601,672 + 20,669,013 = 55,745,771
4. 84,795,861 + 32,967,192 = + 51,828,669
5. 87,406,205 - 13,637,138 = 73,769,067
6. 50,239,521 - 35,309,180 = 14,930,341
7. 2,894,597 + 67,326,957 + 25,182,673 = 95,404,227
8. 14,934,502 + 39,512,851 + 8,466,070 = 62,913,423
9. 55,851,647 + 1,936,268 + 20,145,509 = 77,933,424
10. 34,925,772 - 19,869,528 = 15,056,244
11. 64,624,690 - 38,849,823 = 25,774,867
12. 44,318,243 - 38,736,013 = 5,582,230

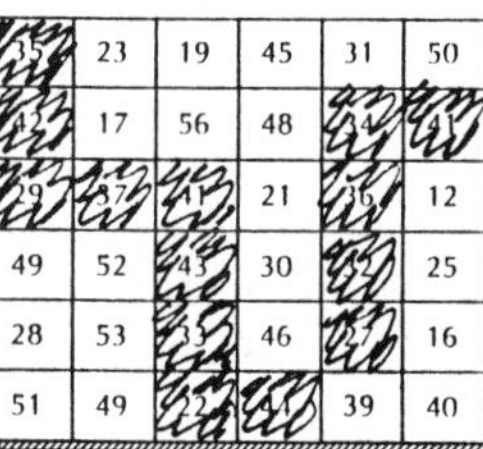

ON MAY 25, 1935, JESSE OWENS ACHIEVED THE BEST ONE DAY SHOWING IN TRACK HISTORY!

Digits	Event	Tally	Total
0,5	swimming and diving	𝍸 𝍸 11	12
1,6	lifting	𝍸 𝍸 11	12
2,7	parallel bars and horse	𝍸 𝍸 1111	14
3,8	(track and field)	𝍸 𝍸 𝍸 𝍸	20
4,9	ice skating	𝍸 𝍸 1	11

Page 67

Picking a Way Through the Orchard

Name ____________

Harvest Time

Solve each percentage problem. Then refer to the Coordinate Key to find the coordinate location of a tree in the orchard. Using one color for the answers to the odd-numbered problems and another color for the even-numbered problems, shade each tree. Four trees in a row; horizontally, vertically, or diagonally; is one point. How many points does each team earn?

1. 3% of 900 = 27
2. 12% of 150 = 18
3. 50% of 68 = 34
4. 30% of 40 = 12
5. 4% of 400 = 16
6. 15% of 460 = 69
7. 60% of 80 = 48
8. 16% of 50 = 8
9. 33% of 200 = 66
10. 60% of 400 = 240
11. 10% of 910 = 91
12. 90% of 60 = 54
13. 2% of 50 = 1
14. 7% of 300 = 21
15. 25% of 68 = 17
16. 70% of 120 = 84
17. 55% of 160 = 88
18. 45% of 80 = 36
19. 12% of 200 = 24
20. 75% of 12 = 9
21. 12% of 800 = 96
22. 50% of 6 = 3
23. 80% of 25 = 20
24. 2% of 300 = 6
25. 10% of 70 = 7
26. 25% of 140 = 35
27. 50% of 98 = 49
28. 20% of 70 = 14

Coordinate Key

1 (3,4)	18 (3,2)	49 (6,0)
3 (5,3)	20 (5,5)	54 (4,5)
6 (5,2)	21 (4,6)	66 (1,1)
7 (5,1)	24 (1,3)	69 (1,4)
8 (0,5)	27 (2,1)	84 (3,6)
9 (5,4)	34 (2,2)	88 (4, 0)
12 (2,3)	35 (2,5)	91 (4,2)
14 (0,3)	36 (6,6)	96 (6,3)
16 (4,1)	48 (3,1)	240 (5,6)
17 (4,3)		

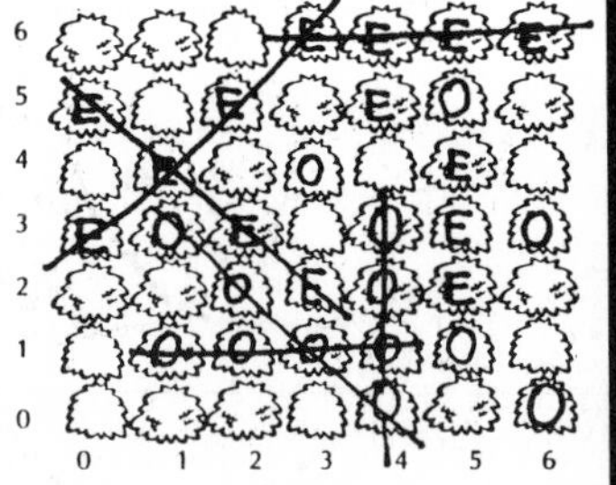

Points: 3 (even) 3 (odd)

Page 68

Through the Orchard

Name ____________

Harvest Time

Solve each problem. Shade each box whose answer has a 4 in the hundredths place to find the pathway through the orchard.

Start

36.021 x .251 = 9.041271	50.596 x 1.25 = 63.245	325.14 x .022 = 7.15308	67.381 x .36 = 24.25716
92,394 x .145 = 1,339.713	243.69 x 46 = 11,209.74	30.145 x .0082 = .247189	4,723 x .08 = 377.84
81.89 x 3.7 = 302.993	6523.1 x .12 = 782.772	20.046 x 44 = 882.024	1.392 x 45 = 62.64
952.1 x 2.4 = 2,285.04	37,114 x .06 = 2,226.84	43.64 x 8.2 = 357.848	4,806 x .074 = 355.644
768.11 x .008 = 6.14488	52,123 x .007 = 364.861	354.01 x 2.5 = 885.025	82.235 x .09 = 7.40115

Page 69

Plant Those Apple Trees!

Name ____________

Harvest Time

Solve each problem and order the sums from least to greatest. Write the letter of each problem in the same order on the lines below. Find out which historical character is responsible for planting apple trees across the United States.

1. 4,269,812 + 6,922 + 358,189 = 4,634,923 J
2. 1,620,803 + 2,811,249 + 4,053,525 = 8,485,577 P
3. 3,405,000 + 1,598,762 + 46,909 = 5,050,671 H
4. 985,136 + 6,168,523 + 6,508 = 7,160,167 H
5. 3,641,805 + 56,123 + 983,057 = 4,680,985 O
6. 58,921 + 7,934,600 + 846,773 = 8,840,294 M
7. 1,843,277 + 3,462,915 + 3,610 = 5,309,802 N
8. 867,426 + 1,473,916 + 7,406,205 = 9,747,547 N
9. 6,235,403 + 62,407 + 1,548,522 + 136,403 = 7,982,735 A
10. 3,947,601 + 89,053 + 624,109 + 4,861,756 = 9,522,519 A
11. 66,385 + 5,281,923 + 801 + 942,564 = 6,291,673 C

J O H N

C H A P M A N

Page 70

Scarecrows

Name ____________

Harvest Time

Circle the scarecrows head that you predict will translate to the fraction $\frac{1}{5}$. After you complete the page, shade the head, body, and legs that go with the fraction $\frac{1}{5}$. Write each as a decimal.

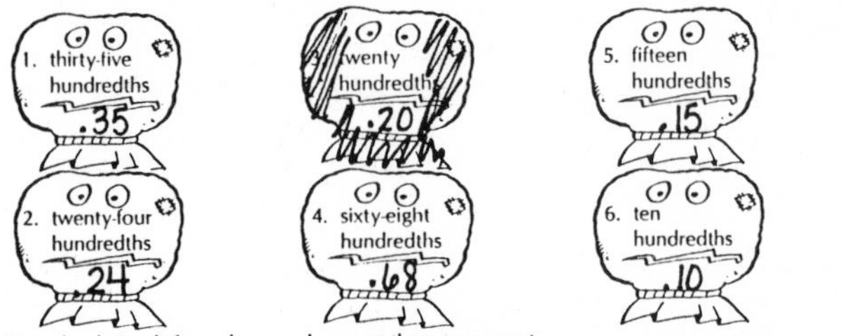

Copy the decimals from above and convert them to percents.

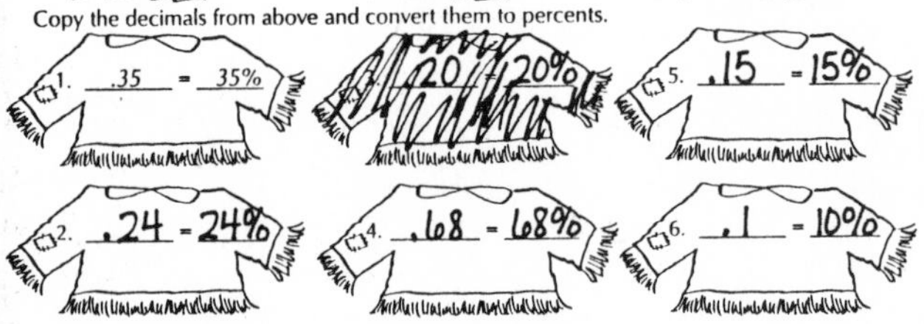

Write the above percents as fractions. Simplify to lowest terms.

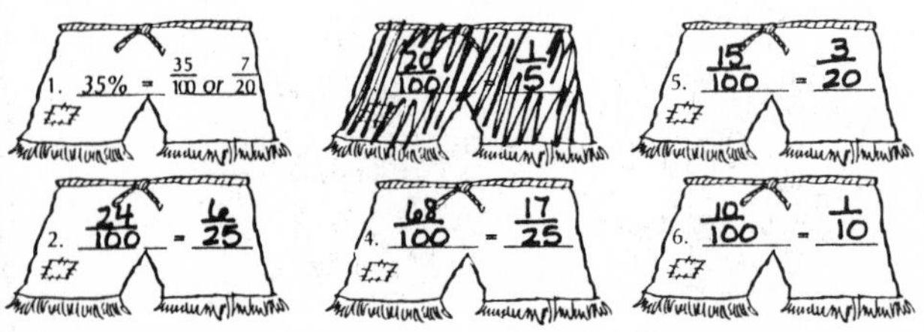

Page 71

Great Food

Name ____________

Harvest Time

Find the square roots. Write the corresponding letter with the matching answer below to answer the question.

1. $\sqrt{.49}$ = .7 B
2. $\sqrt{.0196}$ = .14 H
3. $\sqrt{729}$ = 27 L
4. $\sqrt{2.89}$ = 1.7 A
5. $\sqrt{1.44}$ = 1.2 R
6. $\sqrt{.0081}$ = .09 G
7. $\sqrt{121}$ = 11 Y
8. $\sqrt{2.25}$ = 1.5 S
9. $\sqrt{1,024}$ = 32 E
10. $\sqrt{.25}$ = .5 A
11. $\sqrt{144}$ = 12 M
12. $\sqrt{.36}$ = .6 D
13. $\sqrt{169}$ = 13 N
14. $\sqrt{529}$ = 23 I
15. $\sqrt{.0064}$ = .08 E
16. $\sqrt{6.25}$ = 2.5 V
17. $\sqrt{676}$ = 26 F
18. $\sqrt{8,100}$ = 90 T
19. $\sqrt{.16}$ = .4 U
20. $\sqrt{.0004}$ = .02 S

What did the farmer harvest?

MORE THAN HALF OF THE WORLD'S POPULATION IS ENGAGED IN FARMING!

Compare the Harvest

Name ____________

Harvest Time

Solve each problem. Write the difference in the correct portion of the Venn diagram. Don't forget to use the outside set.

1. 887.245 − 265.9 = 621.345
2. 567.597 − 541.256 = 26.341
3. 857.445 − 256.104 = 601.341
4. 647.258 − 321.144 = 326.114
5. 561.9353 − 25.8941 = 536.0412
6. 367.996 − 341.55 = 26.446
7. 1,132.425 − 483.125 = 649.3
8. 461.477 − 325.446 = 136.031
9. 847.191 − 246.25 = 600.941
10. 234.8315 − 225.8899 = 8.9416
11. 688.778 − 542.818 = 145.96
12. 308.6191 − 254.3651 = 54.254
13. 762.96 − 130.554 = 632.406
14. 1,021.232 − 56.1859 = 965.0461
15. 941.509 − 250.168 = 691.341
16. 965.415 − 520.694 = 44.721

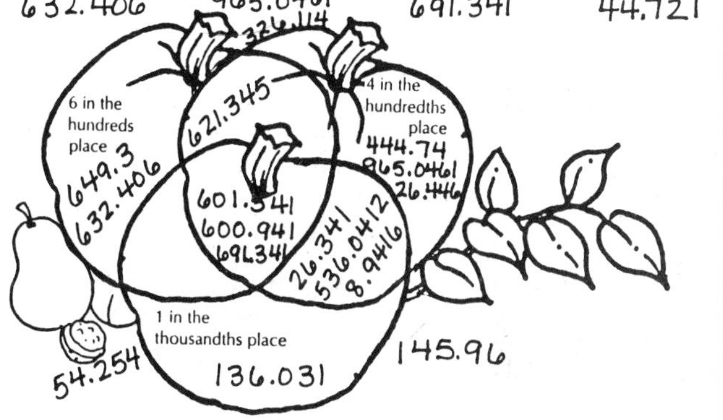

6 in the hundreds place: 649.3, 632.406

4 in the hundredths place: 444.74, 965.0461, 26.446

6 in the hundreds place and 4 in the hundredths place: 621.345, 326.114

6 in the hundreds place and 1 in the thousandths place: 601.341, 600.941, 691.341

4 in the hundredths place and 1 in the thousandths place: 26.341, 536.0412, 8.9416

1 in the thousandths place: 136.031

Outside set: 54.254, 145.96

Fill that Basket

Name ____________

Harvest Time

Solve each problem and shade each answer in the produce baskets to determine who has the largest amount of produce.

1. 13.86 ÷ 6 = 2.31
2. 370.4 ÷ 8 = 46.3
3. 21.264 ÷ 4 = 5.316
4. 8.4 ÷ 24 = .35
5. 60.48 ÷ 36 = 1.68
6. 405.42 ÷ 87 = 4.66
7. 17.64 ÷ 49 = .36
8. 20.772 ÷ .3 = 69.24
9. 6.152 ÷ .8 = 7.69
10. 13.684 ÷ .04 = 342.1
11. 3.8116 ÷ .52 = 7.33
12. 2.7735 ÷ .86 = 3.225
13. 380.68 ÷ 6.2 = 61.4
14. 3.468 ÷ 3.4 = 1.02
15. 1.9206 ÷ .06 = 32.01
16. 118.02 ÷ 2.1 = 56.2
17. 261.66 ÷ 4.2 = 62.3
18. 1.932 ÷ .14 = 13.8
19. 21.315 ÷ 2.9 = 7.35
20. .37284 ÷ .013 = 28.68

Bases Are Falling

Name ____________

National Bookkeeper's Day

Complete the base table on the right. Use the tables to answer the problems.

Base 10	Base 8	Base 6	Base 3
1	1	1	1
2	2	2	2
3	3	3	10
4	4	4	11
5	5	5	12
6	6	10	20
7	7	11	21
8	10	12	22
9	11	13	100
10	12	14	101
11	13	15	102
12	14	20	110
13	15	21	111
14	16	22	112
15	17	23	120
16	20	24	121
17	21	25	122
18	22	30	200
19	23	31	201
20	24	32	202
21	25	33	210
22	26	34	211
23	27	35	212
24	30	40	220
25	31	41	221
26	32	42	222
27	33	43	1,000
28	34	44	1,001
29	35	45	1,002
30	36	50	1,010
31	37	51	1,011

1. $132_6 + 11_6 =$ 12_6
2. $222_3 + 201_3 =$ 1200_3
3. $15_8 + 35_8 =$ 52_8
4. $115_6 - 31_6 =$ 44_6
5. $46_8 - 14_8 =$ 32_8
6. $112_3 \times 11_3 =$ 2002_3
7. $102_3 + 10_3 =$ 112_3
8. $25_6 + 40_6 =$ 105_6
9. $21_8 - 12_8 =$ 7_8
10. $12_3 \times 12_3 =$ 221_3
11. $13_8 \times 5_8 =$ 67_8
12. $120_6 + 12_6 =$ 10_6
13. $101_6 - 24_6 =$ 33_6
14. $11_8 + 23_8 =$ 34_8
15. $11_3 \times 101_3 =$ 1111_3

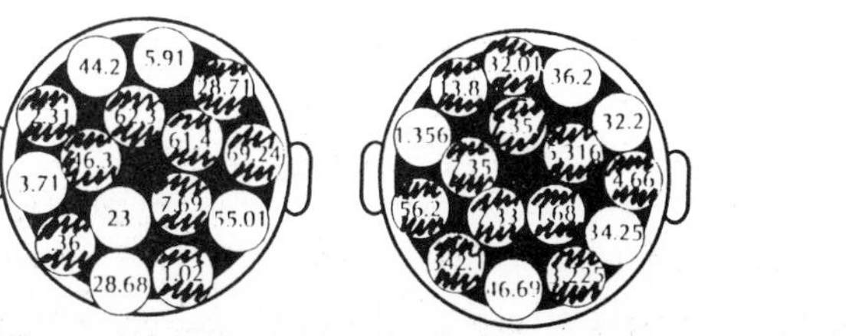

YOU ARE SO TOTALLY, LIKE, JOKING, RIGHT?

Base 10	Base 8	Base 6	Base 3
32	40	52	1012
33	41	53	1020
34	42	54	1021
35	43	55	1022
36	44	100	1100
37	45	101	1101
38	46	102	1102
39	47	103	1110
40	50	104	1111
41	51	105	1112
42	52	110	1120
43	53	111	1121
44	54	112	1122
45	55	113	1200
46	56	114	1201
47	57	115	1202
48	60	120	1210
49	61	121	1211
50	62	122	1212
51	63	123	1,220
52	64	124	1221
53	65	125	1222
54	66	130	2000
55	67	131	2001
56	70	132	2002
57	71	133	2010
58	72	134	2011
59	73	135	2012
60	74	140	2020
61	75	141	2021
62	76	142	2022

The Ships of Columbus

Name ____________________

Columbus Day

Columbus requested ships from several kings and queens before getting financing for his trip. On a separate sheet, design a ship for Columbus. Be sure to include the following geometric items, and tally the number of times you used each one.

ANSWERS WILL VARY.

triangles	______	quadrilaterals	______
circles	______	pentagons	______
ovals	______	open figures	______
hexagons	______	polygons not listed above	______

Use the data you gathered to make a graph in the space below. Once the graph is made, write at least three statements regarding your data. For example: I used twice as many circles as triangles. Some vocabulary you may choose to use includes: more, most, greater than, fewest, less, and compared to.

triangles | circles | ovals | hexagons | quadrilaterals | pentagons | open figures | polygons not listed above

CHRISTOPHER COLUMBUS WAS BORN IN 1451!

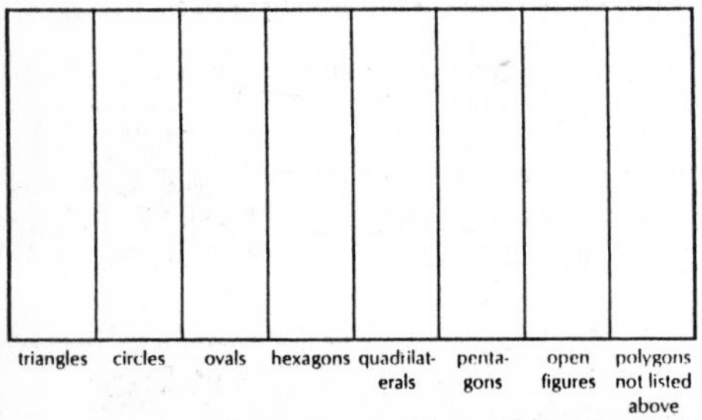

ANSWERS WILL VARY.

____

____

____

____

Page 76

Columbus Sails

Name ____________________

Columbus Day

Shade all fractions that are equivalent to the eight fractions listed below to find the year Christopher Columbus sailed to the Americas.

$\frac{1}{2}$ $\frac{2}{3}$ $\frac{3}{4}$ $\frac{3}{5}$

$\frac{5}{6}$ $\frac{5}{8}$ $\frac{2}{9}$ $\frac{1}{4}$

[illegible]/10 (shaded) 1/2	1/6	[illegible]/16 (shaded) 1/4	2/16 1/8	10/16 (shaded) 5/8	4/5	30/50 (shaded) 3/5	6/9 (shaded) 2/3	75/100 (shaded) 3/4	6/11	15/20 (shaded) 3/4	3/6 (shaded) 1/2	[illegible]/12 (shaded) 2/3
25/30 (shaded) 5/6	7/9	9/15 (shaded) 3/5	4/5	[illegible] (shaded) 1/2	3/9 1/3	10/45 (shaded) 2/9	4/12 1/3	15/24 (shaded) 5/8	9/10	10/21	4/7	2/8 (shaded) 1/4
18/20 (shaded) [illegible]	10/18 5/9	16/24 (shaded) 2/3	18/24 (shaded) 3/4	[illegible] (shaded) 1/4	8/29	[illegible]/72 (shaded) 2/9	30/60 (shaded) 1/2	18/30 (shaded) 3/5	6/20 3/10	3/8	35/42 (shaded) 5/6	10/100 (shaded) 1/10
20/32 (shaded) 5/8	2/6 1/3	1/9	6/11	18/27 (shaded) 2/3	7/10	21/23	40/50 4/5	60/80 (shaded) 3/4	70/90 7/9	22/88 (shaded) 1/4	34/40 17/20	90/95 18/19
8/36 (shaded) 2/9	6/7	4/12 1/3	20/50 2/5	9/18 (shaded) 1/2	17/80	14/16 7/8	2/10 1/5	6/10 (shaded) 3/5	4/9	10/12 (shaded) 5/6	6/27 (shaded) 2/9	17/34 (shaded) 1/2

I WASSA JUST LOOKIN' FOR A DECENT CHEESEBURGER, THASSA ALL!

Page 77

It's That Time of Year

Name ____________________

Autumn

Find each product. Use the last three digits in each answer to solve the code.

1. 32,426 x 63 = 2,042,838 O
2. 56,841 x 145 = 8,241,945 Y
3. 241,650 x 21 = 5,074,650 E
4. 45,186 x 62 = 2,801,532 A
5. 451,736 x 57 = 25,748,952 U
6. 35,086 x 83 = 2,912,138 B
7. 47,214 x 47 = 2,219,058 M
8. 176,256 x 172 = 30,316,032 H
9. 316,520 x 33 = 10,445,160 D
10. 160,544 x 72 = 11,559,168 N
11. 59,186 x 112 = 6,628,832 R
12. 862,411 x 40 = 34,496,440 T
13. 72,443 x 231 = 16,734,333 L
14. 650,333 x 29 = 18,859,657 G
15. 59,627 x 301 = 17,947,727 S

What are students saying this time of year?

I'M OUTTA HERE!!

G	O	O	D	–	B	Y	E		S	U	M	M	E	R...
657	838	838	160		138	945	650		727	952	58	58	650	832

H	E	L	L	O		A	U	T	U	M	N
32	650	333	333	838		532	952	440	952	58	168

Page 78

Fall Festival

Name ____________________

Autumn

Solve each problem. Use the answers in any order to fill in the blanks so the stories make sense.

$326x = 1{,}304$ x = 4 | $\frac{900}{p} = 6$ p = 150 | $45t = 585$ t = 13 | $\frac{h}{30} = 20$ h = 600

150 students each collected 4 dollars for the Fall Festival decorations. The committee used the 600 dollars to buy 13 rolls of crepe paper and other supplies.

$12y = 540$ y = 45 | $\frac{m}{25} = 9$ m = 225 | $\frac{z}{5} = 13$ z = 65 | $2s = 720$ s = 360

The food committee spent 225 dollars on 45 pies which could be cut into eight pieces each. They decided to charge 65 cents for each of the 360 pieces of pie in order not to lose any money.

$\frac{306}{r} = 34$ r = 9 | $84g = 672$ g = 8 | $7f = 504$ f = 72 | $\frac{1{,}152}{v} = 18$ v = 64

Square activity booths were set up along one wall of the gymnasium. 72 feet of wall space was divided into equal spaces for 9 booths. Each booth had 8 feet along the wall. The area of each booth was 64 square feet.

$23p = 690$ p = 30 | $90 \times 7 = n$ n = 630 | $\frac{i}{5} = 127$ i = 635 | $\frac{882}{w} = 42$ w = 21

635 students enjoyed the activities planned for Fall Festival. Planning for the Festival required 30 students, ten from each grade level. A total of 630 hours went into the planning, with each student contributing 21 hours.

Page 79

Fall Fruits

Name ____________________

Autumn

Change each fraction to a decimal. Then find the decimal answers in the tic-tac-toe games. Draw an apple over answers of odd-numbered problems and an orange over answers of even-numbered problems.

1. $\frac{7}{20}$ = .35
2. $\frac{12}{25}$ = .48
3. $\frac{1}{4}$ = .25
4. $\frac{3}{4}$ = .75
5. $\frac{5}{8}$ = .625
6. $\frac{2}{5}$ = .4
7. $\frac{3}{10}$ = .3
8. $\frac{11}{16}$ = .6875
9. $\frac{9}{10}$ = .9
10. $\frac{3}{8}$ = .375
11. $\frac{4}{5}$ = .8
12. $\frac{3}{25}$ = .12
13. $\frac{1}{8}$ = .125
14. $\frac{1}{2}$ = .5
15. $\frac{9}{20}$ = .45
16. $\frac{7}{40}$ = .175
17. $\frac{3}{5}$ = .6
18. $\frac{7}{8}$ = .875
19. $\frac{1}{5}$ = .2
20. $\frac{17}{20}$ = .85
21. $\frac{11}{50}$ = .22
22. $\frac{19}{40}$ = .475

.25	.4	.625
.33	.35	.48
.3	.13	.75

.12	.5	.6875
.7	.125	.8
.9	.642	.375

.2	.45	.85
.01	.875	.22
.475	.6	.175

Page 80

First Report Card

Name ____________________

End 1st Marking Period

Find the mean, or average, of each student's scores. Round to the nearest whole number and record the scores in the last column. Answer the questions below based on this table.

Asia	93	88	97	100	100	97	100	96
Dunn	55	60	56	72	43	52	60	57
Jorge	88	90	95	100	85	90	90	91
Meg	100	100	92	80	100	100	95	95
Payne	78	83	79	99	87	92	99	88
Shae	97	95	88	100	91	93	98	95
Zia	95	100	100	98	95	100	100	98

57 88 91 (95) 95 96 98

Use the students' cumulative scores to answer the following five questions.

1. What is the mean of these cumulative scores? 89
2. What is the range of these scores? 98-57=41
3. What is the mode of these scores? 95
4. What is the median of these scores? 95
5. Who had the median score? Shae + Meg

THAT'S ONE MEAN REPORT CARD, DUDE!

Use individual student's scores to answer the following questions.

6. What is the range of Dunn's scores? 29
7. What is the mode of Payne's scores? 99
8. What is the median of Meg's scores? 100

Page 81

Ghosts and Bats

Name ____________________

Halloween

Solve each problem and find the answers in the tic-tac-toe games. Draw a ghost over the answers for the odd-numbered problems and a bat over the answers for the even-numbered problems.

1. 56 ⟌ 27,384 = 489
2. 36 ⟌ 23,472 = 652
3. 15 ⟌ 9,450 = 630
4. 33 ⟌ 14,619 = 443
5. 57 ⟌ 10,203 = 179
6. 23 ⟌ 12,489 = 543
7. 47 ⟌ 12,549 = 267
8. 61 ⟌ 16,043 = 263
9. 82 ⟌ 12,218 = 149
10. 76 ⟌ 25,156 = 331
11. 42 ⟌ 33,264 = 792
12. 59 ⟌ 37,937 = 643
13. 27 ⟌ 16,146 = 598
14. 80 ⟌ 34,240 = 428

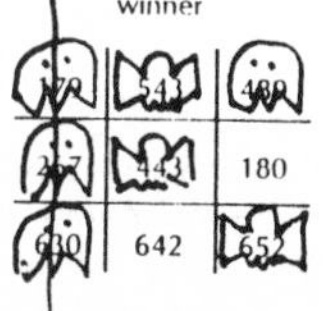

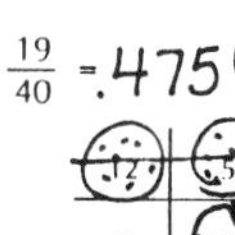

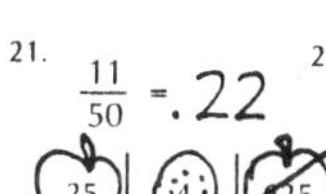

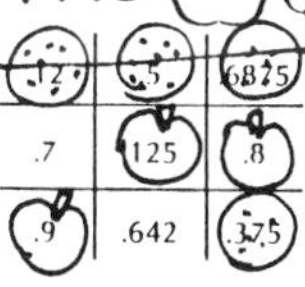

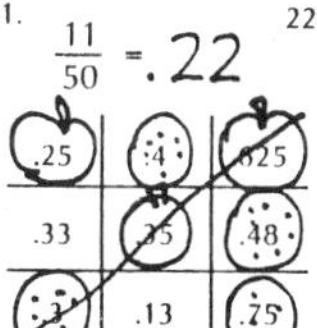

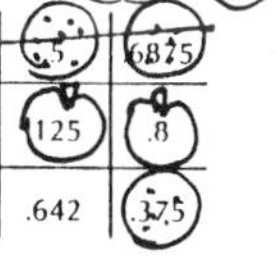

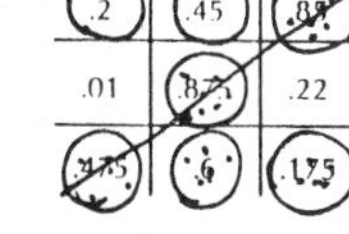

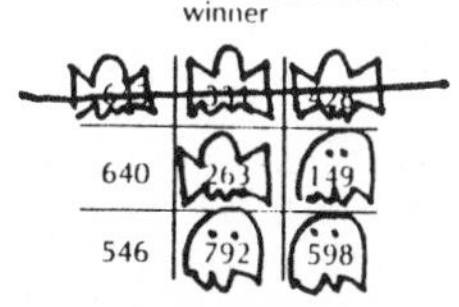

THAT ABOUT WRAPS IT UP!

winner

179	543	489
267	443	180
630	642	652

winner

643	331	428
640	263	149
546	792	598

Page 82

Pumpkins

Name ____________________

Halloween

Organize the addends provided in the pumpkins below. Then solve for each sum. Order the sums from greatest to least by placing a number in the box inside each pumpkin.

Work Space

Pumpkin A: 45.236, 2.8947, 571.4, .0498, 9.5046 — [8] — 629.0851

Pumpkin B: 106.753, 98.5812, 209.0049, 158.601, 66.145 — [2] — 639.0851

Pumpkin C: 25.8815, 41.6888, 138.4076, 6.485, 421.5963 — [5] — 634.0592

Pumpkin D: 316.6118, .9842, 64.0215, 254.168, 3.2145 — [3] — 639

Pumpkin E: 75.6431, 66.03403, .60287, 6.5842, 490.25 — [1] — 639.1142

Pumpkin F: 39.1804, 308.6666, 41.0648, 234.942, 5.4862 — [7] — 629.34

Pumpkin G: 59.8276, 64.721, 105.2047, 3.6487, 400.661 — [4] — 634.063

Pumpkin H: 311.814, 71.3541, .0489, 34.2105, 213.5621 — [6] — 630.9896

Page 83

Let's Get Costumed

Name ____________________

Halloween

Use the data given on this page to answer the questions.

1. Make tree diagrams to show all of the possible combinations for the clown costume.

Hair	Suit
purple	polka dots
red	large stripes
blue	swirls
green	solid
orange	

LET'S EAT!

2. How many combinations are there? 20
3. What is the probability that Yancy will have red hair and a suit with large stripes? 1:20
4. What is the probability that Pearl will have a suit that is a solid color? 5:20 or 1:4
5. What is the probability that Wolfe will have blue hair and a suit with polka dots or blue hair and a suit with swirls? 2:20 or 1:10
6. What is the probability that Barrie will have purple or green hair? 8:20 or 2:5

Pearl has a candy bag to go with her clown suit. In the bag are mini candy bars. There are 7 solid milk chocolate bars, 5 bars with almonds, and 3 candy bars with caramel. With the bag full, what is the probability of . . .

- choosing a solid milk-chocolate bar? 7:15
- choosing a candy bar with caramel? 3:15 or 1:5
- choosing a piece of gum? 0:15
- choosing a candy bar with almonds? 5:15 or 1:3

If Pearl returns the candy bars to the bag each time, what is the probability of . . .

- choosing a candy bar with caramel if she makes 30 picks? 6:30 or 1:5
- choosing a solid milk-chocolate bar if she makes 75 picks? 35:75 or 7:15

Page 84

Costume Party

Name ____________________

Halloween

These seven friends went to a costume party dressed as seven different book characters. Use the clues and matrix to determine who was dressed as which character.

1. Sig's character sailed the seas.
2. Jean went as the spider in E.B. White's book and Tia went as the spider's pig friend.
3. Jay's character lived while the west was being settled.
4. Bob's character tried to catch Moby Dick.
5. Tom's character had a blue ox.

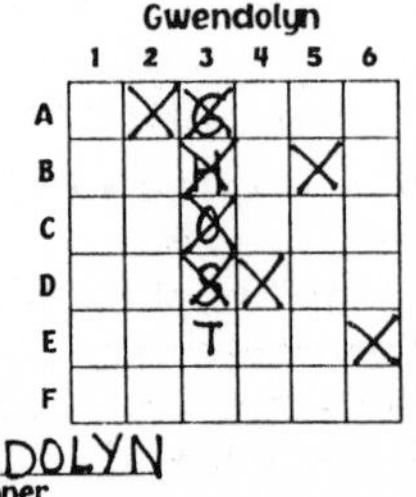

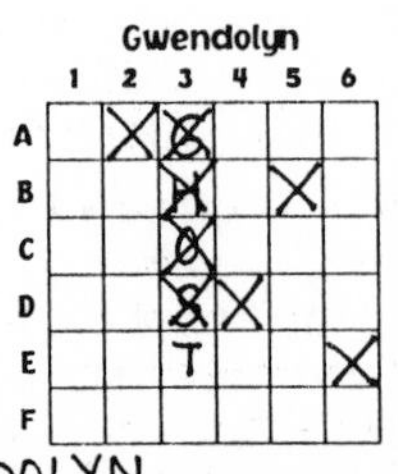

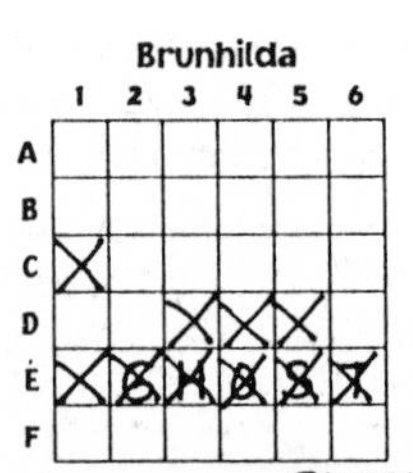

MOBY DICK WAS FIRST PUBLISHED IN 1851 MATEY!

	Captain Ahab	Paul Bunyan	Charlotte	Blackbeard	Laura Ingalls	Tinkerbell	Wilbur
Bob	YES	X	X	X	X	X	X
Jay	X	X	X	X	YES	X	X
Jean	X	X	YES	X	X	X	X
Mae	X	X	X	X	X	YES	X
Sig	X	X	X	YES	X	X	X
Tia	X	X	X	X	X	X	YES
Tom	X	YES	X	X	X	X	X

Bob was CAPTAIN AHAB

Jay was LAURA INGALLS

Jean was CHARLOTTE

Mae was TINKERBELL

Sig was BLACKBEARD

Tia was WILBUR

Tom was PAUL BUNYON

Page 85

Capture the Ghost

Name ____________________

Halloween

Brunhilda and Gwendolyn are playing a game similar to Battleship in which each tries to capture the other's ghost. Brunhilda uses the answers to the odd problems and calls positions on Gwendolyn's board. Gwendolyn uses the answers to the even problems and calls positions on Brunhilda's board. Use the answers to locate the squares called. Place an **X** on each coordinate as it is called. The first to capture the other's ghost wins.

1. -2 + -6 = -8
2. +10 + -4 = +6
3. +1 - -8 = +9
4. -13 - -10 = -3
5. +3 - +8 = -5
6. +1 + +9 = +10
7. -14 - -8 = -6
8. +4 + +4 = +8
9. -4 + -7 = -11
10. +13 + -6 = +7
11. -5 - -8 = +3
12. -1 + +3 = +2
13. -5 + +4 = -1
14. +10 - +5 = +5
15. -4 + -3 = -7
16. +14 + -2 = +12
17. +2 + -4 = -2
18. -4 - +5 = -9
19. +8 - +4 = +4
20. -1 + -9 = -10

Coordinates

-11	D-4	+2	E-4
-10	E-6	+3	A-3
-9	E-5	+4	D-3
-8	F-1	+5	E-2
-7	B-3	+6	C-1
-6	E-6	+7	D-4
-5	B-5	+8	D-3
-3	D-2	+9	C-2
-2	C-3	+10	E-3
-1	A-2	+12	E-1

Brunhilda

	1	2	3	4	5	6
A						
B						
C	X					
D			X	X	X	
E	X	G	H	O	S	T
F						

Gwendolyn

	1	2	3	4	5	6
A		X	G			
B			H		X	
C			O			
D			S	X		
E			T			X
F						

GWENDOLYN
Winner

Page 86

Ghouls and Goblins

Name ____________________

Halloween

Ghouls and Goblins are trying desperately to figure out mathematics that involve letters, but can't seem to do so. They want to work with numerals only. Read the directions and help them solve each request.

Write the algebraic expression for each word expression.

1. eight less than p — p-8
2. q decreased by five — q-5
3. fifteen divided by c — $\frac{15}{c}$
4. m and seven — m+7
5. nine more than j — j+9
6. f times three — 3f

Write the word expression for each algebraic expression.

7. 10r — ten times r
8. s ÷ 2 — s divided by 2
9. v + 6 — v and 6
10. 19 - h — 19 subtract h
11. 24 ÷ d — 24 divided by d
12. y - 9 — y subtract 9

Solve the expression *7r* for each given value of *r*.

13. r = 10 — 70
14. r = .08 — .56
15. r = 3,645 — 25,515

Solve the expression *s - 11* for each given value of *s*.

16. s = 8 — -3
17. s = 27.42 — 16.42
18. s = 1,400 — 1389

Solve the expression *g ÷ 2* for each given value of *g*.

19. g = 65 — 32.5
20. g = .6 — .3
21. g = 42.361 — 21.1805

Solve the expression *6 + m* for each given value of *m*.

22. m = .3 — 6.3
23. m = -12 — -6
24. m = 99,999 — 100,005

Page 87

Happy Halloween

Name ______________ Halloween

Solve for each letter. Then use the code to find out when the Halloween festivities begin.

OCTOBER 31 WAS THE LAST DAY OF THE CELTIC YEAR! BOO!

1. n - 6.97 = 5.59
   n = 12.56
2. 35.15 - c = 15.85
   c = 19.3
3. 3.46 + s = 14.04
   s = 10.58
4. 234,567 + w = 833,108
   w = 598,541
5. l - 98,674 = 157,640
   l = 256,314
6. 6.012 - r = 2.024
   r = 3.988
7. 1.645 + m + 29.403 = 47.647
   m = 16.599
8. 64.008 - d = 25.767
   d = 38.241
9. 364,825 + k = 857,531
   k = 492,706
10. 3.041 - 1.183 = e
    e = 1.858
11. .042 + h + .566 = 1.257
    h = .649
12. g - 8,734 = 5,891
    g = 14,625
13. t + 57.68 = 84.62
    t = 26.94
14. 5.203 - i = 2.536
    i = 2.667
15. 23,546 + o = 53,392
    o = 29,846

W H E N   T H E
598,541 .649 1.858 12.56   26.94 .649 1.858

C L O C K
19.3 256,314 29,846 19.3 492,706

S T R I K E S
10.58 26.94 3.988 2.667 492,706 1.858 10.58

M I D N I G H T
16.599 2.667 38.241 12.56 2.667 14,625 .649 26.94

Page 88

Food Drive

Name ______________ Thanksgiving

During "No-one-Hungry-on-Thanksgiving Week," Marion Middle School students held a food drive to compliment the turkeys donated by a local grocery store. Use the graph to answer the questions.

IN CANADA, THANKSGIVING IS THE 2ND MONDAY IN OCTOBER! LET'S EAT!

Thanksgiving Food Drive

Number of items: 0, 25, 50, 75, 100, 125, 150, 175, 200, 225, 250, 275, 300

canned vegetables, paper products, boxed mixes, soups, beverages, other

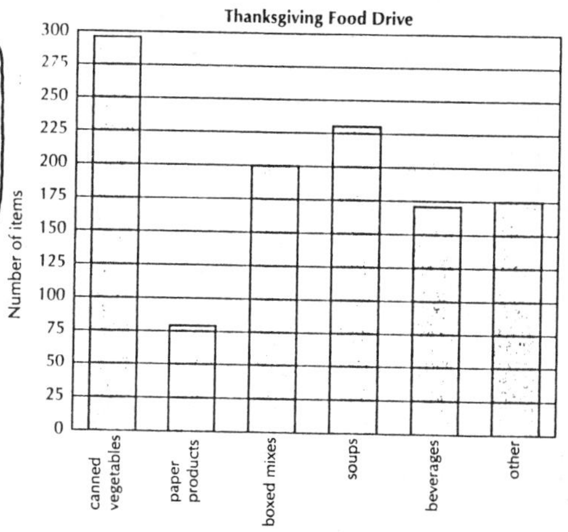

1. Which item did the students collect the greatest number of? Canned veges
2. Of which item did the students collect 230 pieces? Soups
3. Were more beverages or mixes collected? Boxed mixes
4. Write a statement comparing the paper products and soups. Less paper products were collected than soups.
5. About how many items were collected all together? 1150

Page 89

On with the Feast

Name ______________ Thanksgiving

Use the data given on this page to answer the questions.

Beverage	Dessert
milk	pumpkin pie
water	mince pie
cola	brownie
	apple crumble

1. On the back of this sheet, make a tree diagram to show all of the possible combinations at Thanksgiving dinner.
2. How many combinations are there? 12
3. What is the probability that June will have milk and pumpkin pie? 1:12
4. What is the probability that Mick will have milk with his dessert? 4:12 or 1:3
5. What is the probability that Tory will have water and apple crumble or water and mince pie? 2:12 or 1:6
6. What is the probability that Rafe will have a brownie? 3:12 or 1:4

Use the frequency table for desserts ordered with school lunch the day before Thanksgiving break to answer the questions. Use the data to make a bar graph.

Frequency Table

Dessert Chosen	Frequency
pumpkin pie	155
apple pie	75
chocolate chip cookie	60
pumpkin bars	95

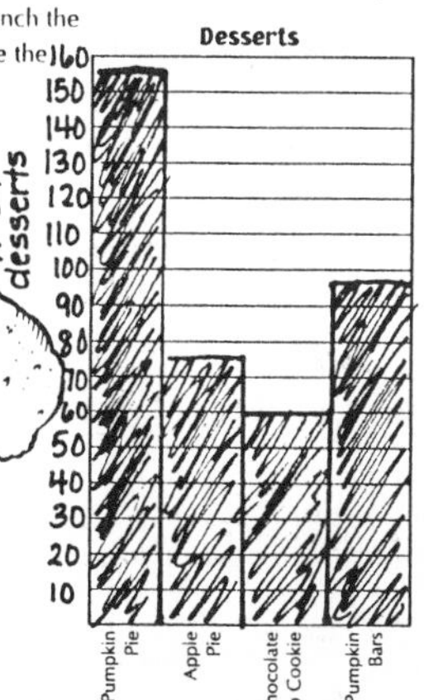

7. What is the greatest number in the frequency table? 155
8. What is the least number in the frequency table? 60
9. Which numerical scale will be easiest to read, one with intervals of 2, 5, or 10? 5 or 10

Page 90

Baskets of Produce

Name ______________ Thanksgiving

Plums	Apples	Pumpkins
Cherries	Beans	Carrots

Write the fraction for the white portion of the produce. Simplify to lowest terms.

plums 1/8   apples 3/10   pumpkins 1/6
cherries 8/15   beans 5/15   carrots 5/12

Write the fraction for the black portion of the produce. Simplify to lowest terms.

plums 2/8 or 1/4   apples 2/10 or 1/5   pumpkins 2/6 or 1/3
cherries 2/15   beans 7/15   carrots 3/12 or 1/4

Write the fraction for the dotted portion of the produce. Simplify to lowest terms.

plums 5/8   apples 5/10 or 1/2   pumpkins 3/6 or 1/2
cherries 5/15 or 1/3   beans 3/15 or 1/5   carrots 4/12 or 1/3

Write a fraction addition sentence for each and solve. Simplify to lowest terms.

white and dotted plums 1/8 + 5/8 = 6/8 = 3/4
white and black apples 3/10 + 2/10 = 5/10 = 1/2
white and black pumpkins 1/6 + 2/6 = 3/6 = 1/2
dotted and black cherries 5/15 + 2/15 = 7/15
black and dotted beans 7/15 + 3/15 = 10/15 = 2/3

Page 91

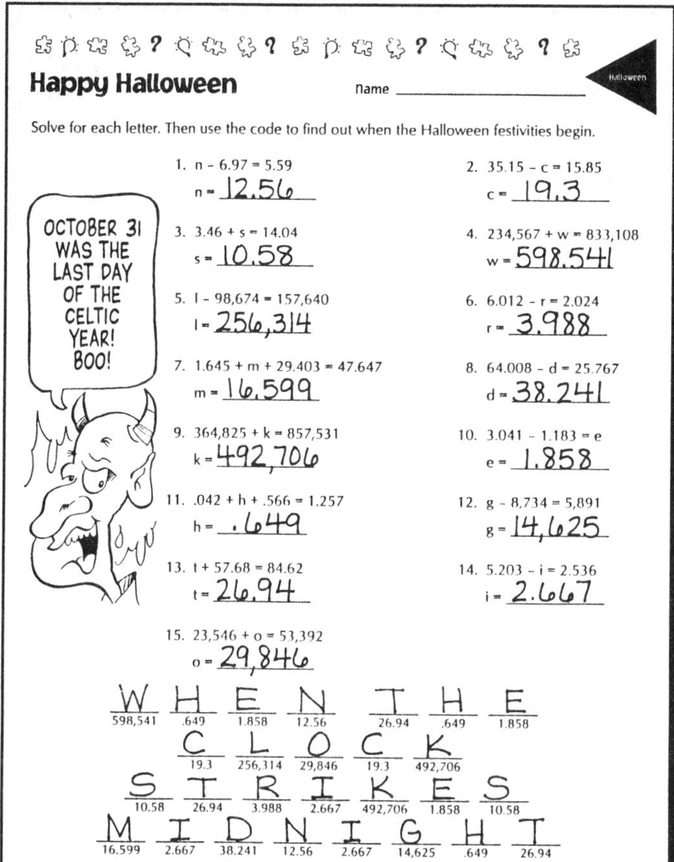

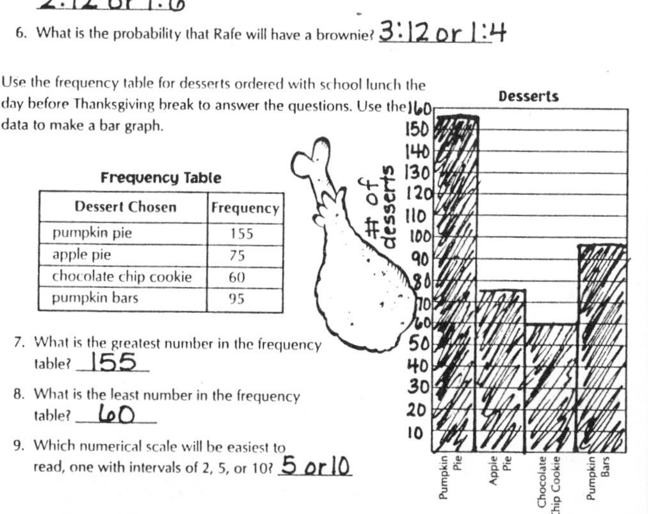

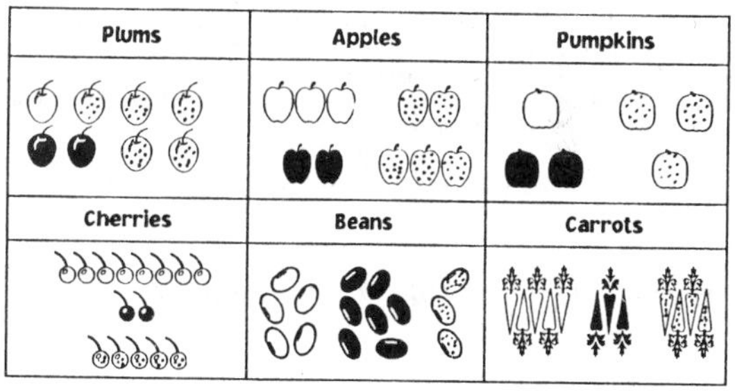

Fabulous Feast

Thanksgiving

Name ____________________

Ms. Kelly's cooking classs decided to put together a Thanksgiving feast for the school's early childhood center. Each student prepared a different dish to complete the meal. Use the clues and matrix to determine what dish each of the seven students made.

1. Sage made a pie.
2. Mia's contribution was a vegetable.
3. Mac used Granny Smiths to make his product.
4. Greer mashed a tuber.
5. Nat did not make a pie but did make a fruit-based dish.
6. Brit made a green vegetable.
7. Abia picked the small fruit for her dish from a tree.

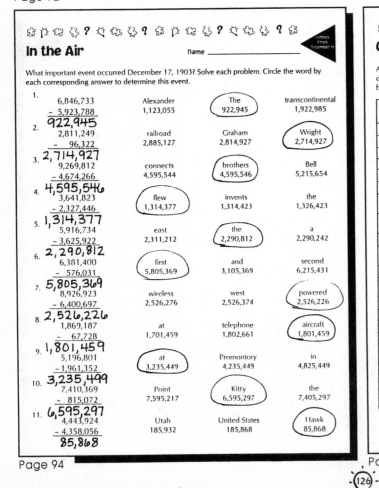

THE FIRST AUTO RACE IN THE UNITED STATES WAS HELD ON THANKSGIVING DAY IN 1895!

	Pumpkin Pie	Apple Pie	Cherry Pie	Corn	Potatoes	Apple-sauce	Beans
Abia	X	X	YES	X	X	X	X
Brit	X	X	X	X	X	X	YES
Greer	X	X	X	X	YES	X	X
Mac	X	YES	X	X	X	X	X
Mia	X	X	X	YES	X	X	X
Nat	X	X	X	X	X	YES	X
Sage	YES	X	X	X	X	X	X

Abia made CHERRY PIE
Brit made BEANS
Greer made POTATOES
Mac made APPLE PIE
Mia made CORN
Nat made APPLESAUCE
Sage made PUMPKIN PIE

Page 92

Pick A Pie

Thanksgiving

Name ____________________

Change the unlike fractions in each pie to like fractions. Then number them from least to greatest.

1. $\frac{1}{5}=\frac{6}{30}$ (4), $\frac{1}{6}=\frac{5}{30}$ (3), $\frac{1}{3}=\frac{10}{30}$ (5), $\frac{1}{10}=\frac{3}{30}$ (2), $\frac{1}{15}=\frac{2}{30}$ (1)
2. $\frac{5}{8}=\frac{15}{24}$ (2), $\frac{5}{6}=\frac{20}{24}$ (5), $\frac{7}{12}=\frac{14}{24}$ (1), $\frac{2}{3}=\frac{16}{24}$ (3), $\frac{3}{4}=\frac{18}{24}$ (4)
3. $\frac{4}{5}=\frac{16}{20}$ (5), $\frac{3}{4}=\frac{15}{20}$ (4), $\frac{3}{10}=\frac{6}{20}$ (1), $\frac{1}{2}=\frac{10}{20}$ (2), $\frac{11}{20}=\frac{11}{20}$ (3)
4. $\frac{3}{4}=\frac{9}{12}$ (4), $\frac{1}{2}=\frac{6}{12}$ (2), $\frac{5}{6}=\frac{10}{12}$ (5), $\frac{2}{3}=\frac{8}{12}$ (3), $\frac{1}{4}=\frac{3}{12}$ (1)
5. $\frac{2}{3}=\frac{24}{36}$ (3), $\frac{1}{4}=\frac{9}{36}$ (1), $\frac{7}{9}=\frac{28}{36}$ (4), $\frac{5}{6}=\frac{30}{36}$ (5), $\frac{11}{18}=\frac{22}{36}$ (2)
6. $\frac{1}{2}=\frac{8}{16}$ (2), $\frac{5}{8}=\frac{10}{16}$ (3), $\frac{3}{4}=\frac{12}{16}$ (5), $\frac{3}{8}=\frac{6}{16}$ (1), $\frac{11}{16}=\frac{11}{16}$ (4)

Page 93

In the Air

Famous Firsts December 17

Name ____________________

What important event occurred December 17, 1903? Solve each problem. Circle the word by each corresponding answer to determine this event.

Problem	Answer			
1. 6,846,733 − 5,923,788 = 922,945	Alexander 1,123,055	**(The 922,945)**	transcontinental 1,922,985
2. 2,811,249 − 96,322 = 2,714,927	railroad 2,885,127	Graham 2,814,927	**(Wright 2,714,927)**
3. 9,269,812 − 4,674,266 = 4,595,546	connects 4,595,544	**(brothers 4,595,546)**	Bell 5,215,654
4. 3,641,823 − 2,327,446 = 1,314,377	**(flew 1,314,377)**	invents 1,314,423	the 1,326,423
5. 5,916,734 − 3,625,922 = 2,290,812	east 2,311,212	**(the 2,290,812)**	a 2,290,242
6. 6,381,400 − 576,031 = 5,805,369	**(first 5,805,369)**	and 3,105,369	second 6,215,431
7. 8,926,923 − 6,400,697 = 2,526,226	wireless 2,526,276	west 2,526,374	**(powered 2,526,226)**
8. 1,869,187 − 67,728 = 1,801,459	at 1,701,459	telephone 1,802,661	**(aircraft 1,801,459)**
9. 5,196,801 − 1,961,352 = 3,235,499	**(at 3,235,449)**	Promontory 4,235,449	in 4,825,449
10. 7,410,369 − 815,072 = 6,595,297	Point 7,595,217	**(Kitty 6,595,297)**	the 7,405,297
11. 4,443,924 − 4,358,056 = 85,868	Utah 185,932	United States 185,868	**(Hawk 85,868)**

Page 94

Christmas Shopping

Christmas

Name ____________________

As an early Christmas gift your parents gave you a checkbook and $100. Mom and Dad have decided that you will purchase all of your Christmas gifts to give this year. Balance the checkbook by adding deposits and subtracting debits. Keep a running total.

Date	Check #	Transaction and Reason	Debit	Deposit	Balance
12/1		Deposit–gift from Mom and Dad		$100.00	$100.
12/4		Deposit–babysitting Smiths		$16.00	$116.
12/5	101	Clothes House–jacket	$84.32		$31.68
12/7	102	Pizza Palace–lunch	$6.46		$25.22
12/8	103	Toys and More–craft set for Sammi	$16.89		$8.33
12/8		Deposit–shoveling Cruz		$15.00	$23.33
12/8		Deposit–shoveling our house and Grandma T's		$20.00	$43.33
12/9		Deposit–shoveling Cruz, Vinn, Snich, Van Don		$50.00	$93.33
12/10	104	Bath Stuff–gifts for Grandma T and M	$19.87		$73.46
12/10	105	Men's Den–gifts for Dad, Grandpa T and Grandpa M	$56.82		$16.64
12/12		Deposit–babysitting Smiths		$24.00	$40.64
12/13		Deposit–shoveling Cruz, Vinn, Snich, Van Don		$50.00	$90.64
12/14	106	Rich's Jewelry Store–gift for Mom	$26.89		$63.75
12/14	107	Hamburger Hut–lunch	$4.77		$58.98
12/14	108	Toys and More–art set for Randi	$15.73		$43.25
12/15		Deposit–babysitting Cruz		$17.50	$60.75
12/16		Deposit–shoveling our house and Grandma T's		$20.00	$80.75
12/17		Deposit–shoveling Cruz, Vinn, Snich, Van Don		$50.00	$130.75
12/19	109	Steele's Steaks–gift certificate for Mom and Dad	$30.00		$100.75
12/19	110	Pizza Palace–slumber party with friends	$23.88		$76.87

Page 95

In the Package

Christmas

Name ____________________

Fill up the package by writing the multiples for each number in the table.

1	1	2	3	4	5	6	7	8	9	10	11	12
2	2	4	6	8	10	12	14	16	18	20	22	24
3	3	6	9	12	15	18	21	24	27	30	33	36
4	4	8	12	16	20	24	28	32	36	40	44	48
5	5	10	15	20	25	30	35	40	45	50	55	60
6	6	12	18	24	30	36	42	48	54	60	66	72
7	7	14	21	28	35	42	49	56	63	70	77	84
8	8	16	24	32	40	48	56	64	72	80	88	96
9	9	18	27	36	45	54	63	72	81	90	99	108

Use the table to write common multiples for the following number pairs. Circle the Least Common Multiple (LCM).

1. 8 and 6 (24), 48
2. 5 and 3 (15), 30
3. 2 and 3 (6), 12, 18, 24, 30, 36
4. 7 and 2 (14), 28, 42, 56, 70, 84
5. 4 and 6 (12), 24, 36, 48, 60
6. 9 and 6 (18), 36, 54, 72, 90, 108

Page 96

Fill it and Wrap it

Christmas

Name ____________________

Find the volume of each gift box listed below. Also find the surface area to help with wrapping paper purchases. The unit of measurement is inches. Hint: determine the area of all 6 sides, then add up the square units.

6x2x4

Determine the volume: 48 cubic inches

What is the surface area? 88 square inches

7.5x2.5x12

Determine the volume: 225 cubic inches

What is the surface area? 277.5 sq. in.

8x8x8

Determine the volume: 512 cubic in.

What is the surface area? 384 sq. in.

4x6x11

Determine the volume: 264 cubic in.

What is the surface area? 268 sq. in.

Page 97

Greetings

Christmas

Name ____________________

Find the common denominators for each of the fractions listed. Write them on the lines below.

$\frac{15}{24}$ $\frac{1}{6} = \frac{4}{24}$ $\frac{3}{4} = \frac{18}{24}$ $\frac{1}{4} = \frac{6}{24}$ $\frac{1}{2} = \frac{12}{24}$ $\frac{11}{12} = \frac{22}{24}$ $\frac{5}{6} = \frac{20}{24}$

$\frac{3}{8} = \frac{9}{24}$ $\frac{2}{3} = \frac{16}{24}$ $\frac{7}{12} = \frac{14}{24}$ $\frac{1}{8} = \frac{3}{24}$ $\frac{5}{12} = \frac{10}{24}$ $\frac{1}{3} = \frac{8}{24}$

Order the fractions using like denominators:

3/24 4/24 6/24 8/24 9/24 10/24 12/24 14/24 15/24 16/24 18/24 20/24 22/24

Now, order the fractions with unlike denominators and use the Message Key to write a holiday greeting.

1/8 1/6 1/4 1/3 3/8 5/12 1/2 7/12 15/24 2/3 3/4 5/6 11/12

THE ANCIENT ROMANS CELEBRATE THE FEAST OF THE INVINCIBLE SUN ON DECEMBER 25!

Message Key

- A 1/6, 3/4
- D 2/3
- H 1/8, 5/12
- I 15/24
- L 7/12
- O 1/2
- P 1/4, 1/3
- S 11/12
- Y 3/8, 5/6

Write the message:

H A P P Y   H O L I D A Y S

Page 98

Holiday Message

Christmas

Name ____________________

Write each fraction in the simplest form. Then shade each answer in the puzzle to find a holiday message.

1. $\frac{9}{27} = \frac{1}{3}$
2. $\frac{24}{32} = \frac{3}{4}$
3. $\frac{24}{28} = \frac{6}{7}$
4. $\frac{31}{62} = \frac{1}{2}$
5. $\frac{28}{35} = \frac{4}{5}$
6. $\frac{15}{39} = \frac{5}{13}$
7. $\frac{24}{54} = \frac{4}{9}$
8. $\frac{12}{30} = \frac{2}{5}$
9. $\frac{28}{48} = \frac{7}{12}$
10. $\frac{24}{27} = \frac{8}{9}$
11. $\frac{9}{45} = \frac{1}{5}$
12. $\frac{12}{21} = \frac{4}{7}$
13. $\frac{7}{28} = \frac{1}{4}$
14. $\frac{15}{33} = \frac{5}{11}$
15. $\frac{12}{54} = \frac{2}{9}$
16. $\frac{6}{36} = \frac{1}{6}$
17. $\frac{9}{15} = \frac{3}{5}$
18. $\frac{16}{24} = \frac{2}{3}$
19. $\frac{20}{24} = \frac{5}{6}$
20. $\frac{36}{56} = \frac{9}{14}$
21. $\frac{22}{30} = \frac{11}{15}$
22. $\frac{18}{48} = \frac{3}{8}$
23. $\frac{28}{52} = \frac{7}{13}$
24. $\frac{27}{60} = \frac{9}{20}$
25. $\frac{8}{56} = \frac{1}{7}$
26. $\frac{18}{60} = \frac{3}{10}$
27. $\frac{45}{55} = \frac{9}{11}$
28. $\frac{12}{45} = \frac{4}{15}$
29. $\frac{33}{48} = \frac{11}{16}$
30. $\frac{37}{51} = \frac{9}{17}$
31. $\frac{20}{32} = \frac{5}{8}$
32. $\frac{20}{36} = \frac{5}{9}$
33. $\frac{20}{48} = \frac{5}{12}$
34. $\frac{14}{32} = \frac{7}{16}$
35. $\frac{14}{20} = \frac{7}{10}$
36. $\frac{26}{44} = \frac{13}{22}$
37. $\frac{78}{120} = \frac{13}{20}$
38. $\frac{4}{40} = \frac{1}{10}$
39. $\frac{12}{66} = \frac{2}{11}$

[illegible]	5/3	2/15	[illegible]	3/2	7/8	[illegible]	[illegible]	9/10	7/6	[illegible]	[illegible]	[illegible]	5/4	[illegible]	2/7	6/11
[illegible]	[illegible]	2/13	[illegible]	8/11	[illegible]	1/9	3/3	[illegible]	1/11	[illegible]	3/16	4/13	1/33	[illegible]	5/7	2/15
[illegible]	1/16	[illegible]	[illegible]	2/17	[illegible]	11/6	1/19	[illegible]	1/9	[illegible]	[illegible]	10/9	6/5	[illegible]	1/32	2/61
[illegible]	5/4	1/21	[illegible]	1/8	[illegible]	3/13	5/16	[illegible]	1/22	[illegible]	3/23	1/43	5/2	[illegible]	8/11	1/13
[illegible]	3/2	1/12	[illegible]	6/5	1/17	[illegible]	[illegible]	4/25	5/21	[illegible]	[illegible]	[illegible]	1/9	[illegible]	[illegible]	[illegible]

Page 99

Hang the Stockings with Care

Christmas

Name ____________________

Each stocking is filled with a different function machine. Determine the missing functions and fill the stockings with number goodies.

Rule add $2\frac{1}{4}$

$4\frac{3}{4}$	7
$6\frac{1}{4}$	$8\frac{1}{2}$
$7\frac{3}{8}$	$9\frac{5}{8}$
$3\frac{1}{3}$	$5\frac{7}{12}$
$5\frac{5}{12}$	$7\frac{2}{3}$
$1\frac{5}{8}$	$3\frac{7}{8}$
$2\frac{1}{5}$	$4\frac{9}{20}$
$10\frac{1}{2}$	$12\frac{3}{4}$
$8\frac{5}{6}$	$11\frac{1}{12}$
$3\frac{7}{10}$	$5\frac{19}{20}$

Rule + 1 ÷ 3

8	3
5	2
29	10
17	6
14	5
11	4
20	7
23	8
26	9
32	11

Rule ÷ 2

6	3
25	12.5
18	9
15	7.5
15.2	7.6
40	20
96	48
2	1
.75	.375
10	5

Page 100

Christmas Symbol

Christmas

Name ____________________

Solve each problem. Find the answers below and write the corresponding grid coordinates.

1. (2, 4) $\frac{5}{6} - \frac{1}{6} = \frac{2}{3}$
2. (6, 0) $\frac{5}{9} - \frac{2}{9} = \frac{1}{3}$
3. (6, 8) $\frac{9}{15} - \frac{6}{15} = \frac{1}{5}$
4. (9, 4) $\frac{7}{8} - \frac{5}{8} = \frac{1}{4}$
5. (5, 10) $\frac{15}{16} - \frac{3}{16} = \frac{3}{4}$
6. (7, 6) $\frac{19}{20} - \frac{3}{20} = \frac{4}{5}$
7. (10, 2) $\frac{11}{16} - \frac{5}{16} = \frac{3}{8}$
8. (0, 2) $\frac{14}{21} - \frac{8}{21} = \frac{2}{7}$
9. (1, 4) $\frac{17}{18} - \frac{7}{18} = \frac{5}{9}$
10. (2, 6) $\frac{1}{2} - \frac{1}{10} = \frac{2}{5}$
11. (6, 2) $\frac{3}{4} - \frac{2}{3} = \frac{1}{12}$
12. (0, 2) $\frac{1}{5} - \frac{1}{6} = \frac{1}{30}$
13. (8, 6) $\frac{2}{3} - \frac{1}{2} = \frac{1}{6}$
14. (4, 0) $\frac{5}{6} - \frac{5}{8} = \frac{5}{24}$
15. (4, 8) $\frac{7}{10} - \frac{3}{5} = \frac{1}{10}$
16. (8, 6) $\frac{2}{3} - \frac{2}{5} = \frac{4}{15}$
17. (8, 4) $\frac{5}{6} - \frac{7}{9} = \frac{1}{18}$
18. (7, 8) $\frac{7}{8} - \frac{2}{3} = \frac{5}{24}$
19. (4, 2) $\frac{8}{11} - \frac{5}{22} = \frac{1}{2}$
20. (3, 8) $\frac{3}{4} - \frac{2}{5} = \frac{7}{20}$

0,2	6,2	6,0	4,0	4,2	10,2	8,4
$\frac{2}{7}$	$\frac{1}{12}$	$\frac{1}{3}$	$\frac{5}{24}$	$\frac{1}{2}$	$\frac{3}{8}$	$\frac{1}{18}$
9,4	7,6	8,6	6,8	7,8	5,10	3,8
$\frac{1}{4}$	$\frac{4}{5}$	$\frac{1}{6}$	$\frac{1}{5}$	$\frac{5}{24}$	$\frac{3}{4}$	$\frac{7}{20}$
4,8	2,6	3,6	1,4	2,4	0,2	
$\frac{1}{10}$	$\frac{2}{5}$	$\frac{4}{15}$	$\frac{5}{9}$	$\frac{2}{3}$	$\frac{1}{30}$	

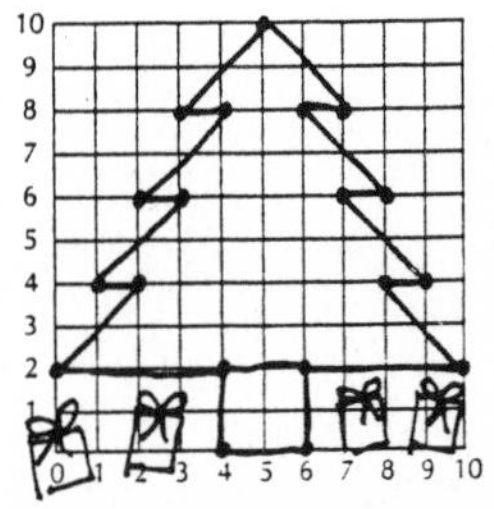

Page 101

Factor Trees

Christmas

Name ____________________

Develop a factor tree for each of the composite numbers listed below. Any factor tree with 5 or more factors is large enough to be cut as a Christmas tree. Outline the trees ready for cutting.

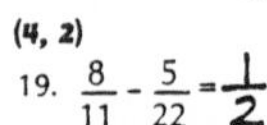

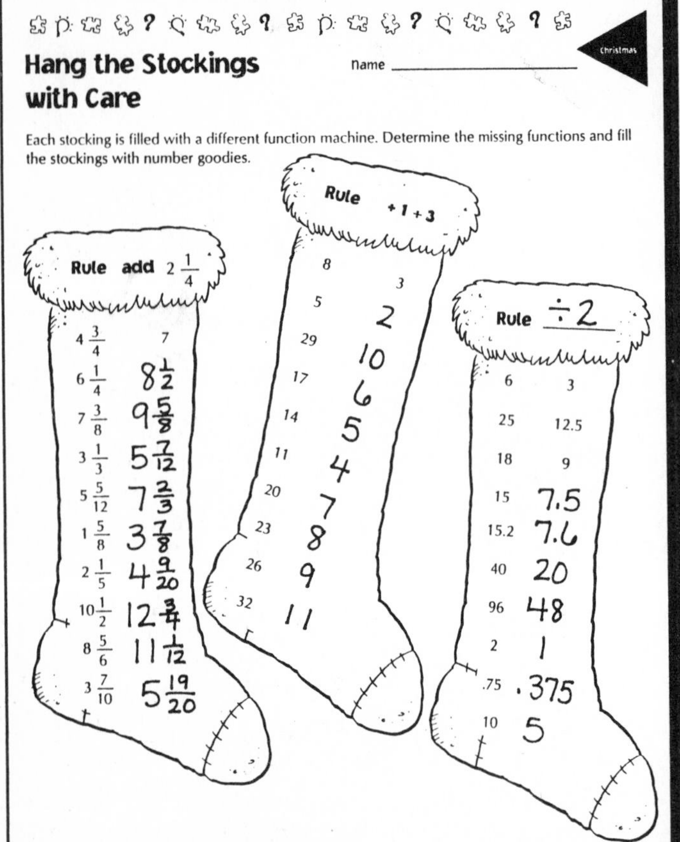

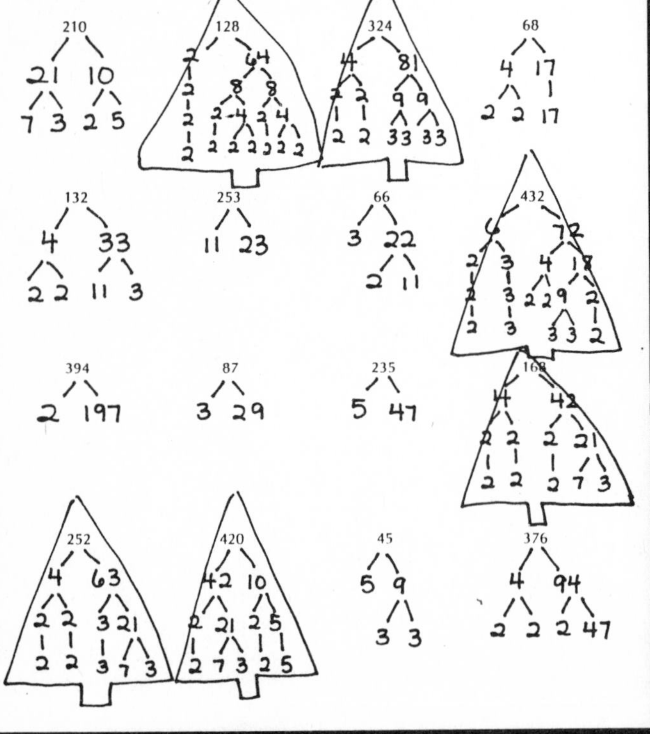

Page 102

Holiday Traditions

Kwanzaa

Name ____________________

Kwanzaa honors African American people and their past. It begins on December 26 and lasts until January 1. It was first celebrated in 1966 by Dr. Maulana Karenga so African American people could learn about their history and customs. Following are some words associated with Kwanzaa. Use the matrix and clues to determine the definition of each word.

1. Ted explained that the Mkeka is not flown or eaten.
2. Jala used Mazao to make a wonderful fruit salad as part of the Karamu.
3. Theo wore his Dashiki.
4. Ashanta lit the Mishumaa Saba, the seven candles of Kwanzaa, that were in the Kinara.
5. Zawadi are more meaningful when they are created or made with the giver's own hands or mind.
6. The green, black and red Bendera was hung for guests to see.

	Bendera	Dashiki	Karamu	Kinara	Mazao	Mkeka	Zawadi
place mat for table						YES	
African American flag	YES						
candle holder				YES			
gifts given on the last day of Kwanzaa							YES
fruits and vegetables of the harvest					YES		
special feast			YES				
piece of clothing		YES					

Bendera AFRICAN AMERICAN FLAG
Dashiki PIECE OF CLOTHING
Karamu SPECIAL FEAST
Kinara CANDLE HOLDER
Mazao FRUITS + VEGETABLES OF HARVEST
Mkeka PLACEMAT FOR TABLE
Zawadi GIFTS-LAST DAY OF KWANZAA

Page 103